212733

ESSAYS IN CRITICAL DISSENT

F. W. Bateson

ESSAYS IN CRITICAL DISSENT

Longman

LONGMAN GROUP LIMITED
London
Associated companies, branches and representatives throughout the world

First published 1972

ISBN 0 582 48409 X

Printed in Great Britain by
Western Printing Services Ltd
Bristol

To Henry W. Sams

of Pennsylvania State University, U.S.A.,

most considerate of chairmen,

friendliest companion

Contents

Oh God! Oh Montreal! Oh Oxford!

Miscellaneous Antipathies

Acknowledgements

Critical Quarterly Society for 'The Indispensable Weekly Essay' from *The Critical Survey* 1 (1962); The Journal of Education for a slightly adapted version of 'The Literary Artifact' by F. W. Bateson from *The Journal of General Education* Volume XV No. 2 (July 1963); Macmillan, London and Basingstoke for 'The Poetry of Pseudo-Learning' from *Eliot in Perspective* by T. S. Eliot—A symposium edited by Graham Martin; New Statesman for 'Oxford English' by F. W. Bateson from the *New Statesman* 17 Dec. 1965; Prentice-Hall Inc. for 'The Poetry Emphasis' by F. W. Bateson from *A. E. Housman—A Collection of Critical Essays* © 1968 Reprinted by permission of Prentice-Hall Inc. Englewood; Quelle and Mayer for 'Shakespeare's Laundry Bills' —The Rationale of External Evidence (very slightly revised) from *Shakespeare Jahrbuch 98*, Heidelberg 1962; The Times for an untitled article by F. W. Bateson from *The Times Educational Supplement* 28th Nov. 1969; Francke Verlag for 'Modern Bibliography and the Literary Artifact' (slightly adapted) from *English Studies Today*, edited by G. A. Bonnard; and Yale University Press for 'Linguistics and Literary Criticism' by F. W. Bateson from *The Disciplines of Criticism* edited by Peter Demetz.

Preface

I was not thinking of Newman's *An Essay in Aid of a Grammar of Assent* when I selected a title for the much less ambitious essays and articles that are collected here. Over forty years have passed since I subjected myself to those subtle and elegant sophistries, making, as I remember, a careful précis of each chapter as I proceeded. Nevertheless the echo of Newman in my title has a certain antithetical appropriateness. Revisiting his pages recently I realized that I was never a Newmanite—*could* never have been a Newmanite, even as a very young man. Where he assents, I dissent. My Victorian master, so far as I have had one, has always been Matthew Arnold. Indeed, for the last twenty years I have been editing and publishing, originally alone and now with two co-editors, a quarterly literary journal that I called *Essays in Criticism* specifically in Arnold's honour. (Several of the essays here reprinted originally appeared in its pages.) I even welcomed there his notorious prophecy—first made in the curious symposium called *The Hundred Greatest Men* (1879)—that religion is in process of being superseded by poetry. If by poetry we mean literature in the widest sense of the word, including its social roots and political context as well as the actual words on the page, I believe Arnold will eventually be proved to have been right; the Newmans live in a world of hypostatized metaphors. If hell is abandoned, as apparently it is now, why should Heaven survive?

To Arnold, however, the omnipresent enemy was not such transcendentalists but the Philistine. Arrayed as often as not in a self-protecting or self-consoling armour of conventional Christianity, philistinism (which the Marxists now call capitalism) is at heart an aggressive materialism, subduing whatever it touches to its peculiar and debased mystique of avarice. Against avarice a Newman fights in vain because he is not credible. The Philistine preens himself on being pragmatically *right*; he can only be routed if he is shown to be ridiculous in error, contemptible and a laughing stock because he is incapable either of simple logic or of simple arithmetic. In his own time and tone Arnold was an expert at the refutation of such creatures by ridicule. But with the advancement of science materialism has been provided with new weapons and more sophisticated tactics. Arnold's literary criticism did not have to meet the challenge of the computer or the collating machine—or the weird technologies employing these or similar instruments like the newest bibliography and textual criticism or our so-called structural linguists. It has become necessary to discredit any such inhumane specialization, however elaborate and ingenious, that is not a direct extension of the traditional values of literature. In my first and longest section in this collection, which I have called 'The Philistinism of "Research"', I have tried to combine an Arnoldian approach with the tools of a modern scholar-critic in a resistance to some of the more recent encroachments of anarchy on culture.

The other essays extend the critical attack. They are almost all by-products of my years as a university lecturer and college tutor at Oxford, a strenuous period which did not begin for me in polemical earnest until 1947. Between the end of my undergraduate period at Oxford (where like Newman and Arnold before me I just 'missed my First') and the beginning of my career as a don over twenty years had elapsed.

I spent those years partly at Harvard, then in getting married and settling in Italy, before finally transferring myself to an English village where I have busied myself in local government, politics and sport, editing *The Cambridge Bibliography of English Literature*, and with the coming of the war becoming the Statistical Officer of the Buckinghamshire War Agricultural Committee and the agricultural correspondent in turn of the *Observer* and the *New Statesman*. I give these personal details to explain why, when I re-met it in 1947, Oxford did not impress me at all. It was with a shock of disillusionment that I discovered—or thought I did—that, whereas I had changed with the changing climates of external opinion, Oxford had remained absurdly the same. The Faculty of English Language and Literature, to which I found myself attached, had even reverted to some of its pre-1914 barbarisms. As an undergraduate, for example, I had only been expected to translate four hundred lines of *Beowulf*; my poor pupils, who with the great majority of their contemporaries reading 'English' had opted for 'literature' rather than 'language',

found themselves compulsorily committed to a minimum of sixteen hundred lines of that overrated epic in what is virtually a
foreign language. They had also to familiarize themselves, as we
never did, with *Beowulf's* many linguistic and textual cruxes.
I found the conscientious student spending ten times as many
hours on those sixteen hundred lines as on the whole of Shakespeare, many of whose plays and poems he could at best skim.
And as an absurd logical consequence English literature had to
'end' officially in 1830. More recently, to those *in statu pupillari*
it has gradually extended to 1900, and blessedly and surprisingly
the terminus is now 1940—with the ration of *Beowulf* once again
reduced to translating four hundred lines.

Some specimens of those Oxford battles will be found in the
section headed 'Oh God! Oh Montreal! Oh Oxford!'[1]

Arnold, while dissociating himself from the lost causes and
forsaken beliefs that still flourished in the Oxford of his day,
excused their persistence there because the University had at
least not surrendered to the philistines. But he wrote in 1865; the
Oxford English School did not come into being until 1894 when
Arnold was safe in his grave. What distressed me most about the
English School, of which I got myself made the first secretary
and as such was able to organize for the first time the regular
terminal meetings of the Faculty demanded in the University's
Statutes, was its combination of apathy and complacency. If
things are better today with Oxford 'English' it has perhaps been
partly my doing. I failed, however, to effect a reform of the
grotesque examination system—with its Final Examination by
torture in a week-long series of invigilated three-hour papers, two
a day. The system had been borrowed from the grammar schools,
where it still has no doubt some justification, but at university

---

[1] All reprinted from the *Oxford Magazine*, now, alas defunct (one more
example of Oxford's complacent apathy). I have not included my earliest
article there, in which I applied a 'Who's Who test' to the results in three
of Oxford's largest schools, 1400 results being compared to the future
success of the candidates in 'real life' as measured by their inclusion in—or
more often exclusion from—*Who's Who* twenty-five years later. It was
reassuring to find that of the total number of those who had achieved
'Firsts', especially in 'Greats', rather more (in terms of percentages) reached
the relative eminence of a *Who's Who* entry, but the difference was a
narrow one, especially in the case of those who had taken English Literature
as their Final School, and in any case was quite incommensurate with the
glory popularly attached to a 'First'. A curious discovery was the number of
professors who had only been awarded a 'Third' for the B.A.

level it inevitably turns even the best tutors into part-time cram-
mers. Its success in distinguishing the sheep from the goats
reading 'English' may be judged by the following awards in the
late 1920s:

> *2nd class:* John Butt, G. Wilson Knight, Kenneth Muir,
> Geoffrey Tillotson
> *3rd class:* W. H. Auden, Geoffrey Grigson

Of the 'Firsts' in the same period (1925–29) I can only think of
two of comparable quality—the charming and eccentric J. B.
Leishman, who had an almost photographic memory (I tutored
him in Anglo-Saxon) and Mrs Geoffrey Tillotson.

This is not the place to elaborate the scandal of the Oxford
English School. To some extent it was done as long ago as 1937
by Stephen Potter (who obtained *his* 'Second' in 1923) in *The
Muse in Chains,* a book even funnier in places than his *Games-
manship* or *One-Upmanship.* If I may seem to take the philistinism of Oxford's examination system too solemnly, it is because
I know from my own pupils' experience the unnecessary distress
its inevitable injustices can cause. Nor, of course, is the system
confined to Oxford's English School or even to Oxford. Except
for a few enlightened post-war universities—York, for example—
no serious attempt at either examination fact-finding or examination experimentation seems to have been made in the United
Kingdom, though both are common exercises in America.

The grossest fallacy in the English system of grading achievement in the Final Examination by 'classes' is that it masks the
real intellectual difference between the good 'First' or 'Second'
and the man who just squeezes into these classes. The division
between a good 'First' and a low 'First' is far greater than that
between the low 'First' and the good 'Second'. So too with
'Thirds' and 'Fourths', etc. Tutors' expectations demonstrate in
my article below, even in subjects as different from each other
as Mathematics, French, German, Jurisprudence and English
Literature, that tutors tend to be consistently 'wrong' to almost
exactly the same degree (about 30 per cent). The error is clearly
in the system rather than in the peculiarities of individual
examiners or candidates (where the differences tend to cancel
each other out). What is so deplorable is the University's contentment or unawareness of the extent of this disagreement between
tutors, who have normally supervised an undergraduate's work

for two or often three years, and the marks on nine or ten scripts that is all the examiner has to go on—and which he prudently destroys before the class-lists are made public. An analysis of four mark-books revealed a similar degree of disagreement (about 33 per cent) between two independent examiners of each script—mainly, as might be expected, over the borderline cases between each class. But such often minimal differences become absurdly exaggerated when translated into classes. Stephen Potter may well have been right in recommending a total abolition of the Final Examination—at any rate in English literature.

The monstrous regiment of examiners have made me more continuously angry than any other academic abuse, but there is a critical gimmick much in use both in examination papers and in ambitious critical studies from which I dissent with an almost equal vehemence. This is the method known in England as 'practical criticism' and in the United States as 'explication'. The ablest exposition of its theoretical basis is not, in my opinion, I. A. Richards's *Practical Criticism* (1929), indispensable though that is, but a well-known essay with the pleasantly dogmatic title 'The Intentional Fallacy' by William K. Wimsatt and Monroe C. Beardsley, which will be found in Wimsatt's *The Verbal Icon* (1954).

Reduced to its simplest terms the Wimsatt/Beardsley doctrine asserts that the meaning of a work of literature cannot be usefully equated with what the author intended because what he intended in the process of composition is unknowable—even at a later period by the author himself. (Strictly speaking, it is not, indeed, *fully* knowable by the author himself even in the process of composition, as subconscious elements are always likely to be present.) And no doubt all this is true, but the conclusion that Wimsatt and Beardsley draw from these impeccable premises, namely, that the critical reader should only concern himself with the meaning of the separate words and sentences, if necessary looking them up in the dictionary or a grammar, without paying any attention to what may be inferred about the author's meaning from his other writings, his biography or the social order to which be belonged, is obvious nonsense. A responsible reader will always attempt to identify himself as far as he can with his author at the moment when the particular words were being selected. That will be the work's 'correct' meaning historically, even when the reader for reasons of his own refuses to respond

to the meanings and attitudes apparently expected by the author.
But is a 'correct' meaning necessarily the 'best' meaning? It is at
this point that the critic must intervene. An appeal may appropriately be made here to Aristotle: 'It is a thing very difficult if
not impossible for a man to be a good judge of what he himself
cannot do.'[1] Ben Jonson has given the proposition a literary turn
in his *Discoveries*: 'To judge of Poets is only the facultie of Poets;
and not of all Poets, but the best.'[2] T. S. Eliot said much the same
thing in his first essay on Milton; earlier, it is true, though at first
'inclined to take the extreme position that the *only* critics worth
reading were the critics who practised, and practised well, the
art of which they wrote', he withdrew from this exposed position
because he found that he 'had to stretch this frame to make some
important inclusions'.[3] Nevertheless, the best critics of English
poetry have almost all been eminent poets—Sidney, Dryden,
Johnson, Wordsworth, Coleridge, Keats, Arnold, Hopkins, Eliot
himself, Empson, Donald Davie—though it is not necessary for a
critic, apparently, to be one of the *best* poets. I think immediately
of Addison, Lamb, Leigh Hunt, Arthur Symons, Yvor Winters
and a dozen others. Aristotle's requirement—to judge nothing
that you cannot do yourself, however imperfectly—would seem
a sufficient qualification.

The late Geoffrey Tillotson prefixed to his *Essays in Criticism
and Research* a short poem of his own which provided a sort of
implicit guarantee that he could be trusted to talk about poetry,
to some extent at any rate, *from the inside*. It seemed a good idea
to me, and so when I published my *English Poetry; a Critical
Introduction* in 1951 I followed his example by prefixing a poem
of my own written specially for the occasion. I do not claim that
it is a particularly good poem, but it is certainly not just versified
prose. I have in fact written a number of other poems, most of
which have been published in reputable weeklies, and writing
them has unquestionably made it easier for me to 'feel my way'
into an English poet's intention with more certainty than any
dictionary can provide. It may be pharisaic to remark that such
eminent contemporaries as F. R. Leavis, L. C. Knights, W. K.

[1] *Politics* 1340b (Leob translation).
[2] Jonson's aphorism is a literal translation from the Latin of the younger
Scaliger.
[3] *On Poetry and Poets* (1957), p. 139; *Selected Essays* (1932), p. 31; the
frame had to be stretched to include Remy de Gourmont. See p. 161 below.

Wimsatt and Northrop Frye, all critics I admire this side of idolatry, have as far as I know given no such public evidence of their creative metal.

The poet's personality then, or its creative equivalent in the literary genres, cannot be left out by the critic. In the pieces of Chaucer, Housman and Eliot that I have collected here I have made a special point of bringing the author in—even though *all* the facts one would like about him are inevitably not available. But there is a further and more difficult problem for the critic to face and one that is all too often evaded. This is the ultimate *basis* of critical evaluation. A certain writer, a certain book, a certain passage, even perhaps a single line or half-line is pronounced good (or bad). Who or what has vested the critic with the authority to make such a pronouncement? The critic is not just saying 'I like this book'; he is at least implying 'I am right to like this book—and you ought to like it too'. It is no good therefore appealing to formulas like Coleridge's 'balance and reconciling of opposite and discordant qualities', because the whole question is the degree of success and the general relevance of the particular balances and reconciliations. The critic must somehow acquire a representative function, and this is not so much a matter of telling us a bit more about the successes we are already familiar with as of those we want to know about and experience *without realizing that we want to know them.*

As Arnold never ceased to argue, the poet today must also be a *vates.* Our civilization, such as it is, indeed any civilization, is bound together and encouraged to survive by an agreement on 'values', which with the development of the sciences has become decreasingly dependent on supernatural sanctions. No doubt we have our false prophets as well as our true ones, but the competent critic, because he is necessarily to some extent a creative writer as well as a critic, will have the feel of the future in his bones. He has begun to speak for it as well as for us, and a part of his prophetic responsibility will be to know when to say 'I dissent.'

I take my own example, claiming no greater infallibility, from Francis Jeffrey of the *Edinburgh Review.* 'This will never do' was how Jeffrey boldly began his review of Wordsworth's *Excursion*—and on the whole, with the exception of Book I (which is simply *The Ruined Cottage* of 1797/8 resuscitated), *The Excursion* has not done. Today, will such things as Professor

Fredson Bowers's 'biblio-textual' methods, or the class system of examination by three-hour invigilated papers, do either? I beg to disagree.

F. W. BATESON

Corpus Christi
Oxford

The
Philistinism
I # of 'Research'

The New Bibliography and the 'New Criticism': a Lecture at Lausanne•

My concern today is with what might be called the Higher Bibliography (*bibliology* would be a better word), and in particular with the superior historical certainty increasingly claimed for such investigations. Here, as a sample, is a characteristic recent pronouncement:

> When bibliography and textual criticism join [*sc.* in the editing of a definitive text], it is impossible to imagine one without the other. Bibliography may be said to attack textual problems from the mechanical point of view, using evidence which must deliberately avoid being coloured by literary considerations. Non-bibliographical textual criticism works with meanings and literary values. If these last are divorced from all connection with the evidence of the mechanical process that imprinted meaningful symbols on a sheet of paper, no check-rein of fact or probability can restrain the farthest reaches of idle speculation.[1]

• *English Studies Today: second series* (1961).
[1] Fredson Bowers, *On Editing Shakespeare and the Elizabethan Dramatists*, Philadelphia, 1955, pp. 34-5.

On the contrary, I shall argue, the only check-rein on idle critical speculation is critical speculation that is *not* idle. To look for mechanical evidence to prove or disprove literary meanings and values is to confuse two separate orders of truth, or—as I prefer to put it—to misunderstand the nature of the literary artifact. Unfortunately bibliography is in good company in its errors. That the Bibliographical Fallacy flourishes so today is largely attributable, I shall also argue, to a similar misunderstanding in certain respected critics whose masterpiece is 'The Intentional Fallacy'[1] by W. K. Wimsatt and Monroe C. Beardsley. This critical misunderstanding might be called the Formalist Error. To some extent, indeed—if I am to be frank—the illusions of modern bibliography are for me a mere stalking-horse, from behind which I hope to bring down, or at any rate alarm, this much bigger game.

This being so, my refutation of the Bibliographical Fallacy may be restricted to a representative specimen, which will raise the main theoretical issues. I have chosen for it to take up the challenge made by Fredson Bowers some years ago, at a meeting of the English Institute in New York, that he could prove 'on physical evidence not subject to opinion' that Shakespeare wrote *sallied flesh* and not *solid flesh* in *Hamlet* I, ii, 129. Bowers has argued out his case at length in the 1956 *Shakespeare Survey*, the 'physical evidence' adduced being entirely bibliographical. Here, then, is a problem of distinct literary interest that has been specially chosen by an expert bibliographer to advertise the certainty obtainable in textual criticism by such methods. If the claim fails here, on bibliography's home ground, as it were, it is perhaps not likely to be made good elsewhere.

Let us agree, to begin with, that this crux cannot be explained away as a case of Shakespeare revising an earlier reading. The forms *sallied* (the reading of both the 'reported' Q1 and the 'good' Q2) and *solid* (the F reading) are so nearly identical that they must go back to a single original in Shakespeare's MS, though that word need not, of course, have been either *sallied* or *solid*. It could, for example, have been *sullied*, as Dowden and Dover Wilson independently conjectured; in the Elizabethan 'secretary' hand used by Shakespeare the loop at the top of a small *a* is often left unclosed, and *a:u, u:a* misprints are therefore frequent. It is now agreed that for Act I the Q2 text was 'con-

[1] Printed in *The Verbal Icon: studies in the meaning of poetry* (1954).

taminated' in some way by Q1, and since Q1 is full of obvious
errors the presence of *sallied* (which seems to make little sense in
the context) in Q2 as well might be due to a mishearing of *solid*
by the Q1 'reporter' that was carelessly repeated by Q2. On the
other hand, if the word Shakespeare wrote was not *solid* but
sullied, all we need posit is a misprint in Q1. The Q2 *sallied*
could also be explained as a simple misreading by the Q2 printer
of *sullied* in the 'foul papers' that were probably the main source
of the Q2 text. But the word Shakespeare wrote may just as well
have been *sollid,* as C. J. Sisson has suggested. In that case the
F reading—whether derived directly from the prompt-book or
from a copy of Q2 corrected either by it or by the autograph—
may well be the correct one, leaving *sallied* a compositor's error.
To judge by the three pages of *Sir Thomas More* in Shakespeare's
handwriting his *o* could look at times like an *a* as well as a *u.* In
other words, to summarize textual opinion before Professor Bowers
intervened, the disputed readings are all possible—and palaeo-
graphically one is just as likely to be right as either of the others.

The bibliographical solution of the crux proposed by Bowers
depends (i) on the Q2 spelling *sallies* in Polonius's line to
Reynaldo (II, i, 39),

> You laying these slight sallies on my sonne . . .

and (ii) on minute differences in the running titles used by Q2,
which make it certain—the evidence of the running titles is
confirmed by certain differences of spelling—that Q2 was divided
between two different presses, the compositor who set

> O that this too too sallied flesh would melt . . .

not being the man responsible for

> You laying these slight sallies on my sonne . . .

Bowers's argument then is that two different compositors, each
working for a separate press (though within the same printing-
house), are not likely to make exactly the same misprint. One of
the two readings, *sallied* or *sallies,* is almost bound to be right,
and if Shakespeare's MS had the *a* spelling in one passage it
would be natural to expect it in the other. Q.E.D.

This is ingenious, but far from conclusive. For one thing it
commits Bowers to the desperate hypothesis of a hitherto un-
recorded word *sally* (from French *sale*) that is identical in
meaning with *sully* (from French *souiller*); the philological

improbability of this has been shown up by Kökeritz in a devestating article in *Studia Neophilologica*.[1] But apart from this Bowers seems to be guilty of a *suppressio veri*. He conveniently forgets that, though Polonius uses the *a*-form in Q2, he has the *u*-form in F. And as it happens the F compositor responsible for *solid flesh* was not the compositor who set *slight sulleyes*. Supposing Bowers is right in thinking Shakespeare used the *a*-form, what happens now to his criterion of two compositors not making the same mistake? F's *solid* (compositor B) + *sulleyes* (compositor A or C) seems to cancel out Q2's *sallied* (compositor X) + *sallies* (compositor Y). Bowers has also ignored the odd—and for 1623 archaic—way in which F's *sulleyes* is spelt, a spelling in marked contrast to the *-ies* ending in the spelling of all similar syllables by the same compositor elsewhere in *Hamlet*, viz. *necessaries, Allies, forgeries, modesties, Trophies*. For the compositor to have adopted the unusual termination *-eyes* he must have been following his copy 'blindly'; no doubt the word, still a rare one at that time, was unfamiliar to him. And if he was so careful to reproduce the end of the word correctly, it is a reasonable assumption that he got the first syllable right too. The word turns up in eight other places in Shakespeare, including a Shakespearian scene in *The Two Noble Kinsmen*, and the first editions spell it with a *u* six times, an *o* once, and an *a* also only once. Seven to one! In short, Bowers's *sally* is a 'ghost', an apparition in at least as questionable shape as Hamlet's father.

I need not labour a moral. Clearly, in this case at any rate, the importation of bibliographical evidence has not provided any 'physical evidence not subject to opinion' of a kind to clear up the textual crux. The physical fact that two sets of running titles were used in Q2 is not disputed; nor is the physical inference, that two presses—and therefore at least two compositors—must have been involved. These historical certainties have not been married, however, to the linguistic problem 'Which word is Shakespeare most likely to have used?', still less to its aesthetic extension 'Which was the *right* word for Shakespeare to have used?'

But, if bibliography has failed us, must we then share Kökeritz's pessimistic conclusion at the end of his article that 'the problem of *solid-sallied* will never be solved'? This seems unnecessarily defeatist. But the crux needs to be tackled with the appropriate tools, which are stylistic rather than bibliographical

[1] 30 (1958), 3–10.

or philological. Let us start with Coleridge's formula. The image of Hamlet's flesh melting, thawing and resolving (= dissolving) into dew requires, to be metaphorically effective, an opposite or discordant quality against which the imagination can balance or reconcile it. But *flesh*, in ordinary usage, is not the opposite of *dew*. Flesh at once suggests blood, which is already liquid, whereas the metaphor requires a substance that has *not* already melted, thawed and dissolved, though capable of melting, thaw and dissolution. And since the process of liquefaction is described in three main verbs and a noun, the preceding non-liquid condition needs, to achieve balance, an equally emphatic description; Hamlet's flesh must be supremely rigid, *frozen stiff*. 'too too solid' is therefore exactly what the immediate verbal context requires: it provides the right amount of emphasis, and it prevents *flesh* from suggesting softness or liquidity. On the other hand, 'too too sullied', though perhaps defensible in general terms of the play, lets the metaphor down here by removing any effective relationship between its two terminal points; flesh that is sullied calls for *cleaning*, not *melting*.

An almost exact parallel to the *Hamlet* passage will be found in *2 Henry IV*, III, i, 47–49, which also hinges on the words *solid* and *melt*. The King is moralizing here to Warwick on political mutabilities, 'the revolution of the times', which can

> Make mountaines levell, and the continent
> Weary of solide firmnesse, melt itself
> Into the sea, . . .

In these lines the reduction of mountains to level ground prepares us for a similar process which will dissolve the 'continent' (= terra firma) into sea-water. And to avoid an anti-climax the vaguely descriptive *continent*—which could mean coasts of sand just as much as coasts of rock—has to be reinforced by the emphatic 'Weary of solide firmnesse', which restores the balance between the two elements in the metaphor as 'too too solid' does in *Hamlet*. Solid rock *is* an opposite of sea-water, and its conversion into its opposite (like the conversion of solid-flesh into liquidity) *can* be appropriately compared to the melting of ice.

All in all the stylistic conclusion must be that, though *sullied flesh* is a possible reading (unlike *sallied flesh*), it weakens the metaphor disastrously: *solid flesh* is better English, better Shakespeare, better poetry.

What theoretical deductions can be drawn from the elucidation of this crux? I will ask you to note, first of all, that bibliographical considerations have not entered in any way into the solution I have just proposed, which is entirely stylistic. Dramatic and theatrical evidence in its support exist, but they are less decisive, in my opinion, though they too confirm the superiority of *solid flesh*. Secondly, even if we accept *sally* as a genuine form and drop the point about the F compositors, the bibliographical solution propounded by Bowers will still be invalid. This is because the premiss that two compositors working separately will not make the same misprint is a psychological probability and not a typographical law. Bowers is not claiming that two compositors *never* make the same misprints. And in that case neither he nor anyone else can distinguish *a priori* between the rare occasions when they do and the more frequent occasions when they do not. Unless such a criterion can be produced, one which will enable an editor to distinguish between the Bowers rule and its exception, the rule is not worth having. Of course, if other evidence is available the improbability of compositors making an identical misprint may reinforce it, but on its own, in its own right, differences in the psychology of printers can never resolve a textual problem.

What it amounts to is that bibliographical evidence—in the strict sense of the term—does not *mesh*, as it were, with stylistic evidence. As Alice Walker, the shrewdest of the 'biblio-textualists', has recognized, one of the great fallacies of twentieth-century editorial theory has been 'the assumption that fuller knowledge about transmission would establish which readings were right and which were wrong'.[1] We now know much more than our fathers did about the transmission of the texts of Shakespeare's plays. We talk learnedly about a Ralph Crane transcription, or an F text set up by Compositors A, B, C or E (the apprentice) from a particular Q that had been corrected by a prompt-book or the 'foul papers' (or a copy of either or both). And this information has its own interest and importance. But the new knowledge has made extraordinarily little difference to the actual text in which we read Shakespeare.

Why is this? Why does 'physical evidence not subject to opinion' break in the bibliographer's hand, when he tries to apply it to a textual crux? There is a theoretical problem here that is

[1] 'Principles of Annotation: Some Suggestions for the Editor of Shakespeare' in *Studies in Bibliography*, 9, 1957, 96.

often evaded. It is not as if *all* physical evidence was irrelevant or unusable. Rhyme, the coincidence or approximation of two or more groups of sounds, can be a thoroughly reliable textual tool. Let me cite a simple example. The octave of an early sonnet by Wordsworth—which has only survived in a letter into which his sister had copied it—rhymes *lane-way-hay-wain—gain-book-look-unseen*. This leaves *unseen* without a rhyme, which suggests that *gain* is a slip by Dorothy for *glean*, since the rhyme-scheme then conforms to the Bowles-type octave Wordsworth generally used as a young man: ABBACDDC. Here, then, the physical sound *unseen*, by the mere absence of a similar sound earlier in the sonnet, has called irrefutable attention to a defective rhyme. Physical and stylistic evidence have meshed, whereas the physical evidence turned up by bibliography does not attach itself directly to literary considerations. An imperfect rhyme can be, under certain circumstances, an intrinsic part of a poem's meaning; a misprint, on the other hand, is always extra-literary, an external accident that may get in the way of a poem's meaning but that is not a real part of the poem itself.

We have a theoretical clue here of the first importance. A literary artifact's essential physical basis is not, it seems, black ink-shapes on white paper but human articulations. The ink and paper—and the various uses and abuses to which they can be put by writer, printer, reader and bibliographer—have no literary significance *in themselves*, because the written word is a *translation*, for storage purposes, as it were, of what has already been expressed orally and temporally into visual and spatial equivalents. A book bears the same imperfect relationship to the original literary artifact that your photograph does to you. You can go through life without being photographed, as ballads or obscene limericks can persist in oral tradition for generations without ever being recorded in print or manuscript. Nor, of course, is writing the only mode of literary transmission available; tape-recording, broadcasting and the cinema are among the alternative possibilities.

Bibliography battens on man's superstitious reverence for the written word. *Litera scripta manet*, especially when distributed in printed editions. But the survival of reproductions is not much consolation for the loss of the original. The literary artifact belongs to a different order of values, an altogether superior order, from its 'photograph' in the manuscript or printed version,

which are only useful in so far as they enable us to reconstruct
the oral original. Literary scholarship has still to adjust itself to
these fairly elementary considerations. What is it an editor edits?
According to Greg's formula, based on McKerrow, 'The aim of a
critical edition should be to present the text, so far as the available evidence permits, in the form in which we may suppose that
it would have stood in a fair copy, made by the author himself,
of the work as he finally intended it'.[1] The formula begs more
than one fundamental question of method, but all I want to ask
now is: What is the fair copy a copy of? Greg and McKerrow
were no doubt thinking of those 'foul papers' that are normally
the penultimate stage of literary composition. In fact, though,
does an author merely transcribe into his fair copy the words he
had finally decided on in his earlier drafts, with a little secretarial
tidying here and there? Surely, as he prepares his fair copy, the
sentences in the rough drafts in front of him, instead of staying
put on the paper, come to a second life in his mind, to be tested
there against his inner ear as they re-enact themselves in his
imagination. What he is really copying is this oral drama of the
mind in its definitive form, and it is this that the modern editor
must do his best to reconstruct and transliterate. The original is
speech—in Shakespeare's case the best speech Elizabethan and
Jacobean London made possible. And speech is as far as the
author's own direct responsibilities go *qua* author. To insist on
the editor inflicting his author's 'accidentals' of spelling, capitalization and punctuation on the modern reader, as Greg and
McKerrow do, is to confuse the function of an author with that
of his copyist. It is true most authors are their own copyists, but
the talents and training required in the two functions are quite
distinct. Yeats, Wordsworth and Hand D in *Sir Thomas More*, to
cite three notorious instances, all punctuated like poor Poll.

Perhaps I may now proceed to the parallel I have proposed
between the Higher Bibliography and the New Criticism. Both
errors of emphasis can be traced to our general reluctance to
realize that the literary original exists physically in a substratum
of articulated sound and therefore in the dimension of time. The
Formalist Error reduces itself, for me, to a single key-word, the
word *structure*: literature as a verbal structure, a symbolic structure, even an organic structure. For René Wellek, to whose
brilliant chapter on 'The Mode of Existence of a Literary Work

[1] *The Editorial Problem in Shakespeare*, 2nd edn., 1951, p. x.

of Art' in *Theory of Literature* this essay is deeply indebted, literature is a structure of stratified norms (by which I think he really means a *linguistic* structure).

What I deplore in the structural metaphor is that it ignores or denies by implication the primacy of time in the literary artifact. We go to the Shakespeare Memorial Theatre at Stratford just before 7.30 p.m. and we come out at 10.30. Our mental experience during those three hours, excluding the intervals, *was* the play *Hamlet*. Or we start reading *Lycidas* at twelve noon and we finish it at 12.15. What occurred to the reader psychologically in that quarter of an hour *was Lycidas* for him. A 'structure', on the other hand, exists in space—as does a Well-Wrought Urn or a Verbal Icon. The suggestion of solidity and immobility such words convey makes them misleading metaphors for a psychic activity that is essentially mobile.

At this point I must introduce two refinements. The first is to extend the notion of an overall temporal dimension from the unit of the individual play, poem or novel, to such larger literary units as the whole corpus of a writer's work, or a whole literary movement like Romanticism, or a literary *genre* like the epic. As it is of the essence of *Hamlet* that its fifth act follows the fourth, so it is of the essence of Shakespearian tragedy in general that *Hamlet* was preceded by *Romeo and Juliet* and followed by *Macbeth*. And so *mutatis mutandis* with earlier and later Romanticism, the classical and Christian epic, etc. A time-series is equally discernible in the smallest literary units—single lines or sentences. In our *Hamlet* crux, for example, the progression of meaning from *melt* (a general term applicable to metals or fats as well as ice or snow) to *thaw* (which limits the image to the weather), *resolve* (which completes the process), and *dew* (which converts what had been absorbed into the atmosphere into its reappearance at dawn) is clear and thematic.[1] All of which suggests that, since literary history is precisely the study of such temporal relationships, its role in the profession of literary scholarship must be central and indispensable.

My second refinement is to distinguish between your or my experience when seeing *Hamlet* or reading *Lycidas* and the actual artifacts *Hamlet* and *Lycidas* that were the source or cause of our private aesthetic experience. As the *Mona Lisa* exists both

[1] The synoptic eye of the reader, because it sees the whole sentence as a single spatial block, is liable to take the three verbs as synonymous.

within and outside the various reactions to it by visitors to the Louvre, so there is an objective *Hamlet* behind our individual experiences of it, which enables us to say of a particular performance that it is 'wrong-headed' or 'one-sided'. The fact that we can see a picture, whereas *Hamlet* is invisible, is because the picture's physical basis is spatial and not temporal; it does not affect the general similarity of their aesthetic status. *Hamlet* then is an object; but it is a man-made object and only usable by human beings—like the Constitution of the United States. If it has no Supreme Court, to which we can appeal over differences in its interpretation, the consensus of scholarship is an obvious approximate equivalent to such a Court.

For all these reasons it is useful, I suggest, to call the work of literature a temporal or oral artifact (its speech need only sound to the inner ear). An artifact is any man-made physical object: Coleridge, who was apparently the first to use the word in English, applied it to an inkstand; Gilbert Murray once used it to describe poetry. As artifacts the difference between inkstands and poems is (i) the physical substance out of which man has made them, and (ii) the human purpose they are intended to serve. As for (ii), we can perhaps agree for the moment that the literary artifact's human purpose is likely to be much the same as that of the other fine arts, and as for (i), the physical substance, the analogy of the other arts seems to confirm the conclusion that the case of rhyme has already suggested—namely, that the literary substratum is simply articulated sound. It is true we are usually told that the medium of literature is language. But language is also an artifact, an exceptionally elaborate artifact, and no even approximate parallel to it can be found in the media of the other fine arts. Between them, indeed, and language the difference is absolute: they are brute matter, a language only exists by virtue of the minds using it.

But if language is not the literary artifact's medium, what *is* the role of language in literature? The problem resolves itself immediately, I suggest—it is the crux of my whole argument—if Saussure's seminal distinction between *langue* and *parole* is extended from linguistic to literary theory.[1] *Langue*, you will

---

[1] Modern stylistics has trembled on the edge of the extension more than once. See Pierre Guiraud, *La Stylistique*, Paris, 1954, for examples. No doubt a difference between the *parole* of original composition and the *parole* of each later re-enactment of the original artifact must be recognized, but both can be subsumed under Saussure's general concept.

remember, is the speech-system, the vocabulary, accidence and syntax that a speech-group learns, adjusts and stores away in its individual memories for use when required: *your motor car in its garage.* *Parole*, on the other hand, is the particular speech-act, the words exchanged between A and B in a particular place on a particular occasion: *your motor car on Piccadilly last May.* Saussure did not live to complete the definition of *parole*, and nobody has been able to say where the notion stops. If Aneurin Bevan talking to Jenny Lee is *parole*, why is Aneurin Bevan haranguing the House of Commons not *parole* too? If Bevan's speech in Hansard is *parole*, why exclude from the definition an article in which he makes the same points in similar terms? And if an article why not a treatise? The literary artifact, then, is *parole* extended and elaborated. Its only essential difference from conversation is that it is much more memorable. One may say that it 'wants' to get itself repeated. The extension I am proposing of *parole* necessarily implies a similar elaboration of *langue* into linguistic memorability devices—metre, for example, poetic diction, all the figures of speech, all the conventional literary subject-matter that Curtius has taught us to call 'topoi', and (last but not least) the traditional literary *genres* or 'kinds'.

It is the essential identity of the literary artifact with Saussure's *parole* that overturns the formalist position. A speech-act is not, except by a perversion of language, a structure. It is a communication, an exchange of ideas, a swapping of stories—even if only one member of the group who are conversing achieves memorability, or even utterance. As Samuel Butler put it, if *saying* is going on there must be a *sayee* as well as a *sayer.* Formalist theory has tried to exclude or minimize the function of both author and audience. Hypnotizing themselves with 'the words on the page' the formalists forget that words in *parole*—as distinct from *langue*—can never speak themselves. They must always be spoken by somebody to somebody (even if the audience is an unseen or hypothetical one). The critical reader is one who can identify himself simultaneously with both the original author, as he tells his story or makes his point, and the original audience which had once spurred him on by their intelligent excitement as he foresaw them responding to him. We must re-introduce into the aesthetic act what Saussure called *le circuit de la parole.* To abstract from this human and temporal process 'the best words in the best order' *after* they have left the author and *before* they

reach the auditor, and freeze them into an artificial spatial immobility is to treat *parole* as though it was *langue*. This indeed,
in the final analysis, *is* the Formalist Fallacy. The New Critics
have tended to approach poetry, not as the embodiment of human
values, but as a museum of emphasis and memorability devices,
a kind of syntax. The new explication lesson, with the class busily
parsing the masterpieces of English literature into the modern
rhetoric of symbols and tensions, is not far removed from the old
grammar lesson. And none the worse for that, you will say. I
agree—up to a point. Effective *parole* does depend upon efficient
langue. But do not let us confuse a pedagogic discipline with a
fine art. Literary criticism is *parole* achieving a measure of self-
conscious awareness, sensuous and emotional as well as intellectual, that will enable it to value itself by standards that are
ultimately social and ethical. The acquisition of *langue*, on the
other hand, is a merely cognitive process, though an indispensable
one. You must know English before you can criticize *Hamlet*—
and not only the English language but also the literary and
dramatic extensions of the *langue* of the English Renaissance,
from Senecan tragedy to Senecan prose style, from the pun to the
pastiche.

The Higher Syntax of literary *langue* is not so far removed
from the textual detective work of the Higher Bibliography. For
both the car does not leave the garage; it stays there while our
academic mechanics overhaul it and number each component
part. And for both disciplines, because the artifact is not being
put to its proper human use, there is the danger that the storage
shed of the printed word will come to seem an essential part of
the verbal vehicle. The 'explicator' does not see beyond the words
on the page in their linear arrangements, and the bibliographer
becomes preoccupied with sheets of paper on which a mechanical
process has imprinted meaningful symbols. But the car is only in
the garage for storage purposes, because art is long and memories
are short. When it is in motion, instead of letters and pages, there
are only voices, which are using the devices of *langue*, not for
their own sake, but because in the vicinity of the voices there are
ears—and because in the end we must love our neighbours as
ourselves *or go mad*.

I conclude by descending from these theoretical heights to
examine a particular case—one as typical in its own confident
way of the once 'New Criticism' as Bowers's preference of *sallied*

for *solid* was of the New Bibliography. My specimen is a comment, which has been much admired[1] though it is almost certainly mistaken, by F. R. Leavis on two lines from Keats's 'To Autumn',

> And sometimes like a gleaner thou dost keep
> Steady thy laden head across a brook . . .

These lines, it seems, have a special 'English strength' because 'In the step from the rime-word "keep", across (so to speak) the pause enforced by the line-division, to "Steady" the balancing movement is enacted'.[2] The technical objection to Leavis's interpretation is that a pause at the end of the line is a universal poetic convention similar to the use of two-dimensional space in painting —or the less essential use of a capital letter for the first word of a line. Whether there is enjambment (as in seven other lines in 'To Autumn' to which Leavis's comment does not seem to apply) or not, a line in poetry is necessarily a temporal unit simply as verse, a prosodic *sine qua non,* whether the line has any literary merit or not and whatever its subject matter. Thus the prosodic pause and the balancing gleaner are not *in pari materia.* When the lines are read aloud—translated, that is, into their oral reality —the prosodic pause, as distinct from the grammatical pause, remains the same in every line, just as the number of syllables will usually remain the same.

In other words, Leavis is seeing something that is not strictly there. He had no doubt been misled by the absence of a comma, although considered both prosodically and grammatically it would make no difference if Keats had printed the lines, as Pope might have done:

> And sometimes like a gleaner thou dost keep,
> Steady, thy laden head across a brook . . .

A more serious consequence of Leavis's interpretation remains to be considered. The interpretation is certainly ingenious, but in the careful reader it leaves a feeling of discomfort somewhat similar to that caused by George Herbert's 'The Altar' and 'Easter-Wings'. No one has ever commended the 'English

---

[1] Its influence can be detected in works as poles apart as Mrs Winifred Nowottny's *The Language Poets Use* (1962) and Geoffrey N. Leech's *A Linguistic Guide to English Poetry* (1969), for both of which I have a dissentient admiration.

[2] *Revaluation* (1936), pp. 263–4.

strength' of these pattern-poems, though their use of varying
line-lengths and indentations is certainly ingenious. The critical
objection to Leavis's comment is that this clever but essentially
fallacious notion of the lines 'enacting' what they describe dis-
tracts the reader's attention from Keats's real meaning. A gleaner
balancing her load of corn on her head while crossing a brook is
one of the series of touching vignettes of humble English country
life that Keats introduces as personifications of autumn. A more
democratic equivalent of Ceres is being attempted. The stanza is
memorable because of the range of human sympathies it engages
in us and not because of any verbal or metrical gadgets it may
have in it.[1] I am not wholly convinced by Mrs Nowottny's 'When,
for instance, Keats writes in the Ode to Autumn, "Thy hair soft-
lifted by the winnowing wind", he brings the image of autumn
suddenly and intimately close, as the line's own contour traces
the first soft touch, then the lifting stir, then the lessening tremor
of the "winnowing" as the breeze moves away . . .'.[2] I applaud the
appreciation of a temporal sequence here, though 'contour', a
spatial metaphor, is perhaps an unhappy term. In 'wind' too the
breeze clearly culminates, grammatically as well as by virtue of
being the last word in the line, instead of moving away. But my
most serious misgiving is raised by the paraphrase of 'winnowing', a word that Keats must have meant to bear its literal sense
of 'fanning grain free of chaff' (the personified autumn was
'sitting careless on a granary floor').[3] Here too, as in Leavis's
comment, the primary human sense has been subordinated by
the commenter to the gadget.

In a word, *parole* has been sacrificed to *langue*. But a proper
understanding of literature and a proper response to such understanding demand a fusion of *both* approaches—in the stylistic
critic just as much as in the bibliographer. Sidney's words on
oratory can be applied to our various literary specialists today:

> Undoubtedly (at least to my opinion undoubtedly) I have
> found in divers smal learned Courtiers, a more sound stile,
> then in some professors of learning, of which I can gesse no
> other cause, but that the Courtier following that which by

---

[1] In fairness to Leavis I should add that the essay as a whole, like *Revaluation* as a whole, contains much excellent criticism.
[2] *The Language Poets Use*, p. 116.
[3] A fan is 'an instrument that by its motion artificially causeth Wind useful
in the Winnowing of Corn' (J. Worlidge, *Systema Agriculturae*, 1681, p.
325). See *O.E.D.*

practise he findeth fittest to nature, therein (though he know it not) doth according to art, though not by art: where the other using art to shew art and not hide art (as in these cases he should do) flieth from nature, and indeed abuseth art.[1]

[1] *The Defence of Poesie* (1595), ed. Albert Feuillerat, 1923, p. 43.

2

What is Bibliography?•

I

'"What is bibliography?" says the jesting critic, and stays not for
an answer.' The accusation—typical of the New Bibliography's
self-complacency (it was after all *Christ* whom Pilate stayed not
to answer!)—was made in an anonymous front-page article in
The Times Literary Supplement of 24 March 1966, by a writer
who is clearly an expert in the business. (He is generally believed
to have been Dr David Fleeman, one of the ablest and most
dedicated of the younger Oxford bibliographers.) 'The two
disciplines', this writer continues, 'have coexisted for years past,
those who practise them subsisting on the same raw material,
working and often living in the same place, and yet curiously
detached—each tending to misunderstand or underrate the purpose and technique of the other.'

The detachment must certainly be conceded. What is not so
clear is that literary criticism and bibliography subsist 'on the
same raw material'. The literary critic criticizes literature—books
or parts of books that pretend to a degree at least of the aesthetic

• 'The Literary Artifact' (*Journal of General Education*, Pennsylvania, July
1963), revised and expanded.

qualities found pre-eminently in the best poetry, drama and prose fiction; bibliography, on the other hand, concerns itself with all kinds and manners of books, the good, the bad and the indifferent, the stinking fish and the good red herring. At best—as in such similarly parallel disciplines as linguistics or literary history—there is a certain *overlap* between literature and bibliography. And even in the overlapping areas—in the works of Shakespeare, for example—the questions that a critic and a bibliographer address to the common 'raw material' tend to be very different. Criticism cannot do without bibliography altogether, but for bibliography to arrogate to itself more than an occasional or marginal relevance for the study of literature is to display its own essential philistinism. A bibliographer is not required to *read* the books that he describes in such meticulous and sometimes fascinating detail; professionally, considered simply as a bibliographer, he is, or does his best to be, *illiterate*.

The *TLS* article from which I have quoted gives two elaborate examples of the use of bibliography. One is an octavo edition of Farquhar's collected plays with the imprint 'London, Printed in the Year 1710'; this is believed to be a Dutch piracy of the genuine first edition of 1710 (which *was* printed in London), which it follows closely. In several copies, however, *The Recruiting Officer* is found both with cancelled and uncancelled sheets. This unusual bibliographical condition is cited to make a point against Fredson Bowers's *Principles of Bibliographical Description*; but the edition itself seems to have no literary interest. The second example is the four reprints of Cowper's *Poems* that appeared in 1798, and here a typographical connection is demonstrated between an Edinburgh piracy and the authorized seventh edition. In this case too, what bibliography has contributed is simply to supply a more detailed differentiation between editions in which the author himself had no hand at all, Farquhar because he was dead, Cowper because he was mad. This is 'raw material' for a history of the book trade, and its literary relevance is minimal; all that bibliography has added to literary history is confirmation of the popularity of a certain author at a certain time. And this bibliographer is unaware or uninterested in the critical significance even of his modest crumb of new knowledge.

The one area in which such bibliographical refinements can claim a certain literary utility is that of textual criticism. Just as the editor of an autograph manuscript is expected to be able to decipher his author's handwriting correctly, so some degree of familiarity with the contemporary processes of printing and publishing is required in the editor of printed texts. To take a very simple example, the persistence of long *s* (except at the end of words) until *c*. 1800 is a fact that an editor of pre-1800 printed books has to be aware of, because of the similarity of long *s* and lower case *f*; a modern printer when asked to reprint an early text often confuses the two letters. Earlier printers are less likely to do so, but a plausible emendation does sometimes hinge on a confusion of long *s* with *f* or vice versa.

In our time the prophet of bibliographical textual criticism—what Fredson Bowers calls the 'biblio-textual' method—has been Sir Walter Greg (better known as W. W. Greg). Three papers read to the Bibliographical Society—'What is Bibliography?' (1912), 'The Present Position of Bibliography' (1930), and 'Bibliography—an Apologia' (1932)—contain a brilliant exposition of the Greg gospel. They will all be found in his *Collected Papers* (ed. J. C. Maxwell, 1966), with notes that Greg added in 1958.[1] In 'What is Bibliography?' Greg had already reached his central position which was that 'critical bibliography', as he called it, is 'the science of the material transmission of literary texts'. But the argument becomes subtler and bolder in the two later papers, especially in 'Bibliography—an Apologia'. Textual criticism is here identified as the study of failures in the process of transmission, such failures being definable in strictly bibliographical terms 'without any reference to the meaning of the signs or the subject-matter of the text'. Greg admits that there is also an 'intuitional' or 'psychological' aspect to textual criticism— 'judgments of what an author must or should have written'. But the material transmission, Greg insists, is 'logically prior', and a final triumphant conclusion is reached that bibliography 'is in fact the same as textual criticism'.

The logical priority depends—so the argument runs—upon the reader being first confronted in whatever he proposes to read by certain black objects (letters, punctuation marks, etc.) that have been imposed on white paper. These can no doubt be described as 'material'—as can also any later copy or print of them. The fallacy in Greg's thesis is in detaching the physical symbols from their mental or 'psychological' accompaniment, what the symbols symbolize. The writer or printer records those black marks on the

[1] Page references are all to this collection.

paper as a *translation* of words and sentences that already exist orally in his mind. And a similar process of translation operates for the reader who recognizes the series of black marks as conventional representatives of certain already familiar words and word-orders. Greg's exclusion of meaning from the process of literary transmission flies in the face of experience. A reader does not in fact peruse books in a language he does not understand; a printer does not in fact use symbols that have not already a certain mental reality for him. Even, to take an extreme case, a completely unfamiliar symbol—such as a mathematician's *pi* or capital *sigma*—cannot escape *some* meaning for either compositor or copyist simply by virtue of the context of meaning in which it occurs.

The logical priority is therefore with 'meaning'—and its oral embodiment in the physical material of speech—and not with a written or printed word or words. The point would seem an elementary one, but once it is granted the claims of Greg's 'critical' bibliography become very much reduced. As a theory of literature it is tainted by what René Wellek once called 'the superstition of behaviourism', which 'denies the evidence of introspection and empathy, the two main sources of human and humane knowledge'.[1]

Bibliography is, it would seem, in urgent need of re-definition. In the general sense that Greg was rightly demanding for the term it has certainly provided us with a new kind of external evidence. Greg's friend and colleague R. B. McKerrow, unfortunately, is resolutely untheoretical in *An Introduction to Bibliography for Literary Students* (1927), the nearest that he comes to a definition of it in his Preface being 'the evidence as to a book's history which can be gathered from its material form and make-up'. Where Greg's interest was in the physical text, McKerrow's was primarily in the physical book, an even more behaviourist attitude. The chapter of most interest to the textual critic in the *Introduction* is likely to be Chapter Four of Part II, 'On Bibliographical Evidence as to the Order of Editions', which contains the following generalizations.

[1] *Style in Language*, ed. Thomas A. Sebeok 1960, p. 409. Wellek's *Theory of Literature* (written in collaboration with Austin Warren, 1949) cites as evidence of the antiquarianism flourishing in English graduate schools an influential professor who considered the future of literary scholarship was in 'bibliography'—'i.e., the type of textual criticism cultivated by W. W. Greg and Dover Wilson' (p. 285).

Handsomeness of 'get-up' is as a general rule better evidence
of priority than correctness of text, if by 'correctness' we mean
the reproduction of what the author intended. On the other
hand, a handsome edition is as a rule carefully produced and
is comparatively free from *literal* errors. The words in it will
as a rule be real words correctly spelt; but they may not be
the correct words. . . . A most carelessly printed book, abso-
lutely swarming with literals, may contain important corrections, and from an editor's point of view give us the best
text. Indeed if we may imagine an author making improve-
ments from time to time in his own copy of his work (presumably a copy of the original edition) and sending lists of these
to the printer to be inserted in reprints, or even inserting them
in proofs himself, and if these reprints were in other respects
not more carefully supervised than the general run of such
things, we might have a series of editions steadily degenera-
ting in corrections of printing and at the same time steadily
improving in 'readings'.

No doubt the state of affairs imagined by McKerrow does often
obtain. Greg, whose prose style was greatly superior to Mc-
Kerrow's, distinguished between the two levels as 'accidental'
readings, which tend to degenerate in the process of textual
transmission (the degenerations are generally contributed by the
scribe or printer), and 'substantive' readings (for which the
author is normally though not always responsible). *Accidentals* include spelling, punctuation, the use of initial capitals, italicization,
paragraphing and even in the sixteenth and seventeenth centuries
a book's title, which was often the invention of the publisher; *substantives* are 'what the author intended', whatever is meaningful
—though Greg did not deny that spelling (consider the case of
Milton's *thir* for an unemphatic *their*), punctuation, capital letters
(consider Gray's personifications) and even the use of italics (consider the habits of Matthew Arnold) *may* sometimes be meaningful.

But with the admission of meaning as a decisive criterion the
whole case for bibliography as 'the science of the material transmission of literary texts' begins to collapse; psychology, even
'intuition', are now being vindicated. McKerrow's doctrine of
the 'copy-text', a term coined by McKerrow himself to explain
his procedure in his remarkable edition of Nashe (5 vols, 1904–
1910), proved in the end too 'material', too mechanical, even for
Greg. McKerrow had laid it down as an editorial principle in his
Nashe[1] that if a later edition contains some variants attributable

[1] I, 197.

to the author we must accept *all* the alternations in it, apart from obvious misprints or blunders. This might at first sight seem just what the rigour of the bibliographic game demanded, but Greg's comment on the 'principle' in an appendix to be found at the end of F. P. Wilson's reissue of McKerrow's Nashe[1] in 1958 has proved difficult to refute. It runs as follows:

> This will have struck many as doubtful, and it seems to me definitely perverse. It admittedly belongs to what is commonly the 'conservative reaction' against the unprincipled eclecticism of most editors of the eighteenth and nineteenth centuries, and it forms, indeed, but an element in the concerted attempt of a later generation to substitute objective or mechanical rules in place of personal judgement. It seems to me, however, that any such attempt is in its nature mistaken and bound to lead to uncritical results. Judgement must inevitably be exercised alike to detect the presence of authorial alternatives and to eliminate 'obvious blunders and misprints', and there can be no logical reason for refusing to exercise it likewise to discriminate between alterations for which the author must be considered responsible and those due to some other agency. . . . The truth is that no critical principle can be devised that will relieve an editor of ultimate responsibility, and the risk of overlooking some authorial corrections is no excuse for an editor including in his text readings that he himself believes to be of no authority at all. Essential as it is to eschew the excesses of eclecticism, any attempt to evade the responsibility of individual judgement is an abdication of the editorial function.

This remarkable retraction lays a quite new emphasis on 'judgement'. The 'obvious blunders and misprints' that McKerrow blithely corrected in his Nashe had not corrected themselves automatically by the application of some mechanical 'principle'; without realizing it McKerrow recognized that each to a greater or less degree was *meaningless*—or at best bad or clumsy English. Meaning, though expelled by the fork of the New ('material') Bibliography, inevitably returned.

What is curious is that it was only at the end of his long life that these fairly elementary critical realities began to dawn on a man as intelligent as Greg. Thus 'The Function of Bibliography in Literary Criticism Illustrated in a Study of *King Lear*' is typical of his earlier work in its combination of local brilliance and a pervasive theoretical self-contradiction. This paper, which is

[1] V, 33.

generally considered one of Greg's best, was originally published
in 1933—one year, that is, after 'Bibliography—an Apologia'. It
begins on the same lines:

(i) 'A knowledge of the true text is the basis of all criticism' (p.
268) and so 'textual criticism is at the basis of all literary
study' (p. 270).

(ii) The 'attack on textual problems' is best made, not 'through
speculation as to what we fancy may have been in an author's
mind', but through bibliography, 'the study of books as tan-
gible objects', which is 'not concerned with their contents in a
literary sense' but with 'the signs and symbols they contain
(apart from their significance)'.

These general propositions are then illustrated—this at least is
Greg's claim and the *raison d'être* of the paper—by a close
examination of the textual problems raised by *Lear*.

Pre-bibliographical critics had already discovered that there
were two quarto editions of *Lear*, each with different readings,
but both dated 1608. Shakespearian bibliography achieved one of
its most sensational triumphs when it was able to demonstrate on
the basis of watermarks in the paper and a common framework
on the titlepages that several of the plays were reprinted together,
some with false dates, in 1619. One of these misdated plays was a
'1608' *Lear* which has since been accepted as Q2. Q1 survives in
only twelve copies, with 167 variants distributed erratically between them. Bibliography may also claim the credit for explaining the origin of these variations, viz. that corrections were made
in the formes after the printing had begun, the corrected sheets
being then assembled with uncorrected sheets.

What, however, was the relationship of the texts of Q1 and
Q2? How are they connected with the very different text in the
First Folio (1623)? And what was the nature of the 'correction'
carried out in Q1? These are the essential problems for the textual
critic, and bibliography cannot resolve them. Greg airily concedes
that sometimes 'the compositor had merely made a slight mistake
in reading his copy, and that when the press-reader altered the
word to something quite different, he was merely guessing and
did not trouble to consult the manuscript at all'. But the manuscript is not extant, and the only basis Greg has for distinguishing
the respective nature of Q1, Q2 and F1—whether the result of a
compositor's error, a press-reader's guess or a press-reader's con-
sultation of the manuscript—is the degree of 'sense' the editor

attributes to each variant. Which reading provides the best words in the best order? Which supplies the best *meaning*?

It is because Q1 of *King Lear* fails over and over again to satisfy this requirement that it is now generally classified as a 'reported' text—one either recorded in shorthand during a performance, or else, as Greg later considered more probable in *The Shakespeare First Folio* (1955), one compiled by the actors from what they remembered of their parts in the absence of the prompt-book (perhaps on a provincial tour). The 'official', though by no means infallible text, is that in F1, which seems to have been prepared by correcting a copy of Q1 to conform as far as possible with the prompt-book.[1]

What is surprising in view of the emphasis laid earlier in the paper on the irrelevance of content and significance is Greg's total dependence on internal evidence in determining the textual relationship of Q1 to F1. Bibliography proves to be a *muta persona*. On the contrary, as Greg himself now puts it, 'it is the verbal variants of the two texts that supply the most ample evidence of reporting' (287). Among the many examples he cites is the Folio's 'true Shakespearian phrase'.

> Close pent-up guilts,
> Rive your concealing Continents, and cry
> These dreadful Summoners grace.

'The Quarto's "rive your concealed centers"', Greg adds, 'makes neither verse nor sense' (288). At one point too in a discussion of the theory that F1 is a revision of Q1 he comments with splendid forthrightness: 'If anybody can see revision in this passage his conception of poetical composition must be radically different from my own' (289). Later he praises the superior 'pregnancy and vigour' of the Folio text (297).

So far, then, from Greg's study of the text of *King Lear* illustrating the function of bibliography in literary criticism, as his title had proclaimed, it turns out that literary considerations alone, apart from the one trivial matter of the misdating of Q2, determine the probable route of transmission of the play's text. The crucial issues of (i) the 'reported' character of Q1, and (ii) the authoritative nature of the manuscript used to correct a copy of Q1 for the F1 text are decided simply by internal 'psychological' evidence. Literary criticism has in this case provided a

[1] Q2 is disregarded textually by modern editors. It is a reprint of Q1 with no independent authority.

basis for bibliography; Greg had in fact put the cart before the horse.

The bibliographical delusion has been responsible for some other textual heresies. One may be called the Old Spelling doctrine. This is the direct descendant of Greg's doctrine that the first concern of the textual critic is with the material transmission of the text he is editing or emending. Greg derived this 'genetic' or genealogical principle from Karl Lachmann, the nineteenth-century editor of Lucretius, but his bibliographical preoccupations compelled him to limit disastrously Lachmann's useful principle. As the issue is put by Greg, the bibliographer, intent on those material pieces of paper that provide his point of departure, always asks himself the question 'What was the nature of the copy that the printer had before him when he was setting up the type?' (274). For Lachmann and his classical followers 'copy' included the readings (or words); for the bibliographer of the school of Greg 'copy' meant, at least theoretically, the arrangement of the sheets of paper (format), their watermarks, and the black marks left on them by the printing press. Since the words' meaning was theoretically irrelevant, the modern editor was expected to reprint as exactly as possible the printed *shapes* of the early edition. Hence the typographical facsimiles of the Malone Series of Reprints to the preparation of which Greg devoted so much of his life.

Greg's ultimate emergence from the illusion that material transmission is the key to textual criticism is reflected in his change of attitude to spelling and the other 'accidentals'. They should be preserved, not because they are an important part of the material transmitted, but because they have some meaning, have in fact become 'substantives'. The change is evident in a sentence in *The Editorial Problem in Shakespeare* (1939): 'In Shakespeare's day a writer's individualities of speech reflected themselves naturally in his spelling, and to alter his spelling is to destroy a clue to his language.'[1] The dictum is not illustrated; it is difficult, indeed, to see how it could be. The three pages of the manuscript play of *Sir Thomas More* (now in the British Museum) that are now agreed to be in Shakespeare's autograph must be among the worst spelt and the worst punctuated in the whole history of English literature. The word *sheriff*, for example, appears in no less than five forms in five consecutive lines: *shreif, shreef, shreeve,*

[1] 2nd edn. (1951), p. li.

shreive, shreve. But what do such aberrations prove? That spelling was badly taught at Stratford-on-Avon? Or what?

Greg does not tell us—although having transcribed the whole of *Sir Thomas More* in 1911 and the Shakespearian pages again in 1923 he must be presumed to have known whatever (if anything) the clues of spelling and punctuation revealed. A careful reading has not revealed anything of significance to me, though it is no doubt always possible that hints of a Warwickshire pronunciation *may* lurk somewhere in the three pages. In any case, Greg's corollary that the proper way to print Shakespeare today is in the spelling and punctuation of the earliest editions will not bear serious cross-examination. For one thing the spelling of the so-called Good Quartos and the First Folio (1623) is only occasionally that of Shakespeare's autograph and the punctuation system used is quite different. Greg was, of course, aware of this, but his position is ambiguous. What he is particularly anxious to preserve is any clue to Shakespeare's own pronunciation, but in the absence of such clues any and every Elizabethanism was still preferable to modernization. 'So long as there is any chance', he writes (*op. cit.*, pp. li, lii), 'of an edition preserving some trace, however faint, of the author's individuality, the critic will wish to follow it: and even where there is none, he will still prefer an orthography that has a period resemblance with the author's to one that reflects the linguistic habits of a later date.' The same point is made in connection with punctuation: 'Just as the language of an Elizabethan author is better represented by his own spelling than by ours, so the flow of his thought is often more easily indicated by the loosely rhetorical punctuation of his own day than by our more logical system' (*ibid.*). This sounds plausible; it ignores two crucial facts—(i) the flow of an Elizabethan's thought was not simply hit or miss like his spelling and punctuation; (ii) the Elizabethan printers' corrections of an author's manuscript look forward directly to our modern uniformity, being the same in kind, if not in degree, as those of a modernizing editor. The typical Elizabethan accepted a printer's changes in the spelling and pointing without protest because they represented an obvious improvement on his own efforts; it is difficult to believe that the printers would not have welcomed modern standardizations if they had known of them. Modern punctuation in particular is far more flexible than Elizabethan punctuation, which is not really 'loosely rhetorical' but loosely logical, i.e., often illogical and meaningless. In any case, rhetoric is not an anti-logic. On close examination its pauses always turn out to be the logical ones too.

But the real objection to an Old Spelling Shakespeare—or to any Old Spelling edition of any author whatsoever (including the spelling cranks like Spenser and Milton)—is the theoretical or artifactual one. An editor's duty is to establish his author's text, and since that text was originally oral and becomes oral again whenever it is properly read, what theory requires is a written text so spelled and punctuated that it can be translated back into an approximation of the oral original with the maximum certainty and the minimum difficulty or delay. Modern spelling offers no difficulty to the modern reader, whereas an obsolete one often does, and modern punctuation is both more precise and more flexible than earlier systems, because our range of stops is so much wider. (We can add colon, exclamation mark, question mark, dash, round or square brackets, and dots to Shakespeare's three: comma, full stop, occasional semicolon.) This is not to deny that passages may occasionally occur when the older spelling and punctuation may suggest a subtlety that modern orthography cannot convey, but such passages—like the obsolete words or archaic usages—can always be elucidated in the editor's notes. Indeed, without such elucidation the modern reader is likely to miss the subtlety anyway.

Old Spelling editors have lacked hitherto the logical courage of their erroneous convictions. If their object really is to retain the peculiarities of their author's spelling and punctuation, then they should simply look much harder at whatever survives in their author's autograph and emend those copyists' and compositors' forms that tend to displace or obscure authorial peculiarities in the first editions. A clear case of such editorial cold feet occurs in the elaborate edition of Thomas Dekker's plays recently prepared for us by Fredson Bowers, who has been one of the noisiest advocates of original 'accidentals' (to employ Greg's omnibus term for spelling, punctuation, capitalization, and hyphening). Now Dekker also contributed a short scene to *Sir Thomas More*, and this autograph passage shows Dekker consistently using the spellings *mee* (8 examples), *bee* (for *be*, 4 examples), *hee* (1 example). The idiosyncrasy is also confirmed by occasional spellings in the first editions. Thus *The Shoemaker's Holiday* (1600), which was printed, according to Bowers, from Dekker's own 'foul papers', or at worst from a copy of them, has in its first act alone *hee* (6), *wee* (3), *shee* (1), *mee* (1). Since Dekker clearly preferred a double *e* in the personal pronouns oughtn't an Old Spelling editor to emend the printer's single *e*'s elsewhere? But Bowers retains the jumble of Dekker and compositorial forms without explanation or apology.

The Bowers edition of Dekker illustrates another textual embarrassment into which Old Spellers are often forced. I take two examples from the first scene of *The Honest Whore*, Part I: 'I pry' (for 'pray', I.i.9); 'Froxen and dried up' (for 'frozen', I.i.27). These are almost certainly misprints, which a modern reader rather resents having to emend off his own bat, as it were; but since neither word occurs in the *More* fragment either or both *may* be genuine Dekkerisms, and so Bowers is compelled by his Old Spelling premises to give them the benefit of such a doubt. There are dozens of similar instances. That their preservation adds anything of literary significance to Dekker's meaning is not clear to me.

An alternative spelling formula would be to use the earlier forms that come closest to suggesting how the plays of Shakespeare and the other Elizabethans were originally pronounced when acted or read aloud. Many editions of Chaucer normalize *his* spelling with some such end in view, and on the face of it the proposal is not an unattractive one—though it could not be put into actual effect in Shakespeare's case until the philologists are in greater agreement than they are today on how people like Shakespeare, Dekker, and Richard Burbage did pronounce their vowels and consonants. But is the project sound theoretically? Does the oral substratum in the literary artifact commit us to a historical reconstruction of either the author's or the original performers' or readers' pronunciations? The former possibility is particularly intriguing. Since William Blake and John Keats both spoke English with a cockney accent it is conceivable that we ought to read 'The Tiger' as follows:

> Toiger, toiger, burnin' broight . . .

And 'Ode to a Nightingale' as follows:

> Theow was not born for death, himmortal bird;
> Now 'ungry generitions tread thee deown!

The conclusion does seem to follow logically from the recommendations already quoted from Greg; the 'individualities of speech' Greg was so anxious to retain, as the context of the passage makes clear, were *primarily* eccentricities of authorial pronunciation.

An author's pronunciation has its snob interest, of course. Until Edison's recordings of 'Come into the Garden, Maud', 'The Charge of the Light Brigade', and other poems were discovered the other day who would have thought Tennyson's speech was so grossly 'non-U'? But nobody has suggested that the modern reader of Tennyson ought to try and copy that rough Lincolnshire growl. The theoretical position is perfectly plain here. The sounds and half-sounds that constitute the physical substratum of the literary artifact originate in the speech of the society to which the author belongs. As such they are public (not private). A particular speaker's private idiosyncrasies—whether they are physical (perhaps he has no roof to his mouth?) or local (he may have been brought up in Germany!)—are extraneous to the public communication he engages in whenever he speaks. If he is to be understood we have, as it were, to subtract the idiosyncrasies, so converting his utterances into good English, the public linguistic medium. In the case of the printed word the position is even clearer. Unless a special spelling is employed, or a special stage direction is inserted, a standard pronunciation is implicitly commanded in the mere fact of publication. The word itself, 'publication', makes that clear.

The bigger theoretical headache is the proper pronunciation today of a literary work composed in the standard English of another period—or indeed of another English-speaking community. (Ought you to read T. S. Eliot with an American or a British accent?)

The commonsense solution—the one we all adopt in practice—is to modernize or anglicize (or americanize) whatever we decently can. Not Chaucer, of course, or *The Playboy of the Western World*, but roughly everything not overtly dialectal written in England since about 1500 as well as everything not specifically marked off as Anglo-Scots, Anglo-Irish, or Anglo-American. And on the whole theory endorses our practice. But the theoretical argument has not been ventilated, as far as I know, and it carries with it important implications about the nature of literary evidence.

I shall use the modern educated reader as my point of theoretical departure, together with his logical correlative the modern educated writer. Readers write; writers read. For both of them the literary process terminates on the printed page, though the writer's *terminus ad quem* is of course the reader's *terminus a quo*.

Moreover, the psychological sequence is the same in both cases, if also in reverse directions. For the reader that complex intellectual emotional response which is literature's real *raison d'être* occurs *after* the eyes' first encounter with the printed series of letters; for the author, however, his creative counterpart, inspiration—the red hot coal of Shelley's image in *A Defence of Poetry*—comes before even the oral symbols have received public utterance. But the crucial events are internal, mental, subjective. They are both difficult therefore to describe; introspection does its best, but the material on which it is working is so fluid and indistinct that a strict analysis finds itself almost helpless. Nevertheless two propositions will probably find general acceptance: (i) The subjective response of a sympathetic reader at the moment of maximum literary intensity is similar in kind if not in degree to what an author experiences in the heat of literary creation; (ii) at the two psychic peaks in the cycle of literary expression and impression the strictly verbal element becomes subordinate. It would be untrue to say that odd phrases (ghosts of 'the best words in the best order') are not present at all in the moment of authorial inspiration or a reader's ecstasy, but at this point the inner speech is a muted language. Compared to what it becomes later for the author in his panoply of rhetoric and to what it has been earlier in all its linguistic complexity for the reader the verbal tissue, both phonetic and semantic, is only half-present. Sound and meaning are subordinate to an inner vision, the moment of 'illusion'.

If this account of the literary experience is accepted, with however many qualifications, it must follow that the precise pronunciation of each syllable, the exact allocation of stress between words or parts of words, do not really matter. Do they ever really matter, except perhaps as the shibboleths of class or material differences? Let me quote to you Saussure, the founder of modern descriptive linguistics:

> The important thing in the word is not the sound *per se* but the phonic differences that makes it possible to distinguish this word from all others. . . . Phonemes are characterized not, as one might think, by their own positive quality but simply

by the fact that they are distinct. . . . Proof of this is the latitude that speakers have between points of convergence in
the pronunciation of distinct sounds. . . . I can even pronounce
the French *r* like German *ch* in Bach, doch, etc., though in
German I could not use *r* instead of *ch*, as German uses both
and must keep them apart.[1]

The phonetic latitude that Saussure was describing in this
passage pinpoints the difference between 'correct' speech and
mere intelligibility. The social overtones of 'good' English are
thought to be part of an author's meaning, but they are not often
heard as such in the intimacies of a reader's inner speech. Grammar tends to go by the board in the same way. A psychologist's
summary may be worth quoting:

> Investigators of the reading consciousness report that inner
> speech during silent reading is practically universal. . . . Most
> of us, in reading, use the inner speech extensively although
> heightening our speech by clipping our words and telescop-
> ing our sentences . . . in reading foreign languages we adopt
> the pronunciation of our native tongue; and, in general, we
> sacrifice enunciation and distinctness to rapidity; words to
> meaning.[2]

Who of us would claim to be guiltless in these matters—not
only in reading the newspaper but in reading Shakespeare or
Milton too? We need not however agree with this psychologist
that such reading represents a sacrifice of anything. The 'enunciation and distinctness' of speech that we are said to sacrifice are
surely supererogatory in inner speech, when there is nobody
listening but ourselves. The clipping of words and telescoping of
sentences can't matter either—provided we have identified the
words correctly and got the proper gist of the sentences. This is
not, as the psychologist says, sacrificing words to meaning (the
two terms imply each other, are two aspects of the same thing),
but simply adjusting outer speech to inner speech. Once the
reader has assimilated the writer's outer speech, the mere
mechanisms of communication fall away and what is left to the
reader is the writer's *essential* meaning, which however is still
basically verbal. At this point, therefore, which is the reader's
terminus ad quem, the reader has penetrated at least in part into

[1] Ferdinand de Saussure, *Course in General Linguistics*, translated [with
minor corrections by me] from the French by Wade Baskin, 1959, pp. 118–
119.
[2] June E. Downey, *Creative Imagination: studies in the psychology of
literature* (1929), pp. 45–6.

the writer's *terminus a quo*, the inner speech of original composition or, if you like, 'inspiration'.

What in the meantime is left of the literary artifact's physical substratum? Not much, it might seem. The aural/oral element that was so prominent in medieval and Renaissance literature with its plays, minstrel-recitations, songs and ballads (as well as the reading aloud in monasteries and churches, the long Protestant sermons, etc.) has been in continuous retreat since the invention of printing. But even in public speech, or in theatrical representation, it seems impossible not to agree with Saussure that the main thing linguistically is not the sound proper but the 'sound-image', the inner psychological imprint of a sound. In learning a language sound-image cannot at first be divorced from sound, but before long the sound-image functions mentally without any actual sound accompaniment at all. It is in sound-images that we do our thinking and the inner speech is conducted primarily in them. Because the sound-image is psychological rather than physical it is necessarily more abstract than outer speech, a fact which explains both the latitude of intelligible pronunciation defined by Saussure and the grammatical looseness described by our psychologist. This essential abstractness of language *qua* language is confirmed by the literary evidence.

The fact, for example, that classical scholars of different centuries and countries have pronounced Latin and Greek in very different ways, most of them demonstrably incorrect, has not prevented them reaching a remarkable degree of uniformity as to who are the best classical authors, which are the best readings in classical texts, even which are the correct interpretations of this or that crucial passage. Even classical prosody—which one might think *must* hinge on questions of pronunciation—seems, except for the *minutiae*, to be within sight of general scholarly agreement. Prosody indeed provides the most conclusive confirmation of the loose, almost abstract, character of oral sound in the process of literary communication. I will confine myself to one example. In Western prosody the basic element is the line—with the underlying metrical pattern consisting in a relationship between adjoining lines either of temporal identity or of some simple arithmetical ratio of it (e.g., 6 to 5 in the Latin elegiac couplet). Thus in the epic, whether it is Greek, Roman, French, Italian, or English, each line is always of the same 'length' (a term admittedly with different meanings in the various languages). This is, I suppose, the basic metrical premise. In linguistic fact, however, line-length—whether it is measured by vowel-length or the number of syllables or stresses—is always being extended or abbreviated by the presence or absence of grammatical pause. For example, the last three lines of *Paradise Lost*, Book I:

> A thousand Demi-Gods on golden seats,
> Frequent and full. After short silence then
> And summons read, the great consult began.

The three lines are of equal length metrically (the same number of syllables, the same total of stresses and half-stresses per line). But both grammar and sense demand a pause at the full stop in the middle of the second line. The pause even receives a sort of onomatopoeic confirmation in the three words following it ('After short silence'), and yet no one could describe this line either as unmetrical or even as a metrical 'licence'. And of course there are hundreds of similar enjambments in every epic or narrative poem. It seems evident then that metre does not measure poetry as it is actually recited or read aloud, but as it exists in our half-spoken inner speech—which is ungrammatically almost continuous, a stream of ghostly sound that permits itself to be marked off arbitrarily in regular lines and then flows illogically over all the weirs and dams of syntax and punctuation. W. H. Auden has described 'the opposition and interplay of the line stop and the sentence stop' as 'a subtlety which can be one of the great charms of poetry'.[1] No doubt he is right. But a literary theorist will want some explanation of the phenomenon. I suggest that Auden's interplay occurs at that point where inner speech (phonetically continuous, though divisible metrically) becomes outer speech (phonetically discontinuous because grammatical). The subtlety is comparable then to a pun or a metaphor: two disparities (the sentence end and the metre's non-end) are coaxed by the poet's art into a surprising coincidence.

I conclude, then, in the light of the philological, psychological, and prosodic evidence, that no literary purpose is served by exact phonetic reproduction in modern editions of the pronunciations current when a literary artifact was originally composed. If the work falls into the Modern English period—or if the difference between writer's English and reader's English is no greater than that between Britain's and the United States's today—I see no

[1] *Poets of the English Language*, ed. W. H. Auden and Norman Holmes Pearson, New York, 1950, II, xviii.

theoretical objection whatever to the editor's adopting the spelling, punctuation, and capitalization of his own age or country. If a word or form is obsolete, he will, of course, become a normalizing Old Speller for that one word or form. But with this exception anything less than total modernization would seem to be pedantry or tushery. Let us leave 'Ye Olde Tea-Shoppe' to Wardour Street and/or Madison Avenue.

II

Greg never recanted in so many words his doctrine of the primacy of material transmission irrespective of a text's meaning. However he comes near to doing it in 'The Rationale of Copy-text' (1949).[1] This important paper begins by acknowledging the force of A. E. Housman's arguments in 'The Application of Thought to Textual Criticism'. Now Housman had conducted that devastating foray into German methods wholly in terms of 'sense' (and nonsense), and the change in Greg's theoretical position can be measured by comparing his attitude to Housman in 'Bibliography—an Apologia'. In 1932 the 'almost mechanical' methods of bibliography were contrasted, very much to their favour, with Housman's 'metacritical' procedure. ('To Professor Housman', he wrote then, in mock-admiration, 'it is the metacritical that is alone worthy of a gentleman and a scholar'.) By 1949, however, the 'attempt to reduce textual criticism to a code of mechanical rules' is the object of Greg's censure. The final McKerrow formula—as elaborated in *Prolegomena for the Oxford Shakespeare*—of taking all the accidentals from the first authoritative edition and all the substantive changes from the last authoritative edition is specified as one such 'mechanical rule'. Here Greg is at his best:

> It is impossible to exclude individual judgement from editorial procedure: it operates of necessity in the all-important matter of the choice of copy-text and in the minor one of deciding what readings are possible and what are not; why, therefore, should the choice between possible readings be withdrawn from its competence? Uniformity of result at the hands of different editors is worth little if it means only uniformity in error; and it may not be too optimistic a belief that the judgement of an editor, fallible as it must necessarily be, is likely to bring us closer to what the author wrote than the enforcement of an arbitrary rule.

[1] In *Collected Papers*, ed. Maxwell, 1966.

The pen is Greg's, but the voice might almost be that of Housman denouncing a blind dependence on the 'best text'. What is particularly exhilarating is the apparent abandonment of 'bibliography' and the once sacred cow of material transmission.

Unfortunately Greg cannot resist one mechanical rule himself. In the case of a later reading that is clearly authorial being substituted for an earlier equally authentic one a modern editor should prefer the later reading 'whether the editor himself considers it an improvement or not' (387). As an example he gives a revision by Ben Jonson in his *Masque of Gipsies*. In the original version 'a wise Gypsie . . . maunds'; in the revised version *maunds* has become *stalkes*—though, Greg adds, 'no reasonable critic would prefer it to the original'.

Just as the ability to spell and punctuate correctly does not necessarily carry with it the ability to write well, in the literary sense, so there is no guarantee that creative talent includes that of revising successfully. Some writers improve their work by revising it—Pope, for example; others, like Wordsworth, tend to spoil whatever they rewrite. There are four versions of Fitz-Gerald's *Rubáiyát*, each in general a deterioration upon its predecessor. Keats's final view, as he gave it to Richard Woodhouse, was that correction of one's text was a mistake, unless it occurred in the process of composition:

> He never corrects, unless perhaps a word here or there should occur to him as preferable to an expression he has already used—He is impatient of correcting, and says he would rather burn the piece in question and write another or something else—'My judgment, (he says) is as active while I am actually writing as my imagination. In fact all my faculties are strongly excited, and in their full play—And shall I afterwards, when my imagination is idle, and the heat in which I wrote, has gone off, sit down coldly to criticise when in Possession of only one faculty, what I have written, when almost inspired.'[1]

The methodological conclusion that textual criticism must clearly draw is that each reading or version should be judged on its merits. And those merits are essentially literary. Exactly the same criteria apply to a reading, provided it can be shown to be authorial, as to the work in which it occurs. 'Is this the best reading?' is simply a miniature form of 'Is this a good work of

---

[1] *The Keats Circle*, I 1948, 128. Abbreviations expanded and deletions ignored. Hyder E. Rollins, the editor of this collection of Keatsiana, dates the conversation July (?) 1820.

literature?' In textual criticism the approach is known as eclecticism, but eclecticism does not deserve the reproach in which it has recently been held. All criticism is necessarily eclectic: some writers are selected by the consensus of informed opinion as better than others. Bibliography, in the widest sense of the word —a sense that includes palaeography, typography and such lesser sciences as bibliopegy (expertise in binding) and the history of paper—has from time to time its contribution to make, but its subordinate character must not be forgotten. To claim more for it is to offend against literature 'as in itself it really is'.

As a colophon to this paper I shall add the closing words of *Textual Criticism* by Paul Maas, an eminent twentieth-century German classicist:

> The core of practically every problem in textual criticism is a problem of *style*, and the categories of stylistics are still far less settled than those of textual criticism. And there is the further danger that the editor in making his recension may fall into the habit of forgetting his responsibility for being continually alive to the author's style. Here I may be allowed to end by recalling a remark of Richard Bentley's in his note on Horace, *Odes* 3. 27. 15, *nobis et ratio et res ipsa centum codicibus potiores sunt.* This remark has always tempted some scholars to misuse it, and it will always continue to do so; but it is true.[1]

The meaning and the facts of the case are worth more to the student of literature than a hundred cancels or compositors. If he is prudent he will acquaint himself with the fundamentals of bibliography, but problems of style must always predominate. Indeed, if we go on reading Greg and neglect McKerrow or Fredson Bowers and their progeny, it is because he wrote such excellent English—muscular, lucid and superbly phrased. And if his textual theorizing was often wrong, especially in his earlier papers, his contempt for mere bibliophily was constant and undisguised. In general, however, bibliography must be considered a by-product or appendage of book-collecting, that 'ritual of conspicuous waste' particularly favoured by English and American millionaires. Pope's Lord Timon (of the *Epistle to Burlinton*) would have recognized his successors in such men as Folger (who did his best to 'corner' the Shakespeare First Folio, finally

[1] Pp 40–1 of the translation by Barbara Flower (1958).

assembling eighty copies) and Henry E. Huntington (who bought everything and read nothing):

> In Books, not Authors, curious is my Lord;
> To all, their dated Backs he turns you round,
> These Aldus printed, those Du Sueil has bound.
> Lo some are Vellom, and the rest as good,
> For all his Lordship knows, but they are Wood.

Appropriately the patron saint of book-collecting today is the forger Thomas J. Wise, who was Greg's and McKerrow's colleague in the Bibliographical Society. By a poetic or bibliographical justice Wise's forgeries of non-existent first editions of the Victorian classics now fetch more in the auction-room than the authentic 'firsts' in mint condition!

3

Shakespeare's Laundry Bills: The Rationale of External Evidence*

Shakespearian scholarship is entitled, like any other reputable human activity, to its own comic mythology. The laundry bills—they are entirely hypothetical objects, of course—are a nice *reductio ad absurdum* of external evidence pursued for its own sake, a sort of *ne plus ultra* of 'pure' literary research. I believe Leslie Stephen was the inventor of this particular conceit. 'It does not follow', Stephen wrote in a review of the Brownings' letters that is reprinted in *Studies of a Biographer*, 'that because I want fact not fiction I therefore want all the facts, big and small; the poet's washing bills, as well as his early drafts of great works.'[1] The mythic figure was revived, or concocted independently, by T. S. Eliot in the penultimate paragraph of 'The Function of Criticism', one of his early essays Dr Leavis most admires. Eliot's central theme is that the critical gift *par excellence* is 'a very highly developed sense of fact':

> And any book, any essay, any note in *Notes and Queries*, which produces a fact even of the lowest order about a work of art is a better piece of work than nine-tenths of the most

* *Shakespeare Jahrbuch* 98 (1962), 51–63.
[1] Ser. 2, III (1902), 30.

pretentious critical journalism, in journals or in books. We assume, of course, that we are masters and not servants of facts, and that we know that the discovery of Shakespeare's laundry bills would not be of much use to us; but we must always reserve final judgment as to the futility of the research which has discovered them, in the possibility that some genius will appear who will know of a use to which to put them.[1]

Since Mr Eliot began a recent lecture ('The Frontiers of Criticism') by reaffirming the doctrines of 'The Function of Criticism' —'I was glad to find nothing positively to contradict my present opinions'[2]—I suppose he sticks to the laundry bills. It may be useful therefore to take up the argument where he has left it. Some issues of considerable practical and contemporary importance are involved.

Opposed to 'fact' in the Eliot schema is 'opinion'. There is a hierarchy of facts, though what distinguishes a fact 'of the lowest order' from one of a higher order is not explained; but opinion, apparently, is always vicious:

> *fact* cannot corrupt taste; it can at worst gratify one taste—a taste for history, let us say, or antiquities or biography—under the illusion that it is assisting another. The real corrupters are those who supply opinion or fancy; and Goethe and Coleridge are not guiltless—for what is Coleridge's *Hamlet*: is it an honest inquiry as far as the data permit, or is it an attempt to present Coleridge in an attractive costume?[3]

I do not propose to attempt a defence of Goethe and Coleridge here; the Romantic interpretation of *Hamlet* is not likely to corrupt much taste in the 1960s that would not be corrupted anyway. It is the status of Shakespearian 'fact' in general that needs investigation and perhaps deflation. The monuments of scholarship raised by McKerrow, Greg and Chambers—are they in retrospect more than impeccable works of reference for the books those intellectual giants never wrote—perhaps, their premises being what they were, never *could* have written?

The laundry bills' claim to scholarly attention is presumably based on the critical doctrine that a poet's style is, or ought to be, the man. It seems to follow, then, that every aspect of Shakespeare the man must connect in some way with Shakespeare the writer. The exact connection awaits that critical genius with the supremely developed sense of fact of Eliot's hypothetical future,

[1] *Selected Essays* (1932), p. 33.
[2] *On Poetry and Poets* (1957), p. 103.   [3] *Selected Essays*, p. 33.

but we can guess how the laundry bills might be used if they were ever discovered. They might demonstrate, for example, that Shakespeare changed his linen every day. I do not deny that such biographical minutiae have a certain interest. What porridge had John Keats? The difficulty is to connect them, directly or even indirectly, with the actual words and word-orders of Shakespeare's or Keats's plays and poems. If it is claimed, for example, that the passion for clean linen would corroborate the absence of sexual cynicism in Shakespearian drama, are we not back in the proscribed area of 'opinion'?

The relationship between external evidence (fact) and internal evidence (opinion) needs restatement. As against the Eliot antithesis between the two procedures the formula I prefer is an interdependence of *relevant* fact and *relevant* opinion. The definition of relevance will vary with the scholarly context, but in Shakespearian studies it seems reasonable to posit as our central criterion a relevance to the meaning of Shakespeare's text. The kind of antiquarianism, therefore, that is symbolized by the laundry bills must prove its right of entry by a demonstration of its textual relevance; equally a Shakespearian critical opinion must survive exactly the same test. Coleridge's interpretation of *Hamlet* on this basis is erroneous, in so far as it is erroneous, not because it is disguised autobiography but because it does not make sense when confronted with the play's text; it is *irrelevant* to it.

But if textual relevance is the criterion that we must apply both to Shakespearian 'fact' and to Shakespearian 'opinion or fancy', this is not to say that relevant textual fact is the same thing as relevant textual opinion. Rather they are two stages, both equally indispensable, in a single process. It might be put this way: an elementary understanding of the separate words, images, theatrical situations, modes of characterization, etc., has to precede an appreciation of the combinations or sequences of such dramatic constituents. In other words, to a greater or less degree Shakespeare, or indeed any other writer, is for all of us a sort of foreign language that has just to be learnt. First of all, then, in the order of logic, we need the facts (external evidence); the relevant opinions (internal evidence) come later. If the logical order of these events is reversed or confused, error or irrelevance is likely to break in.

Suppose, for example, I am challenged to make out a case for the emendation 'a' talked of green fields' (which was proposed by Theobald's 'Gentleman sometime deceas'd'[1] and was supported by Tennyson's friend Spedding, the editor of Bacon) against the Folio's 'a Table of greene fields' and Theobald's own 'a' babbled of green fields'. What evidence am I likely to use? What would the order be in which I ought to call my witnesses?

I shall obviously be well advised to begin with the kind of evidence that would be acceptable in a court of law. My first witness, then, would probably be Hand D's scene in *Sir Thomas More*, which is approximately contemporary with *Henry V* and provides four items of palaeographical relevance:

1. Doll Williamson, a character of the same general type as the Hostess, uses 'a' (so spelled) for the unemphatic form of 'he' ('a keepes a plentyfull shrevaltry, and a made my Brother Arther watchin Serjant Safes yeoman').

2. Commas, like the other stops, are rare in D and always introduce a new clause; the comma in Doll's 'shrevaltry, and a made' would be an exact parallel to the Folio's 'for his Nose was as sharp as a Pen, and a Table of greene fields', if 'Table' is a misprint for a verb like *talked* or *babbled*.

3. Since D reserves its initial capitals for the beginnings of sentences or proper names, the *T* in the Folio's 'Table' must be the compositor's contribution.

4. Theobald's reading assumes that Shakespeare wrote 'babld' which was mis-read 'table'. D's *d* is certainly almost indistinguishable from its *e*, but its initial *ba* is always easily legible (e.g., 1. 75, 'their babyes at their backes') and is not at all likely to be confused with its initial *ta* (e.g., 1. 80, 'taught'), which is also easily legible. On the other hand, D's *k* might be confused with a *b*. A compositor meeting what looked like *talbe* (but was really *talkd*) may be excused for emending it to *table*. (John Munro points out that there are two *b* for *k* misprints in *King Lear*.)[2]

My second witness might well be this Folio compositor—who in this passage, to judge by the spellings, is apparently Jaggard's Compositor A. The obvious objection to 'a Table of greene fields' is that it does not seem to make sense. But sentences that do not make sense are the characteristic failing of Compositor A. Whereas his fellows tended, even in their most careless moments, to look beyond the word to its immediate context, A (a simple-

---

[1] *Shakespeare Restored* (1726), p. 138.
[2] *The London Shakespeare* (1858), IV, 1055n.

minded man) was content if each word made sense by itself. Provided each separate word that he set was a real English word A was satisfied. A specimen of his handiwork is to be found at the end of the Hostess's speech:

> *then I felt to his knees, and so up-pear'd, and upward, and all was as cold as any stone.*

The quartos, F3 and modern editions correct 'up-pear'd' to 'upward', which is obviously the right reading. But for A, proceeding word by word instead of clause by clause, 'up-pear'd' was good enough; it was after all a possible English word. A's methods, half-baked though they may seem, have the great virtue of approximate fidelity to the copy. What he has mis-read was really there; he does not insert words of his own to try and make sense of a passage that has defeated him. We may be certain, then, that something that looked like *a table* was actually in the manuscript from which A was working. Our range of possible emendation is therefore greatly narrowed. Indeed, to the best of my knowledge, *babbled* and *talked* are so far the only alternatives to *table* that have ever been proposed. To those editors, then, who struggle desperately to coax some meaning from the Folio text A's frequent contentment with meaninglessness is, I should say, a sufficient rejoinder.

My third witness is the 'bad' or 'reported' quarto of 1600. Q omits the crucial phrase altogether, rearranging the passage as follows:

> *His nose was as sharp as a pen: For when I saw him fumble with the sheetes, And talk of floures, and smile upon his fingers ends I knew there was no way but one.*

It is worth noticing that F's 'play with Flowers' is corrupted in Q to 'talk of floures': the verb may well be a relic from the lost clause. Now *babble* is a more memorable word than *talk*. If the words omitted had been *babbled of green fields*, would not Q have preferred *babble of flowers* to *talk of flowers*? A significant feature of the passage in Q is that, apart from omissions and changes of word-order, Q's deviations from F are all trivial, such as 'when' instead of 'after'. The one exception is 'talk'—an exception that would prove the rule if F's 'Table' is indeed a misprint of *talkd*.

The three witnesses hitherto called all belong to the honourable department of external evidence known as textual criticism.

And the points that have emerged in the analysis of their evidence
are certainly relevant to the problem to which I am committed,
which *is* a controversial detail of Shakespeare's text. The embarrassing thing, though, about them is the disproportion between
the two short disputed words and the hundreds and hundreds
that my commentary, which is far from complete, seems to
require. A mountain of disquisition and the molehill of *a' talked*!
Unlike the work of the detective in real life, which is normally the
bringing to justice of serious crime, textual criticism does not
carry its own justification with it. After all, what was Compositor
A really guilty of? The peccadillo of momentary carelessness! All
this fuss over two words seems to verge on pedantry.

But I have two more witnesses to call—the dramatic critic and
the literary critic. With them a more humane series of values
enters into the argument. To the dramatic critic the Hostess
(Mrs Quickly in *2 Henry IV* and *The Merry Wives*) is a masterpiece of comic characterization, but a masterpiece in virtue of
what she says rather than what she does. It is her mode of speech
—brilliantly breathless, touchingly domestic and comically mala-
propist—that enchants him. She has an idiom of her own that is
maintained with extraordinary consistency throughout the three
plays. It is the positiveness of this idiom that is fatal, I believe, to
all the various attempts that have been made to retain the Folio's
'and a Table' unemended, or with 'on' substituted for 'and'.
These emendations generally consist in an extension and elaboration of the Hostess's simile: Falstaff's nose is as sharp as a pen *on
a table covered with the green cloth usual in counting-houses*
(Henry Bradley), *and a memorial tablet pointed in Gothic fashion
in the green fields of a cemetery* (Percival R. Cole), *in an engrav-
ing of Sir Richard Grenville* (Leslie Hotson).[1] The pen in these
examples has been the ordinary quill-pen, but it too can be re-
interpreted and for Hilda Hulme it is *a device on a coat-of-arms,
the field vert*, and for John S. Tuckey *a mountain-peak rising
steeply from a tableland consisting of green fields*.[2] The game will
no doubt continue. As ways of making some sort of sense of the
Folio reading such interpretations deserve, I suppose, their modi-
cum of praise. But they lose all their plausibility once they are
put side by side with the Hostess's other similes. Compare these
elaborate and sophisticated analogies with those of *2 Henry IV*

[1] See *London Shakespeare* as above, and *TLS* 6 April 1956.
[2] *Essays in Criticism*, 6 (1956), 117–19, 486–91.

(IV ii): *red as any rose, rheumatic as two dry toasts, and 'twere on aspen leaf.* Or those of *Henry V* (apart from the pen): *honey-sweet, as any christom child, as any stone.* The Hostess's metaphors and similes are always short, colloquial, traditional. She has only one simile in all her appearances that she may be supposed to have made up herself, and that, significantly, is in *The Merry Wives*: 'a great round Beard, like a Glovers pairing-knife'. That paring-knife does not ring quite true to me, but it is naïve compared to the elaborate Wycherley-type witticisms attributed to her by Henry Bradley and the others. She just doesn't talk like that.

The dramatic critic's testimony can be put in peremptory terms: such interpretations have only one defect—*they ruin the Hostess's part.* It would be far better to leave the whole clause out, as Q does, than to spoil her best speech with this sort of laboured and quite uncharacteristic rubbish. No such objection can be raised to *babbled* or *talked.* Both words are probably within the range of the Hostess's vocabulary, though *babbled* (unlike *talked*) does not appear elsewhere in her part. The word may well have been a bit beyond her; it only occurs nine times in Shakespeare, six of these being *babbling,* and it is usually confined to the upper-class characters. (But Dogberry uses it once: 'for the Watch to babble and to talke, is not tollerable'.)

I have one more witness to call—the literary critic. As between *babbled* and *talked,* the first question the critic will want to ask is the exact difference in meaning between the two words at the end of the sixteenth century. The quick answer is that *talk* had much the same range of meanings as today, but that *babble* in all the Shakespearian passages—including two from *Titus Andronicus* which may be pseudo-Shakespearian—meant only one thing, viz., 'to talk excessively or inopportunely, to chatter' (*O.E.D.*). Whereas to *talk* is neutral, the speech may be either silly or sensible, to *babble,* as Shakespeare uses the word, always carries a dyslogistic sense of silly speech. The critical or stylistic problem, then, is whether a neutral meaning or a dyslogistic meaning is more appropriate in the context of this passage. The sentences concerned could, I suggest, be summarized as follows:

> *When I saw him fumbling* (foolishly) *with the sheets, and playing* (foolishly) *with flowers, and smiling* (foolishly) *at his fingertips, I knew he would soon be dead. His nose looked* (ridiculously) *pointed, and he talked* (foolishly) *about green fields.*

The object of this summary is twofold: (i) to make it clear that the five traditional symptoms of approaching death form a continuous series of parallel items; (ii) to show that the five symptoms are all to some degree grotesque and even absurd. And by adding the non-italic adverbs in brackets I have tried to bring out the *implicit* character of the absurdities. The Hostess does not say in so many words that the first four symptoms are foolish or ridiculous, but we certainly respond to them as such; to maintain the continuity of the imagery therefore the fifth symptom must also be only implicitly absurd. To read *babbled* (= talked foolishly) is to break the semantic series by making the comment explicit; no such objection can be made to the apparently neutral *talked*.

I shall rest the case for *a' talked* at this point. My immediate concern is not with the superior plausibility of the Deceased Gentleman's emendation so much as with the general character of the items of evidence on which an emendation such as his must depend. The evidence has been reasonably representative, I think, if by no means complete. One very significant point that emerges in analysis is a difference of objectives in the external evidence (Hand D, Compositor A, and the 'reported' quarto) and the internal evidence (the consistency of dramatic idiom, the stylistics of serial imagery). They cannot be used to prove the same thing. The external evidence has combined to demonstrate *what Shakespeare probably wrote*, namely *talkd*, in the minuscules of the secretary hand; on the other hand, the internal evidence has been concerned to show *what Shakespeare must have meant*, namely a popular and 'neutral' kind of talk that is not brought out satisfactorily in the other interpretations or emendations.

In this instance what was probably written and what must have been meant overlap; they will normally do so. But they do not necessarily coincide, and if a divergence can be established what Shakespeare wrote will have to be corrected, so far as that is possible, by what he must be presumed to have meant.

The point is easily demonstrated. Heminge's and Condell's testimony that 'what he thought, he uttered with that easinesse that wee have scarce received from him a blot in his papers' must mean that Shakespeare's manuscripts showed little sign of revision. But anyone writing *currente calamo* is bound to have some words that have been miswritten, or even left out altogether, and the punctuation is sure to be more or less imperfect. Some revision, however slight, some final tidying-up, is always necessary. Hand D's scene is typical. The number of minims in sequences like *in* or *un* is incorrect seven times in the 147 lines, and there are also, according to Greg, 'slips', 'errors', malformed letters, a word the writer 'forgot to cross out' and another in which 'the writer's intention is quite obscure'.[1] Finally D's punctuation, or absence of punctuation, is wildly erratic and inconsistent. If this scene is typical one must agree with Ben Jonson: 'would he had blotted a thousand'. I do not mean that the scene in *Sir Thomas More* is riddled with textual cruxes. This is not so. The errors and omissions are most of them easily corrected. But it remains true that what Shakespeare meant in this scene has to be recovered from what he wrote by the application of exactly the same methods that editors use with the printed texts of the early editions. An autograph differs only in degree, not in kind, from other texts

Greg's first editorial rule—'The aim of a critical edition should be to present the text, so far as the available evidence permits, in the form in which we may suppose that it would have stood in a fair copy, made by the author himself, of the work as he finally intended it'[2]—stems from the Eliot illusion that 'fact' (external evidence) must be preserved at any cost from the corrupting influence of 'opinion'. An author's final intentions are buried with him and will never be known in their entirety, but even between his penultimate or antepenultimate intentions and the fairest fair copy in which they are written down there is always the possibility of accidental error. The last editorial word must still be with *what Shakespeare must have meant*; it is the final criterion between what is and is not error in *what Shakespeare wrote*. A reading only proves its correctness by its coherence with the context of meaning preceding it. It is true that the point of departure here is external evidence—the letters on the printed page or manuscript that present themselves to the reader as Shakespeare's play. But at this point a two-way process is necessarily started—first from the external text to the internal meanings it communicates to the reader, and then, as the meanings form themselves internally into a coherent aesthetic body, a reversal of direction from the reader's mind to the text, either confirming it or correcting it. A common or garden misprint is a simple example

[1] *Shakespeare's Hand in the Play of Sir Thomas More* (1923), pp. 230–243.
[2] *The Editorial Problem in Shakespeare*, 2nd edn. (1951), p. x.

of the process: we correct a misprint because it doesn't make
sense in its context.

The dead-end into which textual criticism is driven if it ignores
the stylistic core at the heart of every literary problem may be
illustrated by a passage from the trumpet-call against the critics
recently blown by Professor Fredson Bowers of the University of
Virginia:

> not much is changed whether Hamlet's father's bones were *in-
> terred* as in Q 2, or *inurned* as in the Folio (I iv 49). Yet I hold
> it to be an occupation eminently worth while, warranting any
> number of hours, to determine whether Shakespeare wrote
> one, or the other, or both. The decision, if clear-cut, might be
> crucial in the accumulation of evidence whether on the whole
> the Folio variants from the quarto *Hamlet* are corruptions,
> corrections, or revisions. If this is a problem no editor has
> fairly faced, neither should a literary critic be indifferent to
> the question. Depending upon what can be proved, some
> hundreds of readings will be affected if an editor decides that
> Shakespeare revised the text after its second quarto form; for
> in that case the Folio variants should be chosen in all but the
> most obvious cases of sophistication. Or he might decide that
> in only a few cases, where the second quarto compositors have
> corrupted the text, should the Folio readings take precedence
> over the generally authoritative second quarto.[1]

It is impossible not to warm to that 'occupation eminently
worth while, warranting any number of hours'. This is the heroic
spirit of scholarship. But an examination of the problem soon
shows that the respective status of *interred* and *inurned* can only
be finally determined from the internal evidence of style. The
bibliographical evidence is quite indecisive. No doubt Q2 does
derive more or less directly from Shakespeare's autograph, but its
Act I was set up, as Bowers agrees, either from a copy of the
'reported' Q1 partly corrected from the autograph, or (more
probably) from a special printing-house transcript of this corrected copy. Now Q1 also reads 'interr'd' here, and the possibility
must be faced that the reading is simply a mistake of the reporter's carelessly carried over into Q2. The Folio 'enurn'd' is certainly the *difficilior lectio*: whereas *inter* is a common Elizabethan
word, *inurn* has not been traced, I believe, before its occurrence
here and the word is probably a coinage of Shakespeare's. He
was fond of words of this type; the following verbs are not found
before Shakespeare according to the *O.E.D.*: *emball, embound,*

[1] *Textual and Literary Criticism* (1959), pp. 7–8.

enclog, endart, enrank, enridge, enschedule, entreasure, illume, immask, impaint, impleach, impress, inclip, incorpse, inhearse, injoint, inscroll, inship, insinew. In other words, on the textual evidence both readings are just about equally plausible. No more and no less.

Well, even the most cursory stylistic analysis can do better than that. It is clear from the preceding and succeeding lines that the elder Hamlet was buried and not cremated. 'Why thy Canoniz'd bones Hearsed in death, / Have burst their cerements, why the Sepulcher / . . . Hath op'd his ponderous and Marble jawes, / To cast thee up againe?' (F text, but Q1 and Q2 are in substantial agreement with it) can mean nothing else. In the face of these direct references to burial *inurn* can only be defended as a dead metaphor. But to impute to Shakespeare of all people an unconsciousness of the cremation-image latent in the word is indeed a desperate conjecture. When the play was originally written the line must surely have read, as in Q2,

Wherein we saw the quietly interr'd

Nevertheless *quietly inurned* has a very Shakespearian ring. I suspect it is the product of a later revision. It is a characteristic of authorial revision, especially of poetry, that it improves the immediate meaning at the cost of that of the wider context.[1] The ashes implied by *in-urn*, though nonsense in the passage as a whole, do go very nicely with *quietly*. This urn too is a bride of quietness, whereas the corpse that has been merely buried carries with it the faint suggestion of movement—the body disintegrates, the flesh decays, the worms enter on their grisly feast—and even a slight movement is surely incompatible with poetic quietness. Another stylistic consideration also points to *inurned* as a later revision by Shakespeare himself. In terms of style the original passage was not in Shakespeare's best manner. Like so much of his blank verse at this period (*Henry V* is the notorious example) it is 'Parnassian' in Hopkins's sense of the word: the words and images have come rather too easily; Shakespeare is relying too much on a rhetoric that resounds a little mechanically. If we can feel this, Shakespeare must have been aware of it too, and it is at least possible that he tried later on, when his blank verse had recovered from its 'Parnassian' phase, to touch the passage up.

---

[1] Some striking examples of this characteristic will be found in the New York edition of Henry James's collected novels and short stories.

Word for word, just as pure poetry, *quietly inurned* is an improvement on *quietly interred*, as it certainly is on *canonized bones*, and even on *ponderous and marble jaws*. Unfortunately however they make dramatic sense, and it doesn't.

I may be wrong. Even if I am right and *inurned* is a case of revision, that is still no guarantee, of course, as Professor Bowers would like us to believe, that the other Folio variants, apart from the 'obvious' corruptions, are also revisions by Shakespeare. They may be revisions by somebody else, Burbage, for example. Or Shakespeare may have revised just this one line: Professor Bowers's assumption that the presence of one revision guarantees a text's *general* revision is sheer guesswork. Each reading must be considered on its merits, external and internal, and both kinds of evidence must be used together, one as the corrective or supplement of the other. Our external–internal dialogue may often be prolonged and sometimes indecisive. That is the nature of most literary problems. But one thing is certain. Whether the enquiry is decisive or indecisive the last word in it must always be allowed to 'meaning' or 'style', not to Mr Eliot's 'fact' or Professor Bowers's 'bibliography'. Inconvenient though it may be for research purposes, the literary artifact remains obstinately in the last resort 'an intellectual thing', which cannot be pinned down on the laboratory bench. With that proviso we need not reject as points of critical departure even the laundry bills themselves.

4

Elementary, My Dear Hotson!•

The elementary proposition to which I invited Leslie Hotson's assent in 1951—soon after the publication of his *Shakespeare's Sonnets Dated and Other Essays*—was that any interpretation which turns a good poem, or indeed any work of literature, into one that is less good must be mistaken. Unless the new reading is superior *considered simply as literature*, whatever its other attractions may be, it can be dismissed out of hand.

That the sonnet numbered 107 in the first edition of Shakespeare's *Sonnets* is a good poem is not likely to be disputed, although it certainly has its obscurities—particularly in the notorious fifth line,

> The mortall Moone hath her eclipse indur'de.

Who or what is this mysterious moon? Various suggestions have been made, but Hotson was the first to identify it as the crescent formation popularly, though incorrectly, believed at the time to have been adopted by the Spanish galleons in the Armada. On this assumption, which Hotson reinforced by some less plausible hypotheses about two other sonnets, this poem—and with it most

• *Essays in Criticism*, 1 (1951).

if not all of Shakespeare's other sonnets—is re-dated 1588 or 1589 instead of the *circa* 1593 or later that earlier scholars had generally preferred.

On its first announcement the Hotson hypothesis had a considerable success. As Hotson himself put it in a letter to *The Times Literary Supplement*,[1] it 'met with very general acceptance'. A long review in this authoritative weekly had indeed described the new interpretation of the 'mortall Moone' as particularly 'convincing' and the whole essay as perhaps 'the most significant contribution to Shakespeare studies of recent years'.[2] I remember discussing the Armada proposal privately at the time with F. P. Wilson, a learned and humane Elizabethan scholar who was then the Merton Professor of English Literature at Oxford, and to my surprise I found that Hotson had convinced him. And J. G. McManaway, an American expert in the field, came out publicly on Hotson's side ('I think he is right') in the *Shakespeare Survey*, though he changed his mind later.[3]

As long as sonnet 107 is considered merely as a historical document, the phrase can no doubt bear the sense that Hotson attributes to it. In fact the Armada did not form itself into a series of crescents when sailing up the English Channel, but the references collected by Hotson and others make it clear that it was thought to have done so at the time. And the general illusion may well have been shared by Shakespeare. But, of course, the sonnet is only incidentally a historical document. Primarily, it is a poem, a very beautiful poem by the greatest of all English poets, and the final criterion in a disputed passage in such a poem can never be the plausibility of the interpretation of a historical allusion. The criterion must be a literary one. Does the proposed interpretation make good poetry or bad poetry? To put it more precisely, does the meaning now assigned to a particular word, phrase or passage reinforce the aesthetic structure of the work as a whole? It must be said that by this test the Hotson interpretation, ingenious though it certainly is, hasn't a leg to stand on.

As printed in the *Sonnets* of 1609, the only text of the poem with any claim to authority, sonnet 107 runs as follows:

> Not mine owne feares, nor the prophetick soule,
> Of the wide world, dreaming on things to come,

---

[1] 2 June 1950.   [2] *TLS*, 10 Feb. 1950.
[3] No. 3 (1950), p. 31. The change of mind I owe to a private letter from Professor McManaway.

Can yet the lease of my true loue controule,
Supposde as forfeit to a confin'd doome,
The mortall Moone hath her eclipse indur'de,
And the sad Augurs mock their owne presage,
Incertenties now crowne them-selues assur'de
And peace proclaimes Oliues of endlesse age.
Now with the drops of this most balmie time,
My love lookes fresh, and death to me subscribes
Since spight of him Ile live in this poore rime,
While he insults ore dull and speachlesse tribes,
    And thou in this shalt finde thy monument,
    When tyrants crests and tombs of brasse are spent.

In spite of some local obscurities, the sonnet's general meaning is clear enough. As in most of Shakespeare's other sonnets, the structural pattern is one of *parallels* between and within the three quatrains,[1] followed by a *contrast*, or *resolution*, in the final couplet. In 107 the parallels are between the poet's private world and the contemporary public world. The poet's 'true love' (Mr W.H. or the poet's happy relationship with him) has survived the disasters he himself had feared and others had prophesied;[2] the 'sad Augurs' had been similarly disproved in their expectations of the eclipse of the 'mortal Moone' in the public world. Instead of disasters 'peace' and a 'most balmie time' have in fact ensued. The third quatrain carries the parallel one stage further in a fusion of the poet's private and public worlds. All is well now in his relationship with Mr W.H. ('My love lookes fresh') and the poem will achieve literary immortality; in other words, it will be a public success.

[1] The use of parallelism as a central structural device has been demonstrated by Winifred M. T. Nowottny in 'Formal Elements in Shakespeare's Sonnets: Sonnets I–VI', *Essays in Criticism*, 2 (1952), 76–84. One of the best of the later sonnets in the series exemplifies the persistence of the device. This example is 73 ('That time of years thou maist in me behold'). In the first quatrain the poet compares his advanced years to the leafless boughs of a tree in winter; in the second quatrain the same point is made by comparing himself to the period of twilight that follows sunset; the third quatrain compares him to the ashes that are left after a fire has burnt itself out. The parallelism is emphasized by the repetition in each quatrain of the same initial formula: 'thou maist in me behold' (i): 'In me thou seest' (ii); 'In me thou seest' (iii). The final couplet begins with the same formula ('This thou percev'st') but achieves its *contrast* by introducing for the first time in this sonnet the miracle of Mr W. H.'s love for the so much older poet.
[2] The first two lines of the sonnet are paraphrased by W. G. Ingram and Theodore Redpath in their careful edition of *Shakespeare's Sonnets* (1964) as follows: 'Neither my own present fears, nor the premonitory dread which the world at large may have of mutability or impending disaster . . .'

Whatever their precise meanings may be, the parallel between
'prophetick' in line 1 and 'Augurs' in line 6 cannot be missed even
on the most casual reading. In each case the prophecy of woe had
been disproved. But if this is granted a parallel to 'my true love'
of the first quatrain is essential in the second quatrain. The
'Augurs' had made a gross error in prophesying disaster to some
public figure or institution that was dear to the poet *qua* citizen
as Mr W.H. was dear to him as an individual. Unless Shakespeare
has specified what this revered figure or institution was the whole
poetic argument collapses. The Hotson interpretation *must* be
mistaken, because the 'mortall Moone' is the only such figure or
institution metaphorically available in the second quatrain. *A
priori* this moon might be England or the Protestant cause, but
the metaphor would then be a strained one. The traditional
identification of the 'mortall Moone' with Queen Elizabeth is
clearly much more plausible. Elizabeth was often compared to
Diana, the virgin goddess of the moon, and she was a *mortal*
moon unlike either Diana or the physical moon because she was
human and already an old woman whose successor was a continually urgent political problem. I imagine the sonnet was written on the Queen's recovery from a serious illness. The metaphor
of a lunar eclipse had been used by Thomas Cecil in a letter to
Robert Cecil, written 9 July 1595, which appears to refer to
Elizabeth's illnesses that year: 'I left the moon in the wane at
my last being at the Court; I hear now it is a half moon again,
yet I think it will never be at the full, though I hope it will never
be eclipsed.'[1] It is possible that Shakespeare's sonnet was written
in the winter of 1595–96, when the Queen's health had been
completely restored. Or the reference may be to the rumour of a
similar crisis in 1599.[2] G. B. Harrison prefers Elizabeth's survival
of her Grand Climacteric (the sixty-third year, which was then
thought to be especially critical) in 1595–96.[3]

The object of this essay, however, is not to date this particular
historical allusion, but to exemplify the literary conditions that
any such allusion imbedded in a poem or a play must satisfy. As
I have suggested, the essential requirement is that interpretation
must add to—or at least not conflict with—the effectiveness of the

---

[1] *Salisbury Manuscripts*, Historical Manuscripts Commission, pt v (1894) 273.
The reference appears to be to Elizabeth, but is not certain.
[2] See 'The "Mortal Moon" Sonnet' in E. K. Chambers's *Shakespearian
Gleanings* (1944), pp. 130–43.
[3] 'The Mortal Moon', *TLS*, 29 Nov. 1928.

particular artifact considered simply as an aesthetic object. Does the Hotson interpretation satisfy this condition? At this point the stylistic analysis may be taken one stage further.

The Armada's defeat was in itself a *negative* occurrence, a possible disaster that the Queen and her subjects had 'endured' and not succumbed to. Now there is no explicit parallel to any such a disaster in the first quatrain, as we would expect to find if Hotson was right. Similarly, in the second quatrain he provides no *positive* equivalent to the first quatrain's celebration of the continuation of the happy relationship between the poet and Mr W.H. ('my true love').

Thus the anticipation of a structural parallelism between the two quatrains is not fulfilled. In the first quatrain the object threatened is specified, but the source of the threat is left undefined. And on the Hotson interpretation the situation is exactly reversed in the second quatrain. If the 'mortall Moone' is the Armada a threat at the public level is specified but the object threatened—England and England's ruler—has been omitted. And in that case not only is the parallelism not maintained but the whole of the second quatrain becomes a *non sequitur*. Why was it necessary to introduce the Armada at all? The sonnet when Hotsonized loses its poetic coherence.

The Hotson version must be wrong, then, because it denies by implication the structural parallels on which the poem hinges. Even if the sonnet is concerned, as he suggests, with the position in England in 1588, the Armada is still an irrelevance in line 5. Unless there are valid reasons for not positing a general parallelism between the first two quatrains, as is so strongly suggested by the 'prophetick'/'Augurs' sequence, Hotson's case collapses. Such reasons have not been propounded by him—or indeed as far as I am aware by anybody. But until they are produced the verdict of literary criticism must be that this interpretation is improbable *a priori* because it is poetically indefensible.

A more technical objection is Hotson's assumption that the 'mortall Moone' was necessarily a crescent moon. If Shakespeare had wanted the word to bear this sense he would certainly have qualified it with some such epithet as 'horned'. In the Elizabethan references to the Armada's moon-like formation cited by Hotson —'after the maner of a Moone crescent' (Petruccio Ubaldino), 'horned Moone of huge and mighty shippes' (James Lea), 'proportion of a half moone' (Sir William Winter), 'in forma

Semilunij' (Emanuel van Meteran)—a particular phase of the
moon is always specified.[1] Used without qualification the word,
then as now, was as likely to imply a circle as a crescent. In
Shakespeare's plays, indeed, in so far as any shape at all is implied, it is apparently always a circle, when the word is used
without a qualifying epithet. In *Midsummer Night's Dream*, III, i,
203, *Othello*, IV, ii, 77, and *Antony and Cleopatra*, V, ii, 80, the
human eye is compared to the moon (or vice versa); in *Richard II*,
II, iv, 10 and *1 Henry IV*, I, iii, 202, it is the human face. Eyes
and faces certainly suggest a full moon. The one exception is
Macbeth, III, v, 23–4, where Hecate speaks of 'a vap'rous drop'
hanging on 'the Corner of the Moone', which does no doubt imply
a crescent or half-moon shape. But this exception really proves
the rule—and disproves Hotson's basic assumption—because
Macbeth, III, v, is almost certainly an interpolated scene and not
by Shakespeare. In any case the metaphor of an eclipse rules out
the possibility of a crescent shape. A lunar eclipse can only occur
when the moon is full. It is just possible, of course, that Shakespeare may not have known this, but the importance that was
attached to eclipses at the Renaissance makes it most unlikely. If
this is Hotson's contention—he has not discussed the point, as far
as I am aware—the *onus* of proof is surely on him. Unless it can
be shown that an Elizabethan dramatist would be unlikely to
know that a lunar eclipse necessarily involves a full moon, we are
entitled to assume both in sonnet 107 and in the parallel passage
in *Antony and Cleopatra* ('Alacke! our terrene moone Is now
eclips'd', III, xiii, 153–4)[2] the metaphor is not that of a crescent.

On the internal literary evidence, then, the Hotson interpretation can be safely dismissed. If Shakespeare had wished to introduce an allusion to the Armada's crescent formation, he would
certainly not have done it in the particular context of sonnet 107.
Nor would he have called such a formation *tout court* a moon.
And if he had done so it is most improbable that he would have
spoilt his metaphor by introducing the notion of an eclipse.

The implications of the Hotson interpretation in literary history

[1] Hotson cites other early allusions to the crescent formation of the Armada
in an article in *TLS*, 2 June 1950.
[2] Hotson's attempt to interpret the 'moone' in this passage as Antony's
crescent-shaped fleet has been effectively disposed of by Arthur J. Perrett
and G. Wilson Knight. (See *TLS*, 14 June 1950.) The allusion is undoubtedly to Cleopatra—a fact that strengthens the case for identifying the
'mortall Moone' of sonnet 107 with Queen Elizabeth.

are not less fatal to it. The present tenses in lines 5–8 of the sonnet make it clear that the public event referred to is contemporary or almost contemporary with its composition. If there is, as Hotson argues, an allusion to the Armada, sonnet 107 *must* have been written in 1588 or 1589.[1] And this is in fact the desperate conclusion that Hotson reaches. It is a desperate historical conclusion, because it assigns sonnet 107, and by implication most at any rate of the rest of Shakespeare's sonnets, to a period several years before either *Venus and Adonis,* which is usually dated 1592–93, or *Lucrece,* which cannot possibly have been written before 1593, since it is clearly the 'graver labour' referred to in the dedication to Southampton prefixed to the first edition of *Venus and Adonis.* But the style of this sonnet is more mature, not less mature, than that of either *Venus and Adonis* or *Lucrece.* It is easy to see how the writer of the narrative poems will in process of time become the writer of the sonnet. But the reverse process posited by Hotson—from writing poetry like Donne, as it were, to writing like Spenser (that is what it almost amounts to)—is incomprehensible. The point could be established in a dozen different ways. One argument that seems to me decisive is the absence from the sonnet of the rash of verbal antitheses that characterizes Shakespeare's early manner. I have not been able to find four consecutive lines in either *Venus and Adonis* or *Lucrece* without one or more verbal antitheses. A passage of fourteen consecutive lines with only a single verbal antithesis ('Incertenties' 'assur'de') can only be described as a stylistic impossibility for the Shakespeare of the early 1590s. Hotson is therefore committed to the hypothesis that the mastery of sentence structure and verbal phrase evident in every line of sonnet 107 represents a style that Shakespeare had achieved in 1588–89 and then lost for a number of years, only to regain it about 1595 in such plays as *A Midsummer Night's Dream. Quod est absurdum.*[2]

[1] I. A. Shapiro has argued for 1599–1600 as the date of composition on the ground that the allusion to the Armada's crescent formation would have been more intelligible then than in 1588–89, because of its popularization in such works as Stow's *Annales* (1592). (See *TLS,* 21 April 1950.) But this suggestion betrays the same inability to read the sonnet as a poem that Hotson displays. By 'Now' (line 9) Shakespeare cannot possibly have meant 'ten years ago'.

[2] It is perhaps worth noting that the form *incertainty* is only found in this sonnet, *The Winter's Tale* and sonnet 115, whereas *uncertainty* occurs in *A Comedy of Errors* and *1 Henry IV,* an early and earlyish play, as well as in *Coriolanus.* In the same way *incertain* is only found in middle-period and

No, literary detection is a harmless avocation, one 'immeasurably more humane than cock-fighting', as E. E. Kellett once modestly put it in his essay called 'The Literary Detective'.[1] But the game has certain elementary rules. One of them is that in the assessment of clues the primacy must always be accorded to the *literary* fact or probability.[2]

later plays, whereas *uncertain* appears in *Richard III* and *The Two Gentlemen of Verona* as well as in some of the later plays. It would be rash to press the point too far, as 'incertenties' in line 7 may be a misprint, but its occurrence, if genuine, tends to confirm the pre-Hotson view that the sonnet is not earlier than 1596 or so.

[1] *Suggestions* (1923), p. 205.
[2] Hotson's handling of the literary facts—he does not disregard them altogether—borders on the disingenuous. Thus, in arguing against 1603 as the date of sonnet 107's composition, he makes a great deal of the fact that by 1603 the sonneteering vogue was over, as no doubt it was. But when he comes to suggest his own date for the sonnet (1588–89), he conveniently overlooks the fact that the sonneteering vogue, which dates from the publication of Sidney's *Astrophil and Stella* (1591) had not started. *A priori* a sonnet was *less* likely to be written in 1588 than in 1603, when Drayton, Donne and Drummond among others were still writing, or about to write, sonnets.

5

Cui Bono? *A Learned Journal's Irrelevance*•

A learned profession can be presumed to get the technical journals that it deserves. In a sense, they are only *symptoms*; the particular specialization—for our present example, the sub-department of historical scholarship devoted to the English literature of the remoter past—is the *disease*. It is from this clinical point of view that I approach the *Review of English Studies*, that eminent 'Quarterly Journal of English Literature and the English Language', to quote its sub-title, which most of us abbreviate, conventionally and affectionately, to *R.E.S.* (The abbreviation was introduced in the first number and is still retained, although the Americans, with their usual innocent blue-eyed brutality to the English language, now prefer the point-less *RES*.)

The diagnosis proposed here is not, therefore, of what is wrong with *R.E.S.* As compared with *M.L.R.*, for instance, or their American counterparts (*JEGP, MP, PMLA, PQ, SP,* etc.),[1] there

---

• *Essays in Criticism,* 6 (1956).

[1] The abbreviations stand for *Modern Language Review, Journal of English and Germanic Philology, Modern Philology, Publications of the Modern Language Association of America, Philological Quarterly,* and *Studies in Philology.* The American journals have all dropped their points now, *PMLA* even accepting the inevitable and actually calling itself *PMLA.* As between the original pretentious polysyllables and the modern abracadabra there does not seem much to choose.

has never been anything seriously wrong with *R.E.S.* As learned journals go it has always been well edited and well produced. And if no one has ever willingly read the whole of a number of *R.E.S.* from cover to cover, *R.E.S.* is at least no more unreadable than its competitors. On the whole, indeed, the standard of the actual writing, both in the articles and the reviews, is commendably high. It is what is written *about*—let us say, 'The Rights of Beeston and D'Avenant in Elizabethan Plays', to cite a representative specimen from the journal's first number—that is so daunting to the spirit. With the best will in the world even the professional who has not interested himself in that particular subdivision of a subdivision often finds himself gritting his teeth. The right to be bored, the right to refuse the intellectual food that you cannot digest, is after all an inalienable human privilege. Who is it, then, that inveigles the aspiring English scholar to devote his days and nights to the composition of such articles? Not the *R.E.S.* certainly, or its editors as such, or its august Advisory Panel as such. No, if the *R.E.S.* pudding is stodgy, it would be unfair to blame the cooks; the cooks have only followed the recipe that the cookery-books provide. And if one asks who wrote those cookery-books, who it is that is responsible for so arid a concept of literary history, the answer, I am afraid, is that we are all of us implicated. The learned journals are what they are because the historical study of English literature is what it is— and for that all of us who teach the subject in the universities, or who write books with scholarly pretensions about it, must accept a joint responsibility. I for one cannot possibly plead an alibi. I have written many articles and reviews for *R.E.S.*, and I was one of its original subscribers. Nevertheless it is not a bad thing if a profession asks itself from time to time a few ultimate questions. And *R.E.S.* happens to be a particularly faithful mirror in which the practice of English literary history today can be seen as in itself it really so often is.

R.E.S. made its début in January 1925. Its editor then and for the next fifteen years was R. B. McKerrow, who was a joint managing director at the time in the publishing firm of Sidgwick and Jackson. McKerrow had made his name in the world of learning by his edition of Nashe (5 vols, 1904–10), a model of severe scholarship that, in the words of J. M. Manly, 'set a new standard of English editing'. And the well-known *Introduction to Bibliography for Literary Students*, though not published until 1927, was apparently under way at the time of *R.E.S.*'s birth. (The ambitious Oxford edition of Shakespeare, which was still unfinished at McKerrow's death in 1940, was begun in 1929.) It was no doubt McKerrow and his Advisory Panel of twenty-one professors and experts who concocted between them the anonymous statement of policy that leads off the first number. The emphasis here is unequivocally on 'research'. 'To the founders of the Review it seems that research as they understand it is the lifeblood of literary history.' A related word that keeps on turning up in the statement is 'fact'. New 'facts' are all-important, although 'research' as the Review's founders understood it included not only the integration of the new 'facts' into the old 'facts' but also the reinterpretation of old 'facts' by themselves.

> This Review will therefore welcome new facts—however disconnected and in themselves seemingly unimportant they may be—but it will welcome no less cordially attempts to weave such facts into a larger unity, to interpret them in the light of their own time and of ours, and to place them in their true relation to the knowledge that we already possess. The only article that will *not* be welcome is 'the mere compilation which has nothing fresh to say'.

The intentions are admirable, but the programme was extraordinarily unspecific. What constitutes a literary-historical 'fact'? Into what is the 'research' to be directed? What are those larger 'unities' into which the 'facts', new and old, are to be channelled? On all such matters, the cruxes of editorial policy, the statement is diplomatically vague. One ominous sentence, which regretted our forefathers' inconsiderateness in not recording 'a few of the familiar facts about their great contemporaries', appears to suggest that McKerrow and his advisers were really thinking about extra-literary evidence—what T. S. Eliot at just about this time was calling 'Shakespeare's laundry bills'. No doubt too many interests had a hand in the formulation of the statement. An Advisory Panel that included the holders of such incompatible literary creeds as A. C. Bradley, W. W. Greg, George S. Gordon and Henry Newbolt cannot have found much to agree on. But the woolliness of the programme was at least a guarantee that there would be no editorial exclusiveness, and the articles in the first number were in fact agreeably heterogeneous. Apart from 'Elizabethan Stage Gleanings' (E. K. Chambers) and 'Some Notes on Dryden' (G. Thorn-Drury), which were mere sweepings from those eminent scholars' studies, and one or two competent but dullish special studies (such as the one on Beeston and Davenant), there were three articles of great interest to all of us. Pride of place was given to R. W. Chambers, who took the opportunity provided by recent work on the *Ancren Riwle* to adumbrate, tactfully and most persuasively, some of the points that were later elaborated in *The Continuity of English Prose*. Then came 'The Present Value of Byron', a lecture originally given on the centenary of Byron's death, in which Oliver Elton attempted to answer such questions as 'Can he tell a story?', 'Could Byron sing?' and 'What has Byron to say to our sense of beauty?' And then, under the rather unpromising title 'A Note upon Chapters XX and XXI of *The Elizabethan Stage*', an essay by Granville-Barker which raised from a new point of view the whole question of the origins of Elizabethan drama. As against E. K. Chambers, who had overstressed Court and aristocratic influences, Granville-Barker built up here an impressive case for the creative effect of the 'emotional' acting of the inn-yards and early public theatres. (In a nut-shell: Alleyn and Burbage and their fellows were the conditioning stimulus that made Marlowe and Shakespeare write the great plays they did write.) By modern standards the article is a bit up in the air. No use, for example, is made of Fynes Morison's account of the English actors' success at Frankfort Fair in 1592, which confirms and explains the extraordinary quality of Elizabethan 'emotional' acting. But even if Granville-Barker's thesis is too much hypothesis the article is still a splendid example of the wide-ranging generalizations without which the details of scholarship have little or no meaning outside themselves. A journal that saw its function as the dissemination of such different and yet variously valid approaches to the study of English literature as those of R. W. Chambers, Elton and Granville-Barker had made an excellent beginning. What remained to be seen was how far a balance would be maintained between such articles (which were complemented by some substantial reviews, notably Greg's of *The Elizabethan Stage*) and the *minutiae* (those 'disconnected and in themselves seemingly unimportant facts').

But *R.E.S.* did not fulfil the promise of its first number. Almost immediately a process of contraction set in. The 'unities' into which, according to the preliminary statement, the 'facts' provided by 'research' were to be fitted became smaller and more perfunctory. Instead of the wide-ranging hypotheses of R. W.

Chambers and Granville-Barker its articles soon became restricted
to elaborate investigations, often conducted with considerable
skill, into such problems of pre-literary detail as 'The Authorship
of *The Maid's Metamorphosis*' (11 pages of parallel pasages at
the end of which a tentative conclusion is reached that the
author was an unidentified admirer of Peele, Lyly and Spenser),
'Samuel Daniel and the Children of the Queen's Revels, 1604–5'
(8 pages, 4 of them occupied by a complete transcription of two
unpublished documents from the Record Office that confirm the
connection), 'Did Massinger revise *The Emperor of the East*?'
(8 pages: yes, he probably did), or 'Was Bishop William Barlow
Friar Jerome Barlow?' (11 pages: he may well have been). Such
grisly matter as this displaced completely the general critical essay
of the type of Elton's reassessment of Byron. The general diet was
of biographical discoveries, attributions, sources and influences.

I am not sure if McKerrow was aware of the contrast between
the first number of *R.E.S.*, with its refreshing variety of interpretations of what constitutes the literary 'fact', and its pedestrian
successors. If he was aware of it, there is no sign that he regretted
it. McKerrow had been for many years a close friend and associate of W. W. (later Sir Walter) Greg, and Greg's formidable
shadow lies across the journal's early pages. This is not the place
to attempt an appraisal of the revolution that Greg has effected
in English studies in this country and America. Partly by the
force of his exemplary editions and textual studies and partly by
the terror he created by some brilliantly destructive reviews the
thoroughness of our documentation and our standards of accuracy
in the handling of external evidence have risen enormously in the
last fifty years. But Greg's interest in literature has been primarily
non-literary. With the one exception of his early and in places
embarrassingly sentimental *Pastoral Poetry and Pastoral Drama*
he has preferred to catalogue books rather than read them, to re-
edit them rather than to reinterpret or evaluate. In the candid
obituary of McKerrow that Greg contributed to the 1940 Proceedings of the British Academy he has conceded that 'a groping after
some more or less mechanical rule' was the defect of his friend's
qualities, and a similar objection—but the machine is more
intricate, more beautifully precise—can be lodged against Greg
himself. At bottom the ideal of literary scholarship that Greg and
McKerrow and their associates have incarnated has, I suppose,
been an unconscious tribute to the physical sciences. The closer

the literary 'fact' could be reduced to a physical 'thing' the more effective their methods of bibliographical description and analysis become.

It is true, of course, that the process of communication by which an author's meaning reaches his audience's minds is necessarily through physical symbols and devices of one kind or another. The drama cannot do without actors and a place where they can be seen acting. Inevitably the way a play is written depends upon the style of acting and the characteristics of the theatre that the dramatist proposes to utilize. With the displacement of oral recitation by the printed book an equally complex system of intermediaries has also grown up between the writer and the reader. The student of literature cannot know too much about such processes of communication, and he is, or ought to be, properly grateful for the contributions of Greg and his associates to our better knowledge of the Elizabethan stage and the Elizabethan printing-house. But the physical processes derive all their interest and importance from the literary meanings that they communicate and from nothing else, and the literary student cannot be expected to concern himself with Shakespeare's company or Shakespeare's printers except in so far as their behaviour is directly related to his understanding of the meanings of Shakespeare's plays. Except by virtue of such a relationship theatrical history and dramatic bibliography are extra-literary studies. No doubt it is true that an intensive investigation into the habits of Elizabethan printers will occasionally turn up a physical fact that the Shakespearian textual critic can put to good use. It is on such grounds that Gregism, as it may be called, is sometimes defended and applauded. The reader of Wellek and Warren's *Theory of Literature* will remember the 'influential professor', an Englishman, I am afraid, who had 'been heard to say that the future of literary scholarship' lay in the bibliographical method. But the corollary of such a defence of 'pure' bibliography must be a not less intensive concomitant investigation into Shakespeare's meanings. Without such knowledge the investigator will have no criterion by which to decide which one, if any, of the new physical facts has a Shakespearian relevance. In other words, to generalize what seems to be a logical conclusion to the argument, a study of the processes of physical communication must go hand in hand with a study of the literary meanings communicated. Unless the combination is maintained, 'pure' bibliography will soon degenerate into a 'research' that is parasitic upon rather than ancillary to literary history.

No doubt Greg and McKerrow did in fact maintain such a combination—in their own persons at any rate, if not always in the subject-matter of their writings. Greg's prose style, still athletic and incisive even at the age of eighty, provides the best possible evidence of the vigilance of his literary conscience. (That of his indefatigable American heir Fredson Bowers inspires a good deal less confidence.) But *R.E.S.* suffered during the 1930s from McKerrow's unwillingness or inability to translate his own love of literature into a positive or consistent concept of literary history. 'Form and Matter in the Publication of Research' (*R.E.S.*, Jan. 1940), in which he instructs the would-be contributor to a learned journal how to organize and present his material, is as careful as the original statement in the first number of *R.E.S.* to avoid anything approaching a definition of 'research'. The recommendations, all of them eminently sensible, apply equally well to an investigation into any other form of history. It is impossible to resist the suspicion that, if McKerrow had been challenged to explain the difference between literary history and political history, for instance, he could have got much further than the tautology that literary history is the history of literature (just as political history is the history of politics!). The literary equivalents of sovereigns' reigns, the fortunes of rival parties, religious crises or foreign invasions hardly existed for McKerrow and his generation. But in the absence of *genres* and 'schools' or 'movements', contrasted ideologies (romanticism versus classicism, etc.), and foreign influences, even the most elementary literary history is not possible. The weakest, if not the dullest, articles in *R.E.S.* in McKerrow's time were undoubtedly those that ventured into or depended on literary history or criticism. I am thinking of a naïve account of Shenstone as a letter-writer, which seemed totally unaware of the tradition and theory of letter-writing, a discussion of Goldsmith's criticism that neglected entirely the neoclassic background and the French sources (as well as recent American studies), an analysis of the Restoration theory of comedy with most of the same defects, and several decidedly uncritical discussions of sources or influences. A similar suspicion or unawareness of the non-physical seemed to govern the books that were or were not reviewed, and the number of words allotted to each book. *The Use of Poetry and the Use of Criticism, Seven Types*

of *Ambiguity*, *Versions of Pastoral* and *Revaluation* were not
reviewed at all. *The Wheel of Fire* received a not unsympathetic
notice from Miss M. St Clare Byrne, but at a length ludicrously
inadequate to its importance.

Since McKerrow's death *R.E.S.* has been edited by scholars of
a less severe cast—James R. Sutherland (1940–47), John Butt
(1947–54), Peter Alexander and Norman Davis (1954–63), and
J. B. Bamborough (1964–   ). It has been encouraging to watch
the journal's progress from brute fact to literary fact. No doubt
the modern deposition in the general climate of opinion of the
physical sciences by psychology and economics has had a good
deal to do with this. Sources, influences, attributions, rediscoveries
and unpublished documents are still the staple diet of *R.E.S.*, but
they are now presented in more humane terms. In an article by
Norman Callan, for example, on Chaucer's and Gower's use of
the *Metamorphoses* (Oct. 1946) the common source becomes a
point of departure for a comparison of strictly literary qualities.
Some of the articles—J. I. M. Stewart's defence of the blinding
of Gloster (Oct. 1945), Frank Kermode's exposition of Henry
Vaughan's imagery (July 1950), Miss Tompkins's illuminating
discussion of *Pericles* (Oct. 1952)—are to all intents and purposes
just well-informed critical essays. Others, like H. S. Bennett's
survey of fifteenth-century prose (Oct. 1945), Joan Grundy's
'William Browne and the Italian Pastoral' (Oct. 1953), and
S. L. Goldberg's 'Sir John Hayward, "Politic" Historian' (July
1955), have been contributions, or at any rate footnotes, to literary
history. Harold F. Brooks's account of the Restoration 'Imitation'
(April 1949) was perhaps something more, a permanently relevant
piece of *genre* history, as F. T. Prince's 'The Influence of Tasso
and Della Casa on Milton's Diction' (July 1949) was to the study
of foreign literary influences. Occasionally, as in E. C. Pettet's
reinterpretation of *Timon of Athens* (Oct. 1947), Graham Hough's
'The Natural Theology of *In Memoriam*' (July 1947) and A. R.
Humphreys's account of an aspect of eighteenth-century 'sensibility' (July 1948), we have been on the edge of literary sociology
and the history of ideas. The reviews, which seem to me to have
been getting better and better, have also shown an increasing
awareness of the more general literary contexts, critical and
historical, within which 'research' must function if it is not to
become a sterile dead-end.

Nevertheless it is difficult to be entirely happy about the condition of English studies that is reflected in *R.E.S.* today. The tendency to irresponsible atomization, if less shocking than in McKerrow's reign, still exists. Generalizations are still suspect, or at any rate avoided. Indeed the expertness and confidence with which detail, especially pre-literary and extra-literary detail, is handled contrasts distressingly with the clumsiness and amateurishness with which general ideas of all kinds are treated. The impression the reader gets is of intelligent men who somehow do not know how to see beyond the end of their noses. No doubt the anti-intellectualism is more passive than active, but it is almost omnipresent. A. J. A. Waldock's 'The Men in Buckram' (Jan. 1947), a pioneer exploration of the 'levels of reality' in *1 Henry IV*, II, iv, is perhaps the only *R.E.S.* article since C. S. Lewis's brilliant analysis of the revisions in *Comus* (April 1932) which might be generalized into a research method applicable to other literary problems or situations. Elsewhere the bias is almost always, except perhaps in some of the American contributors, towards particularity—the minute examination of one limited aspect of a single author or work. Although the approach is certainly less mechanical than it used to be and the *minutiae* are generally reserved nowadays for the shorter 'Notes', too much of the research is still directed towards information, the sort of thing that would be more appropriate in a work of reference, rather than knowledge. In themselves such discoveries usually have little or no genuine literary interest, but they are among the data of which a future critic or historian may have to be aware if he is to reach valid literary conclusions. They are, to repeat the objection already raised, essentially pre-literary. The underlying assumption seems to be that the reader of *R.E.S.*, out of the fullness of his knowledge of English literature, will be immediately aware of the literary implications of the new 'facts' and so be able to use them without further help to enrich his understanding of the particular work or writer under discussion. But, except perhaps in our own restricted field, are we really such polymaths? A recent example, selected simply because it is typical of dozens of others, will show what I mean. 'The Earliest Influences on *A Shropshire Lad*' (April 1955) is an article that devotes five of its eight pages to the influence on Housman of George Augustus Simcox's *Poems and Romances* (1869). Apparently Housman copied four of these poems into his early notebooks, and there are a number of faint but recognizable echoes of Simcox's diluted

Pre-Raphaelitism in Housman's later poems, though not apparently in *A Shropshire Lad*. The article sets out the parallels at length, lucidly and objectively, and that apparently is that. The 'fact' of an influence of Simcox on Housman has been established. But what is the reader of the article to do with his newly acquired piece of information? Until this moment George Augustus Simcox is likely to have been a mere name to him, if even a name. And supposing that he goes to his local library and conscientiously reads right through *Poems and Romances*, will he be much wiser? Surely, if it is to make any difference to our understanding of Housman, the influence of Simcox must take its place in the general influences of the Pre-Raphaelites and people like Heine and the English Romantics on *A Shropshire Lad* and *Last Poems*. Presumably because the writer of the article takes it for granted that anybody erudite enough to read *R.E.S.* must know it already, he does not provide even a summary of the historical framework into which Housman's admiration of Simcox fits. But such knowledge cannot and should not be taken for granted. No doubt, if we did a little special research ourselves, we *could* at a pinch assemble all the essential facts. That, however, is not the point—which is that the writer has failed to do his duty by his reader and by Housman by excluding the literary context within which his piquant discovery becomes utilizable by all but a tiny handful of Housman experts.

In the case of this article, and every issue of *R.E.S.* has one or two contributions which raise exactly the same problem, the editors should surely have returned it to the author with a request for some such a critical-historical introduction. I cannot help feeling that McKerrow's successors have been too passive. The editorial line of least resistance is to allow the contents of each issue to be determined by the articles that come to him, as it were, out of the blue. If there are enough of such articles of a respectable quality he is likely to feel that he has done all that is required of him. But he will be very lucky if, in fact, he has. At the risk that they may turn out unsatisfactory he must also commission articles on the topics that *ought* to be treated in his journal and that are not covered by the uncommissioned articles. *R.E.S.* ought undoubtedly, I think, to print more articles like those of Waldock and Lewis that exemplify new and promising methods of literary research. Occasionally there should certainly be general articles attempting assessments of the contemporary state of English studies, preferably limiting the discussion perhaps to specific fields or techniques. As it is the reader is fobbed off with a few inadequate sentences—though even they are better, of course, than nothing (I am thinking of Alice Walker's comment in July 1955 on 'the lines along which significant advances in the editing of Shakespeare should be made', and H. S. Bennett's suggestions on the proper editing of Chaucer for G.C.E. in the same issue)— at the beginning or end of a review. It is deplorable, too, considering what A. O. Lovejoy, R. S. Crane, Harry Levin and other American scholars have achieved in this area, that *R.E.S.* has never, as far as I can remember, considered the history of a critical term worth an article. Indeed, we look in vain for the discussion of topics of any degree of generality. Granville-Barker's hypothesis in the first number as to the origins of Elizabethan drama has not had a single successor. And with one or two lonely exceptions—like Wilson Knight's stimulating, though to me unconvincing, essay on 'The Scholar Gipsy' (Jan. 1955)—there have been no reassessments of a major figure or major work on the lines of Oliver Elton's 'The Present Value of Byron' in the same number. The range of the books reviewed should also be extended. Why was *Theory of Literature* not even noticed? (With all its limitations it is a book that every responsible literary scholar *must* read —especially perhaps if he is an Englishman.) Why did Donald Davie's *Purity of Diction in English Poetry* not even achieve a Short Notice?

But it would be wrong to end on too critical a note. Within its own conventions—for which the profession of literary scholarship in England today must be held primarily responsible—many of the articles and most of the reviews in *R.E.S.* could hardly be better. When *Essays in Criticism* announced in its preliminary circular that it would try to tread a middle way between *Scrutiny* and *R.E.S.* it was deliberately setting its sights high. But, although I have a natural prejudice in favour of *Essays in Criticism*, a fairly careful reperusal of *R.E.S.*'s thirty volumes compels me to admit that in its own way *R.E.S.* is a better journal than *E. in C.* It is the *R.E.S.* way of literary life that is so open to criticism—a fundamentally *non-humane* ideal of scholarship that the twentieth century has inherited from the nineteenth, and which we cannot apparently manage to outgrow. But it must be outgrown. The scholar must not continue to be intimidated and demoralized by the machine tools of his profession. Have we not all read *Erewhon*?

6

Linguistics and Literary Criticism[•]

Il y a toujours un qui baise et un qui tend la joue. Mysteriously, in the curious flirtation now being conducted in our groves of academe between the specialists in linguistics and their opposite numbers in literature, the amorous advances have hitherto come exclusively from the linguists.[1] We literary critics and theorists, though naturally flattered by these attentions from our once hereditary enemies, have remained puzzled and more or less passive in the exchanges. Are the gentlemen's intentions *quite* as honourable as they profess them to be? Simpering coyly we have, it is true, occasionally allowed ourselves to be coaxed into a brief and embarrassed cooperation, but it has always been with a noticeable lack of enthusiasm. Perhaps, on the other hand, the whole thing is a colossal misunderstanding.

In this essay I propose to limit myself to the recent linguistic

[•] From *The Discipline of Criticism: Essays Honouring René Wellek* (1968).
[1] I have three recent works particularly in mind: *Style in Language*, ed. Thomas A. Sebeok (1960); *Linguistics and Style*, ed. John Spencer (1964); *Essays on Style and Language*, ed. Roger Fowler (1966). *Style in Language* incorporates papers originally read at a conference 'to explore the possibility of finding a common basis for discussing and, hopefully, understanding, particularly among linguists, psychologists and literary critics, the characteristics of style in language' (Foreword, p. v).

invasion of the once specifically literary area of style, though some of the seeds of doubt I hope to sow may prove to have a wider relevance. If I have a methodological conclusion to offer it is, I am afraid, one of almost total scepticism. A linguist is certainly entitled to investigate works of literature for his own non-literary purposes; what he must not expect, I suggest, is that criticism will derive any but the most marginal benefit from his findings. The premises and ideals of our respective disciplines—the linguist's of objective analytic description (analysis in order to describe), the critic's of intersubjective synthetic evaluation (synthesis in the service of value)—differ *toto caelo*; they cannot and should not be compromised.

The first question I am bound to ask therefore is whether 'language', the apparent common denominator, has the same meaning for the linguist as for the literary critic. John Spencer for one, an English neo-grammarian who has recently edited a slim volume called *Linguistics and Style*, has no doubt about it. He begins his introduction as follows:

> Few literary scholars would suggest that literature can be satisfactorily studied without due attention to its medium, language. Nor would many linguists justify the investigation of literary language without guidance from those who devote themselves to the study of literature. There would, moreover, be a measure of agreement on both sides that the student of literature, whatever his particular interests, ought to be trained in the study of both language and literature. Yet, beneath this appearance of politeness and mutual esteem, discord and tension sometimes manifest themselves between what have become distinct disciplines.

That the 'discord and tension' to which Mr Spencer refers—and which R. H. Robins has also recently deplored as 'a certain sense of rivalry and even at times of hostility expressed between literary pursuits and the study of language in linguistics today'[1]—may derive from a tendency of the two parties to force their own meaning of 'language' on each other does not seem to have occurred to him. But the formula 'language is the medium of literature'—which has a way of turning up whenever a linguist feels it necessary to justify his intrusion into literature—is an ambiguous one. After all, language is also the medium of conversation, of business, of scientific discourse, indeed of every aspect

[1] *General Linguistics: an introductory survey* (1965), p. 368.

of human social intercourse. The immediate practical problem, however, is the kind and quantity of linguistic knowledge that is needed for the understanding and appreciation of, let us say, the plays of Shakespeare or the poems of Milton. If the literary student is a native of an English-speaking country, the quantity of additional linguistic knowledge that he will require can, I believe, easily be exaggerated.

The difference in historical premises is nicely, perhaps decisively, illustrated by the respective habits of linguist and critic whenever we read aloud or quote orally from any non-contemporary work of literature. A linguist will take it for granted, in classroom or lecture hall, that each phoneme in every word used by a Chaucer, Shakespeare, or Milton must be pronounced as far as possible just as it would have been by an educated Londoner of their time. To the critic, on the other hand, such detailed phonetic reconstructions appear an absurd affectation. The performance of one of Shakespeare's plays today as it was originally pronounced at the Globe is unthinkable to him, except as a philological curiosity. And the undoubted fact that Shakespeare himself would have considered the English used in a typical modern revival—or when quoted by a professor of English—to be grotesquely mispronounced does not worry the critic a bit.

The paradox that what is the 'correct' pronunciation historically is not the 'right' pronunciation critically is not affected by the notorious difficulty modern philologists find in agreeing upon exactly what vowel sounds Shakespeare and his actors employed. As long as English is a living language, the natural pronunciation of the works of Shakespeare and Milton—and indeed of any fifteenth- or sixteenth-century English writer (Chaucer is the borderline case)—will always be whatever English is current when they happen to be acted or read. The occasional exception in a rhyme or a pun only proves my general critical rule of continuous oral modernization.

An important theoretical principle is implicit in this paradox. It is right and natural for the native of an English-speaking country to pronounce the English literature of any period as if it had been written yesterday—whatever the historical evidence to the contrary may be—because English literature constitutes a cultural continuum that only changes gradually and very slowly. This is easily demonstrable. Thus it can never be an argument against the interpretation of this or that passage in Shakespeare that a usage is presupposed which did not exist in the English of Shakespeare's time. If the innovation was possible in later seventeenth-century English it must also have been possible in Elizabethan English, because there is no essential discontinuity—apart from the introduction of certain new techniques and industries—between the culture of sixteenth-century England and that of the later period. Although the linguistic evidence will always be relevant, it cannot be the final determining literary factor in such cases. The determining literary factor is *stylistic effectiveness within the general cultural context*.

A simple example of this supra-linguistic principle is the Folio reading of *Macbeth*, II, ii, 63, 'Making the Greene one, Red'. To the obvious emendation, first proposed by Johnson, 'Making the green, one red', C. J. Sisson has objected that 'no contemporary instance has been cited of the use of *one* to mean "totally" (however familiar it may seem today) and we may not without authority gloss *one red* as meaning *total gules*'.[1] He therefore retains the Folio's comma, explaining 'the green one' as Neptune. This is certainly a grammatically possible sense; the objection to it is that it gives a bathetic anticlimax (even if we do not assume colloquial reduction of 'one' in Sisson's sense to ''un'—'green 'un'):

> Will all great Neptune's ocean wash this blood
> Clean from my hand? No, this my hand will rather
> The multitudinous seas incarnadine,
> Making the green one, red.

After the polysyllables of the previous line, the three final monosyllables must clearly all receive the maximum possible stress. To a literary critic the proposition is self-evident. That no contemporary instance of 'one' in this emphatic sense is available is completely irrelevant. If Shakespeare can coin the verb 'incarnadine' in the previous line, a licence Sisson does not seem to object to, why may he not also extend the use of 'one' to mean 'totally'? Both usages were what may be called potential English, and the exact date when either became a formal part of the language has a merely antiquarian interest. What the critic is concerned with is the sentence's cultural significance in the continuum of English literature *from the viewpoint of the present—* not because the twentieth century can see more, or more clearly,

[1] *New Readings in Shakespeare* (1956), II, 197.

than earlier centuries (losses have to be balanced against gains), but because an Englishman who happens to live in the twentieth century is committed to it willy-nilly. To become accessible to us critically, the literature of the past must in fact be translatable into the present tense. When confronted therefore with obsolete words or forms in it our only concern *as critics* is to know what they mean in modern English. The principle applies as much to a reader's own literature as to his reading of a foreign literature— such as that of the Romans or indeed, as I have argued elsewhere, the Anglo-Saxons. If we are to identify empathically with Hamlet, Macbeth, and the others, they must in effect become our con-temporaries and so speak our English. Provided that object is obtained, however approximately and imperfectly, a cultural continuity is assured.

The hypothesis of a literary continuum—in the English case perhaps beginning about A.D. 1200 with works like *The Owl and the Nightingale* (in which language, prosody, style, and genre are essentially those familiar in later English poetry)—is a necessary one if the concept 'English literature' is to have any substantial meaning. And we are then bound in logic, as I have implied, to concern ourselves principally, if not altogether, with those fea-tures of the English language that are *common* to the literature since 1200 or thereabouts.[1] The differences, in other words, must as far as possible be ignored—not because they do not exist but because this degree of anti-historicism is the price that has to be paid for the continuing vitality of an English literary tradition. (A parallel case would be the general implicit agreement, found within any linguistic area, to ignore for ordinary daily purposes of communication all but the grossest differences of class or regional dialect.)

The literary irrelevance that I have imputed in the preceding section to 'diachronic' (historical) linguistics applies equally to 'synchronic' linguistics, i.e. the detailed analysis of a language at any one period in its evolution. But the nature of the objection is different. The point that needs to be made depends, as it happens,

---

[1] *The Oxford Dictionary* excludes Old English, except for purposes of etymological explanation, on two grounds: (1) the failure of so large a part of the O.E. vocabulary to survive after ca. 1150; (2) the O.E. inflections would have meant a wholly different system of entry from that 'adapted to the words which survived the twelfth century' ('General Explanations', 1933 edn., I, xxviii).

on considerations invoked in a classic passage in that fountain-head of modern descriptive linguistics, Saussure's *Cours de linguistique générale* (1916). It will be remembered that Saussure's point of theoretic departure—the distinction between *langue* (the language system) and *parole* (the language occasion)—was based on an analysis of the sequence of events implicit in A addressing a remark to B.[1] The following is a simplified summary of what Saussure called *le circuit de la parole*.

Psychological plane
An idea comes into A's head.
The idea releases the appropriate 'sound-image' associated with it (the idea is verbalized).
The 'sound-image' detaches itself from the idea.

Physiological plane
A's brain transmits the correlative nervous impulse to his vocal chords.

Physical plane
Certain sound waves pass from A's lips to B's ears.
[B then repeats the processes undergone by A in an inverse order; i.e. whereas A's contribution terminates on the physical plane,

Psychological plane

1. An idea enters A's head.
2. A's meaning is verbalized in linguistic 'sound-images.'
3. The 'sound-images' detach themselves from the meaning.

9. A's idea enters B's head.
8. The 'sound-images' release their conventional meanings.
7. The sounds are mentalized as linguistic 'sound-images.'

Physiological plane

4. A's brain transmits the appropriate nervous impulse to the vocal chords.

6. B's ears transmit to his brain the appropriate impulses set in motion by A's sounds.

Physical plane

5. A series of conventional sound waves (the phonemes) are directed from A's lips to B's ears.

[1] 'Place de la langue dans les faits de langage', pp. 27–32 of the 1955 edn.

B's begins on it, B then moving first to the physiological plane and ultimately to the psychological plane, where A's three processes are reenacted in the opposite order.]

It will be seen that A's last stage, which is B's first, is the only one common to them both. It is at this physical level that words, in the ordinary sense, are interchanged, but the conventional series of sounds emitted by A derive, of course, from A's four earlier processes, just as they only 'make sense' for B at the end of his four later processes. In the diagram on p. 73 I have numbered the separate stages so as to make the full temporal sequence clear.

Saussure's details, some of which I may have oversimplified, need not detain us. For literary theory the point of particular interest is B's exact repetition of A's psychological, physiological, and physical processes *in an inverted order*. Whereas A proceeds from a psychological phase to a physical phase, B reverses the process and proceeds from the physical to the psychological. There is also a reversal of direction even on the same level. Thus on the physical plane, as the sound waves leave A's mouth to impinge on B's ears, A 'gives out' and B 'takes in'. It follows that even if communication is completely successful and B reproduces accurately at each phase the exact equivalent of what A has already contributed to *le circuit de la parole*, there is still this difference of direction. For A the sequence is towards increasing externalization, for B towards increasing internalization. Saussure's analysis is, of course, incomplete. In the give-and-take of everyday conversation, what A has to say to B is counterbalanced by what B has to say to A. Question begets answer, as assertion begets either assent or contradiction. But once the cycle of speech is inflated into what may be called the literary cycle ('the *best* words in the *best* order'), and A becomes the author and B the literary audience, the typical situation has changed. The function of the author *qua* author is to externalize all the time, just as the literary audience—once the curtain has gone up or until the book is put down—is internalizing all the time. Whether (i) the author is his own reader or reciter, or (ii) a professional reader or reciter substitutes for him, or (iii) the auditor becomes his own reader or reciter, either aloud or sotto voce, does not affect this basic relationship. Even when we are reading a work of literature to ourselves we are not doing it to externalize a psychological condition of our own, as A or an author 'expresses' himself; on the contrary, our object is still under normal circumstances simply to internalize somebody else's externalizations. We are patients, not agents. The point becomes a crucial one for literary theory when the terminal areas of the linguistic or literary cycle are subjected to a rather different mode of analysis from that of Saussure.

Since we are all readers I shall begin with B (who now typifies the literary audience). B, then, begins his book by reading the first sentence on page 1. The fact that a visual process is super-imposed on that of speech adds a further stage to the cycle of communication but does not affect the direction of the series of impulses; the writer is still externalizing, the reader still internaliz-ing. Having identified the series of black marks at the top of the block of printed matter as so many letters, and the separate groups of letters as so many words, B is able to fill out mentally what Saussure called *le signifiant* in front of his eyes with *le signifié*, a process that requires him to recognize the grammatical relationships between the words in his sentence as well as their separate meanings. At this point, if he is a competent performer, he has 'understood' the first sentence.

But what does 'understanding' imply in this context? It is with this question that the distinction between speech, as it is normally practised, and any form of literature, as the term is normally used, forces itself upon the theorist's attention. There are, no doubt, modes of speech which resemble literature in the silent acquiescence of B (but always B in a plural number) to sentence after sentence from A. The preacher, the political orator, even the teller of a complicated story, or the narrator of an elaborate series of events, are all differentiated from the A of such typical speech phenomena as question and answer or assertion and counter-assertion. In these more elaborate situations the speaker becomes in effect indistinguishable from an author and the auditor from a theatrical spectator or the audience at a reading such as those Dickens used to give of his novels. B for once is now content to leave the role of externalization entirely to A. Social custom does not allow or at least encourage him to answer back or challenge A—not at any rate until the speech is complete or the tale has reached its end. His only defences against A's eloquence are to walk out of the political meeting or to close his ears, physically or metaphorically, to what A is saying.

A, however, in his role of prophet or entertainer, is always

aware, consciously or unconsciously, of the possibility of B's
denial of *le circuit de la parole*; he has therefore developed his
own counter-strategy, which is to *persuade* B to continue silent,
interested, and attentive. The eloquence of the orator must now
become so irresistible, the story must be told so amusingly or so
excitingly, that B 'cannot choose but hear'. In other words,
rhetoric is now added to speech. Unless rhetoric, in its most
general sense, *is* added to speech, the prolongation of A's role in
the speech cycle will tend sooner or later to be resisted or refused
by B. A club bore cannot hold his audience, because his rhetoric
is inferior or non-existent, because he is innocent of the *ars dicendi*.

Literature is therefore committed by the nature of its audience
relationship to the superimposition upon speech of the specially
heightened rhetoric that we call 'style'. Etymologically the word
carries us back to the *stilus* of the scribe, just as 'literature' itself
implies a mode of speech recorded physically in *literae* inscribed
by a *stilus*. In a written work, because a rereading or a reference
back will elucidate the obscurities or ambiguities, the speech can
be heightened, concentrated, elevated, coordinated. The speech
rhythms in a poem have been specially regularized or diversified;
the vocabulary is unusually varied or purified; certain unusual or
artificial 'figures' add colour, balance, and subtlety to the word
order; the subject matter has been sifted selectively; appropriate
attitudes towards the audience and modes of their presentation
(the genres) have been distinguished and elaborated.

This, it will be agreed, is what literature looks like *ab extra*—to
all of us, whether we are linguists or critics. It will be objected no
doubt by a linguist that the traditional categories of prosody and
stylistics are now being revised and reconstructed by descriptive
linguistics with much more precise and up-to-date tools of external analysis. Why is it then, we retort, that so little of critical
interest has so far emerged from modern linguistics? One answer,
I suggest, stares us all in the face in the movements of *le circuit
de la parole*. The linguist must always tend to refer the phenomena of style *back* to their constituents in language (stage 8 in
Saussure's scheme in the second diagram above) rather than
forwards to the post-linguistic or strictly psychological phase
represented by Saussure's stage 9. Language after all is the
linguist's business. But a realistic approach to the problems of
style demands a two-way investigation—not only of the linguistic
constituents of such devices as irony and metaphor, but also of

their psychological origins and their post-linguistic consequences. The essence of *le circuit de la parole*, as we have seen, is its temporal continuity: each phase in the series is being displaced at any one moment by its successor, as word follows word and sentence follows sentence. But, just as the separate letters of each word are immediately lost to sight in the reader's consciousness as he internalizes their total significance, so the separate words, phrases, clauses, and sentences disappear mentally once they translate themselves into the ideas or images that they symbolize. In Saussure's formula, A's idea eventually enters B's head, *le signifiant* having again become *le signifié*.

In the literary cycle, with the intervention of 'style' between Saussure's stages 8 and 9, the process is more complicated. Reduced to its simplest linguistic terms, 'style' can be described as a complex of verbal *repetition*, either overt or disguised. Thus metre is basically the abstraction from the verbal totality of certain syllable patterns which are then repeated; in an accentual system, for example, the 'foot', consisting typically of any heavily stressed syllable preceded by any lightly stressed syllable (the iamb), does not become a 'line' unless it is repeated several times. Other modes or levels of repetition are equally familiar. A sonnet, for example, superimposes on the pattern of syllable recurrence the further pattern of its special rhyme scheme. In the area of figures of speech the repetition is usually a *partial duplication*. Thus in puns, ironies, and metaphors two things are being said at the same time which are in some respects identical, though in others blatantly discrepant or contradictory. A similar combination of identity and difference characterizes such other stylistic devices or categories as connotation, balance, ambiguity, and symbolism. I need not retraverse what is familiar ground.

A crucial point, however, tends to be overlooked in linguistic investigations into the various aspects of style, namely, the effect of such repetitions on Saussure's stage 9. As the separate words and sentences merge in the reader's consciousness into the verbal combinations or patterns that he has learned to associate with literature, *le signifié* changes its nature with *le signifiant*. The context of literary communication is different from that of speech in four respects: (i) A (the author) is invisible and B (the audience) cannot influence him or answer back in any effective way; (ii) A's act of communication may often not be completed until B has spent many hours or days turning many pages; (iii) A's communication is not meant to be confined to a single B but may sometimes have millions of readers, all responding to it in more or less the same way. But the real crux is the fourth difference, which might be described as the new sense of order and significance that the accumulated repetitions of style add to Saussure's stage 9.

In the literary cycle stage 9 can perhaps be called the Aesthetic Moment. As the actual words and stylistic devices recede from the reader's consciousness their place is taken by an illusion of actual experience, one in which the reader shares though without being actively involved in it. An aesthetic distance, as we say, separates the human situation which the reader appears to be contemplating from such a situation in real life. Lessing put it succinctly in Chapter xvii of his *Laokoön*:

> The poet wishes not only to be intelligible, his representations
> ought not only to be clear and perspicuous; with this the prose
> writer may be content. But the poet desires to make the ideas
> which he awakens in us so vivid, that from the rapidity with
> which they arise we believe ourselves to be really as conscious
> of his objects as if they were actually presented to our senses;
> and in this moment of illusion we cease to be conscious of the
> means—that is, of the words—which he employs for this
> purpose.[1]

We can now return to Saussure's stage 1. In *le circuit de la parole* B's process of internalization repeated in an inverted order the phases—physical, physiological, and psychological—of A's externalization. The idea that came into A's head in stage 1 finally reached B's head in stage 9. If we substitute the literary cycle for the speech cycle a similar relationship must be expected to hold. But if stage 9 is the reader's Aesthetic Moment, what are we to call stage 1? The author's Aesthetic Moment? The author's 'moment of illusion'? If the parallel with stage 9 is valid, stage 1 in the literary cycle will at any rate be both pre-stylistic and pre-linguistic. Let us call it the Creative Moment, meaning by the term very much what Coleridge meant by the Imagination and Shelley by Inspiration.

The assumption that an author's progress towards composition follows the same pattern as a reader's towards the Aesthetic Moment but in an inverted order has an important theoretical consequence. It means that literary creation externalizes itself

[1] Translation by Sir Robert Phillimore (1874).

first as style and only secondarily as grammar or language. In style we are nearer to the working of the creative imagination than we are at the linguistic level. It follows that in interpreting literature's stylistic phenomena we shall be well advised to pay more attention to the causes of literary creation, the sources of a particular imaginative act and their correlatives in the reader's part of the cycle, than with the consequences in language.

No doubt this advice will sound suspiciously vague and unpractical, but the parallel between Saussure's *circuit de la parole* and what I have called the literary cycle is once again reassuring. It would not be difficult to discover why under certain circumstances a particular idea came into A's head (he is passing a shop with fresh strawberries displayed in the window)—or what B's reaction might be when he understood what A was saying (the strawberries are five shillings a punnet). The simplest verbal exchange operates in a social or cultural context which is no less real for being tacitly taken for granted. And it will be agreed that the reader's end of the literary cycle presents no special theoretical difficulties. Stage 9 (the Aesthetic Moment) terminates with or soon after the reading of the particular work of literature. But that is not the end, as far as the particular work's particular reader is concerned. As the experience released in the actual process of reading loses its first imaginative freshness it will be followed by a stage 10, which may be called the Emotional Response. (For Aristotle catharsis clearly occurred *after* the tragedy had reached its end.) And a stage 11, that of the Critical Verdict, no doubt comes later still, in most cases many hours or days later. By the time this phase is reached the memory has had an opportunity to discard the trivial and irrelevant elements from the original aesthetic experience, and the emotional consequences can also be seen in a perspective of similar reactions. It follows that when literary criticism begins the originating linguistic stimulus is already very remote.

If the Saussurian formula of an inverted order is equally applicable to the author on this pre-linguistic level, we are presumably left with a creative equivalent of the Critical Verdict as the ultimate origin of a work of literature. Perhaps this origin is some sort of communal value judgment itching to express itself? And instead of the Emotional Response of the reader do we posit an Emotional Explosion within the author resulting from the general originating value judgment? I make these final equations with extreme diffidence. The creative process begins below the level of consciousness, and hypotheses about its origins naturally resist adequate formulation and confirmation.

Nevertheless literary theory must insist that its concern with the pre-linguistic in literary composition and the post-linguistic in the reading of literature is legitimate and essential. To exclude these areas from the literary process, as modern descriptive linguistics is compelled to do, is unscientific as well as arbitrary. The literary cycle is as much a fact of experience as *le circuit de la parole*. Moreover—to reintroduce a concept that I have already applied to 'diachronic' linguistics—both the circuit and the cycle must necessarily be experienced as continuous, if the terms are to have any meaning. In other words, for linguistic or literary communication to take place between them A and B must already be in pre-verbal contact as human beings. The sound waves directed from A's lips to B's ears presume an existing rapport between A and B. I am not invoking any Jungian collective subconsciousness here but the elementary fact that A will not greet B unless some social bond already connects them. I do not say 'How do you do?' to a complete stranger. There is therefore a *social* plane preceding Saussure's psychological plane that is as much a part of *parole* as of *langue*. And what is true of *le circuit de la parole* is equally true obviously of the literary cycle; authors do not write for a non-audience.

Because of its latent premise of discontinuity, linguistics, whether historical or descriptive, can contribute little to the critical study of literature. Some recent attempts to provide linguistic interpretations of poems by Donne, Hopkins, and Larkin have been dismal examples of ingenious irrelevance. Let us therefore follow Socrates's example with the poets, crowning these linguistic invaders of literature with garlands of wool and anointing them with myrrh—*and sending them away to another city.*

The Necessity
7   of Contexts

'Ye gete namoore of me': Chaucer's Merchant's Tale

I

'Blake's poetry', T. S. Eliot has said, 'has the *unpleasantness* of great poetry.'[1] The comment was provoked by *Songs of Experience* and the associated lyrics in Blake's notebook (the so-called Rossetti manuscript), but Eliot extended the criterion not only to Homer, Aeschylus and Villon but also to Montaigne and Spinoza (and 'profound and concealed in the work of Shakespeare'). For Eliot, in effect, the capacity to disturb and discomfort character- izes all supreme literary excellence—and it is not difficult to think of other names to add to his list; Swift, Tolstoy, Baudelaire and Joyce, for example. The paradox is explained by Eliot as the possession by such writers of 'a peculiar honesty, which, in a world too frightened to be honest, is peculiarly terrifying'. (Though terrified the 'honesty' compels us to read on.)

Eliot's disconcerting criterion is at least suggestive. Applied to Chaucer, however, the test may at first sight seem to misfire. If Chaucer has a peculiar quality of his own it is surely not un- pleasantness so much as a fascinating elusiveness—the difficulty

[1] *The Sacred Wood* (1920), p. 137. My italics. The Blake essay is reprinted with two or three minor stylistic corrections in Eliot's *Selected Essays* (1932).

we often have in pinning his ultimate meaning down. How *serious* is he in fact being? Or, alternatively, how *comic*, on reflection, are his comic tales? It is difficult to be certain, for example, how we should respond to the miller's daughter's last words to Aleyn in the *Reeve's Tale* as he leaves her bed before dawn:

> 'And, goode lemman, God thee save and kepe!'
> And with that word almoost she gan to wepe.
>
> (A 4247–48)

And a similar ambivalence characterizes all of the poems, more or less, except the last and best of the *Canterbury Tales*—notably the *Pardoner's Tale* (with its astonishing *Prologue* and puzzling epilogue), the *Wife of Bath's Prologue* and the *Merchant's Tale*. Of the three the *Merchant's Tale* is unquestionably the most 'unpleasant', and it is also the one most free from the 'sly' duplicity of his earlier work. It is probably his last major work. It was apparently written *c.* 1395, though Chaucer did not die until 1400. I imagine he had a stroke or a heart attack soon after completing the *Merchant's Tale*. At any rate only a few trifles survive from the last four or five years of his life. Here, at the very end of his career, he has at last escaped completely from the shackles and perils of a Court audience. I see it, indeed, as basically a final exasperated attack on the values and conventions of Richard II's Court, to which he had hitherto, however reluctantly, been subservient. The tale is therefore best read on its own, detached from the general framework of the *Canterbury Tales*, with which its link by means of the Merchant's short *Prologue* is of the frailest.[1] In the *General Prologue* the Merchant does not make even a passing reference to his wife or to marriage, his one interest being his business; the Merchant of the short *Prologue's* only topic of conversation, on the other hand, is his wife's objectionableness. The *Tale*, however, presents a husband who is, at any rate until the end, among the most objectionable in the whole of literature.

The superficial, almost defiant, 'unpleasantness' of the *Merchant's Tale* is not likely to be denied. What may not be so

[1] Bertrand H. Bronson has pointed out that 'in approximately half of the more complete MSS of the *Canterbury Tales* there is no Merchant's Prologue' (*Studies in Philology*, 58, (1961), 584). He believes the Prologue was an afterthought in a desperate attempt to turn the Merchant into a plausible narrator. Norman T. Harrington (*PMLA*, 86 (1971), 25–31) is unconvincing in his reply to Bronson.

obvious is that the 'honesty' of which Chaucer's 'unpleasantness' (which includes the grossest indecency) is the reflection, is comparable to that of Blake. A better analogy might be with the hideous discovery that Angelo makes of his own nature in *Measure for Measure*—or with the sentimentally happy ending that is almost perversely denied us in *King Lear*. But what differentiates the *Merchant's Tale* even from Shakespeare's 'blackest' plays is that it will allow no concession to the ideal whatever; Angelo is corrupt before he is tempted, as a Cordelia is inconceivable in *Lear's* scheme of things.

Eliot added as a rider to his formula in the Blake essay that the 'honesty' of 'unpleasantness' is accompanied, and indeed guaranteed, by 'great technical accomplishment'.

An analysis of the *Merchant's Tale* will best begin at this level of 'technical accomplishment'. What is most striking in the tale is the variety of genres that the narrative process employs. Whereas most of the *Canterbury Tales* can be categorized under a single heading, such as fabliau, romance, saint's life, parody (*Sir Thopas*), or pastiche (the *Prioress's Tale*), the *Merchant's Tale* employs separate genres in a continuous calculated sequence, a procedure that successfully deflates each of the principal *dramatis personae* and the 'values' that they might be thought to represent. For genre, moreover, Chaucer substitutes a kind of antigenre.

Act I (E 1245–1392), as it may be called, exemplifies the method in the opening lines of the Tale:

> Whilom ther was dwellynge in Lumbardye
> A worthy knyght, that born was of Pavye,
> In which he lyved in great prosperitee . . .

The innocent reader will take this as the promise of a romance. 'Whilom' ('Once upon a time') was the conventional opening formula of a romance, and the remoteness in time is here confirmed by a remoteness of place suggested by the Italian placenames. The *Knight's Tale* had begun in much the same way:

> Whilom, as olde stories tellen us,
> Ther was a duc that highte Theseus . . .
> (A 859–60)

But an unromantic note can be detected as early as the fourth line in the *Merchant's Tale* that is very different from anything in the *Knight's Tale*:

And sixty yeer a wyflees man was hee ...

Why should a man of sixty or more not have married—especially
as he is a knight and a man of substance? The outrageous answer
follows in the fifth and six lines:

> And folwed ay his bodily delyt
> On wommen, ther as was his appetyt ...

This is anti-romance, as the rest of the Act continues to rub in.
Not only is the knight an old fool in expecting to make a happy
marriage at his age, but wives in general are now subjected to a
series of mock eulogics. E 1262–1392 continue the process of
reversing a conventional genre. Instead of an encomium of the
married state Chaucer provides what is in effect an anti-
encomium by the sarcastic tone that accompanies each apparently
eulogistic comment. The whole passage is a masterpiece of contemptuous sarcasm. At times, as the various virtues of a wife are
recited, we may seem to be listening to an authentic *encomium
uxoris*, but any danger of the eulogies being taken at their face
value is averted either by the grotesqueness of the example or its
essential irrelevance. Thus in the catalogue of good wives Judith
makes an unexpected appearance:

> By wys conseil she Goddes peple kepte,
> And slow hym Olofernus, whil he slepte.
>
>   (E 1367–8)

But at the time of her murderous exploit Judith was not a wife
but a widow, and she spent the night (and presumably the bed)
alone with Holofernes in his tent before killing him in his sleep.
Similar hints are dropped throughout the section—notably in the
couplet,

> A wyf wol laste, and in thyn hous endure,
> Wel lenger than thee list, paraventure.
>
>   (E 1317–18)

If Act I is anti-romance followed by anti-encomium, Act II
(E 1393–1708) is anti-disputation. The narrative has been resumed
and we learn for the first time that the knight's name is January,
and that his brothers Placebo and Justinus have similarly semi-
allegorical names. They and other friends are all assembled in
January's house to be told about his matrimonial intentions. The
débat is opened by January who announces his decision in
crudely sexual terms:

> 'But o thyng warne I yow, my freendes deere,
> I wol noon oold wyf han in no manere.
> She shal not passe twenty year, certayn;[1]
> Oold fissh and young flessh wolde I have ful fayn.
> Bet is ' qoud he, ' a pyk than a pykerel,
> And bet than old boef is the tendre veel'.
>
> (E 1415–20)

The very non-academic *disputatio* is continued by Placebo, for
whom everything that January says or decides is right, and then
by Justinus, who deplores January's proposal equally emphatically
—partly perhaps, because as he admits, in spite of his name:

> I have wept many a teere
> Ful pryvely, syn I hav had a wyf.
>
> (E 1544–45)

January is eventually successful in finding a girl, 'of smal degree'
but of 'age tendre', who he decides will do, and the *débat* is
continued. January's principal concern now is that his marriage
will make him so happy here on earth that he cannot expect to go
to Heaven when he dies. Justinus reassures him:

> Despeire you noght, but have in youre memorie,
> Paraunter she may be youre purgatorie!
>
> (E 1669–70)

With the appearance of May the genre changes again and no
more is heard of either Justinus or Placebo. Act III returns us to
anti-romance. These crucial and brilliant lines (E 1709–2020)
present us with the realities of Courtly Love. The description of
May's first night with January was selected by Aldous Huxley for
inclusion in his anthology *Texts and Pretexts*:

> The bryde was broght abedde as stille as stoon;
> And when the bed was with the preest yblessed,
> Out of the chambre hath every wight hym dressed;
> And Januarie hath faste in armes take
> His fresshe May, his paradys, his make.
> He lulleth hire, he kisseth hire ful ofte;
> With thikke brustles of his berd unsofte,
> Lyk to the skyn of houndfyssh, sharp as brere—
> For he was shave al newe in his manere—
> He rubbeth hire about hir tendre face . . .

[1] The text quoted, here and through this essay, is that of F. N. Robinson
(2nd. edn., 1957). Although *twenty* is the reading of the Ellesmere and
Hengwrt MSS, seven of the lesser MSS have *sixtene*. In the Middle Ages and
the Renaissance a girl was conventionally supposed to reach her peak of
beauty at sixteen. Perdita was sixteen, Marina fourteen and Miranda fifteen.

And thanne he taketh a soppe in fyn clarree,
And upright in his bed thanne sitteth he,
And after that he sang ful loude and cleere,
And kiste his wife, and made wantown cheere.
He was al coltissh, full of ragerye,
And ful of jargon as a flekked pye.
The slakke skyn aboute his nekke shaketh
Whil that he sang, so chaunteth he and craketh.
But God woot what that May thoughte in hir herte,
Whan she hym sangh up sittynge in his sherte,
In his nyght-cappe, and with his nekke lene;
She preyseth not his pleyyng worth a bene.

(E 1818–27, 1843–54)

Huxley's comment on this passage—and on May's affair with Damyan that derives from it—is worth quoting.

> What a fearful picture of marriage as it should not be! Chaucer was doing things before 1400 which no other narrative artist did for nearly four centuries. For, in the tale of January and May, there are passages for which one can find no parallel outside modern fiction. For example, when May receives a love letter, she hurries off, in order to read it, to the W.C. Which, is of course, exactly where any one who wanted to be quite certain of privacy would go. But what author before Flaubert would have stated this obvious fact. Except for Chaucer I can think of none.[1]

But Huxley's comparison with the modern novel misses an important point. Chaucer's 'unpleasantness' is not self-sufficient; it is directed at the vague and conventional descriptions of the French romances of his time. The sordid detail is primarily a criticism of the escapist fantasy that the French and English Courts revelled in. What they loved above all was the embellishment of 'rhetoric'. Chaucer therefore provides anti-rhetoric. Here, for instance, is a passage of rhetorical parody immediately following the introduction of Damyan (January's squire who is to be May's seducer):

O perilous fyr, that in the bedstraw bredeth!
O famulier foo, that his servyce bedeth!
O servant traytour, false hoomly hewe,
Lyk to the naddre in bosom sly untrewe,
God shilde us alle from youre aqueyntaunce!
O Januarie, dronken in pleasance

---

[1] *Texts and Pretexts* (1932), 135–6. Huxley's essay on Chaucer in *On the Margin* (1923) is, in my opinion, the best critical appreciation of Chaucer since Dryden's 'Preface' to his *Fables* (1700).

> In mariage, se how thy Damyan,
> Thyne owene squier and thy borne man,
> Entendeth for to do thee vileynye.
> God graunte thee thyne hoomly fo t'espye!
> For in this world nys worse pestilence
> Than hoomly foo al day in thy presence.
>
> (E 1783–94)

A similar passage begins 'O sly Damyan' (E 1869). Neither is to be taken seriously. They are part of the critique of the romance of Courtly Love to which the whole of Act III is essentially devoted. How much Chaucer was ahead of his times here is indicated by the marginal note 'Auctor' opposite both these passages, and also E 2057, E 2107 and E 2125, in the Ellesmere manuscript (and some others). According to F. N. Robinson (1957 ed. p. 694) the scribes added such notes 'to call attention to sententious or otherwise noteworthy utterances—to such quotable texts as were regularly called *auctoritees*'. But Chaucer's whole object, at least in the *Mechant's Tale*, was precisely to satirize such rhetorical exclamations, and he would have been disturbed to have them described as 'noteworthy' or 'quotable'. On the contrary, like the continuous reminder that May was 'fresh' (the epithet is applied sixteen times altogether), they are part of the already obsolete machinery of the courtly romance. January by stimulating and then failing to satisfy Eve's sexual instincts had taken all the bloom from her freshness, and by the time the copulation with Damyan occurs she is already as cynical as a woman of the town. The recurrence of Chaucer's favourite line (used on four other occasions),

> Lo, pitee renneth soone in gentil herte!
>
> (E 1986)

is a similar warning sign and not in the least one of approval at May's instantaneous surrender to Damyan's advances (which would have been most improper in a romance). We remember now that May, far from being a 'gentil', was by birth 'of smal degree', Chaucer's dissatisfaction with the conventional medieval romance is continuously present in this episode. Life, as he had now found out, was cruder, coarser, less rarefied—but also more *real*.

Act IV (E 2021–2139) includes a deflation of a mythological episode. The gods Pluto and Proserine have discovered the

walled garden that January has had made for himself and May,
and they often repair there with their fairy rout. But Chaucer
has vulgarized them, and their domestic quarrels enable the
Merchant's Tale to reach the almost fabliau ending of its Act V
(E 2320–2418). January is blind by now and May and Damyan
have made an assignation in the garden, counting on his not
being able to see them. But as they are 'in the act' Pluto restores
January's sight, feeling sorry for the old man. Prosperine, however, comes to the rescue of May who manages to persuade
January that what he saw was the only way to cure his blindness.
The story is an old one, but as retold by Chaucer the broad
comedy of the incidents merges into pathos. It is almost as if the
carpenter in the *Miller's Tale*, another *senex amans*, should turn
out in the end to be its hero. The humanizing of January like the
humanizing of Pluto, if not exactly cancelling out the mythology
and the farcical conclusion, has given them an extra dimension.
In the terms of genre Chaucer has taken us to the edge of the
novel—and in the process Ovidian mythology and the fabliau
have come to look more than a little inadequate.

II

In the mind of an alert and humane reader January's progress
through the various literary genres leaves him, until the last lines
of the *Tale*, a fool, a hypocrite, a sensualist. January's concern
has been simply to maximize what sexual satisfaction he can
obtain. (Chaucer is discreetly vague on the degree of his impo-
tence.) And until the final episode our continuous reaction to him
is primarily one of fascinated comic disgust. The reluctant com-
passion that we finally extend to him may therefore seem inconsistent, a breach of the *Tale*'s narrative logic. And so no doubt it
is, if the *Merchant's Tale* is detached from the human context of
his private and public life. But is such a detachment ever possible?
Though we know relatively little about Chaucer's biography,
what we do know is as essential a part of the meaning of what he
wrote as is the Westminster variety of London English that he
used as a linguistic medium.

The classic statement of the anti-intentionalist case by Wimsatt
and Beardsley reduced the meaning of a poem to what is dis-
coverable 'through the semantics and syntax of a poem, through
our habitual knowledge of the language, through grammars,

dictionaries, and all the literature that is the source of dictionaries, in general through all that makes a language and culture'.[1]
It is true they add 'the biography of an author' as 'part of the
word's history and meaning',[2] but the reduction of 'biography'
to 'word' is significant. Are not the larger units of literature—the
single poem or play, the series of related poems or plays, an
author's complete works, or even those of a whole 'movement'
or period—equally susceptible of biographical influence? *The
Merchant's Tale* raises the issue in a particularly challenging
form.

It is, Chaucer scholars seem to agree, almost certainly Chaucer's
last poem of any importance. Since it includes a reference to the
Wife of Bath it must be later than her Prologue. If the inferior
Canon's Yeoman's Tale follows it, as is possible, it may still be
considered a farewell to literature of the same sort as *The
Tempest* (which was followed by Shakespeare's collaborations
with Fletcher).

The profounder criterion is simply the degree to which we as
readers—and therefore counterparts of the author—find ourselves
involved. May not both Chaucer's conversion of genres into anti-
genres and the final pity we feel for January have a personal
origin in Chaucer's own experience? May not the extraordinary
force (including the general 'unpleasantness' of the *Merchant's
Tale*) express something that will not be found in grammars and
dictionaries?

Unlike Shakespeare Chaucer had no magical staff to throw
away at the end of his career. Instead he sums up with a special
intensity a problem that had been perplexing his private life
since the death of his wife in 1387. Should he marry again—as
most of his contemporaries in the Court circle would certainly
have done? His own marriage does not seem to have been a
happy one. Philippa, the daughter of Sir Payne Roet, was the
sister of Katherine Swynford, who was first John of Gaunt's
mistress and then his third wife. It has been plausibly suggested
that John of Gaunt, who was notoriously immoral, may have
married Philippa off to Chaucer to conceal the birth of an ille-
gitimate child, perhaps the man later known as Sir Thomas
Chaucer. The details of the evidence need not be repeated here.[3]

---

[1] *The Verbal Icon* (1954), p. 10.   [2] *Ibid.*
[3] The fullest treatment of the problem is by Russell Krauss (New York,
1932).

But the generous gifts showered on Philippa and Thomas compare suspiciously with those received or not received from John of Gaunt by Chaucer himself or his undoubtedly legitimate son Lewis.

Marriage in all its various aspects is certainly a dominant theme in the *Canterbury Tales*. We may be sure that this interest has a connection both with Chaucer's own experience of it and with those of his married friends. Many of them may also about this time have been offering him their daughters' hands, with their youth and beauty compensating perhaps (as with May) for the smallness of the dowry. And Chaucer, who was no hermit, may be presumed to have been interested. But by the time the *Wife of Bath's Prologue* and the *Merchant's Tale* were written he was older and more savagely realistic. The sentimental April of the General Prologue had not restored its 'licour' in every vein of the poet; a re-marriage in 1394 or 1395 would in fact have been to couple a January with a May—with the consequence spelt out in all its appalling aspects in the *Merchant's Tale*. Not to realize the sexual implications of such a marriage would have been a blindness fully justifying the taunts of Justinus; the grim physical fact of old age was an admonition of a specially personal kind. January, who had been the eye-witness of his own cuckolding, is compelled to agree, or pretend to agree, that he had been mistaken; 'lat al passe out of mynde'. Pluto, who had temporarily restored January's sexual potency within the magic garden, was also the god of the Underworld. The mortal death that the mention of this name carried with it would soon be the fate of both January and Chaucer; in avoiding a second marriage Chaucer is well aware that he is not avoiding that ultimate end. And so, with the realization, a degree of sympathy for January's condition—and domestically perhaps Pluto's too—finally mitigates Chaucer's disgust.

If the *Merchant's Tale* was written in 1395, it is at least an intriguing coincidence that one of the shorter poems known as 'Lenvoy de Chaucer a Bukton' (probably written in 1396) is on the same theme. Bukton, who was born in 1350 and was therefore probably re-marrying, is advised (as he would have been by *Punch* later) not to. But Chaucer is careful not to overstate the case against marriage:

> I dar not writen of it no wikkednesse,
> Lest I myself falle eft in swich dotage.

Within four years of his death Chaucer is still not *sure* that he may not commit January's error, though in the ballade's 'Envoy' the advice becomes more specific:

> The Wyf of Bathe I pray you that ye rede
> Of this matere that we have on honde.

The Wife of Bath had already been held up in the *Merchant's Tale* as the best possible argument against marriage, though not by Chaucer in person or as narrator, or even by the hypothetical Merchant, but by Justinus:

> The Wyf of Bathe, if ye han understonde,
> Of mariage, which we have on honde,
> Declared hath ful in litel space.
>
> (E 1685–87)

The passage is the only one in the whole of the *Canterbury Tales* in which a *dramatis persona* in one Tale alludes to another in another Tale. The oddity distinguishes it from the method pursued elsewhere and helps to support the suggestion that the *Merchant's Tale* is different in kind from the others. What is perhaps more significant in this case is that the reference is made by Justinus, whose rough common sense might almost be the moral of the *Tale* itself. Here, instead of the dummy presented to us elsewhere as Chaucer, we are entitled to feel we are close to the sophisticated reality of the author himself. Although not strictly autobiographical Justinus's is *almost* the voice of the authentic Chaucer; it is certainly the bearer of the moral of the *Merchant's Tale*. What is of special interest about that voice is its unabashed 'outrageousness'.

Chaucer, the vintner's son on whom John of Gaunt is at least suspected of passing a cast-off mistress as wife, was at last to speak his mind. And he seized the opportunity with both hands. What a set they were!

8

A Note on Chaucer's 'Rhetoric'●

What is style? What in particular are the relations the ideal
speech of a society ('good English') bears to its greatest literature
(the best English words in the best English order)? Reduced to a
simple formula, some of the principal points of connection are
presumably (i) *speech rhythm* (metre, euphony), (ii) *spoken
vocabulary* (verbal connotations from etymology, learned or
popular use, homonyms and synonyms), (iii) *colloquial syntax*
(degree of elasticity available for the range of semantic differentiation required by the various *genres* and figures of speech), and
(iv) *speech context* (actual or implicit audiences, with modes of
communication, political or philosophical systems, etc., presupposed).

I propose this formula with diffidence; it might be expanded,
qualified, subdivided. But I want to get down to the brass tacks.
My formula is really intended to prepare the way for a critical
look at the first stanza of *The Parliament of Fowls*. As it happens,
D. S. Brewer has brought out a first-class edition of the poem in
Nelson's Medieval and Renaissance Library, which will now
supersede both the text and commentary of F. N. Robinson's
Complete Works of Chaucer. I am therefore able to lean on him

● *Essays in Criticism*, 11 (1961).

when expert assistance becomes necessary. Part of the point of this exercise, however, is to stake a claim in the hitherto specialized area of Chaucer's style for the amateur critic.

The case against most medieval specialists is that they do not know the right questions to ask. The answers that the typical Chaucer scholar, for example, provides, though generally correct, are generally irrelevant—or at best preliminary. In rough rude terms that, or something like it, is my stylistic challenge. Under which King, Chaucerian, 'style' or 'background'?

I quote the stanza in Mr Brewer's text (which differs in l. 2 from those of Robinson, Heath and Skeat):

> The lyf so short, the craft so longe to lerne,
> Th' assay so sharp, so hard the conquerynge,
> The dredful joye, alwey that slit so yerne,
> Al this mene I be Love, that myn felynge
> Astonyith with his wondyrful werkynge
> So sore iwis, that whan I on hym thynke,
> Nat woot I wel wher that I flete or synke.

(L. 3, *slit so yerne* = slideth so quick; l. 7, *flete* = float.)

The stylistic problem that the stanza poses is the rôle of rhetoric in it. Mr Brewer describes it as 'a treasure-trove of rhetorical devices':

> It begins with a *sententia* or striking apophthegm, which is one of the recognized methods of beginning a poem. The *sententia* is in the somewhat unusual form of *contentio* or contrast, and is, moreover, a *circumlocutio*, or roundabout way of expression. The second line contains a metaphor, which is also an example of *circumlocutio*. The first three lines are also an example of *interpretatio*, or different ways of saying the same thing (pp. 48–9).

Comments to the same general effect will also be found in H. S. Bennett's *Chaucer and the Fifteenth Century* (1947), Dorothy Everett's *Essays on Middle English Literature* (1955), and J. A. W. Bennett's *The Parlement of Foules* (1957). Incidentally, the last adds three more figures to Mr Brewer's list: *chiasmus* (l. 2), *oxymoron* (l. 3, dredful joye), *suspensio* (ll. 1–3).

I do not dispute for a moment that these distinguished medievalists are right. The question that must be asked is what is the literary function of this rhetorical density, which looks at first sight like the poetry of art in its extremest form. Why in particular does the rhetoric run out at the end of the third line?

To a lay eye the contrast is remarkable—nine rhetorical devices in ll. 1–3, and out of the dozens recommended by Mathieu de Vendôme and Geoffroi de Vinsauf not one in ll. 4–7? (The metaphor in *flete or synke* is from popular idiom and not from literary precedent.)

The first problem to settle—it has not been raised hitherto, as far as I am aware—is whether the abrupt reversal of style at l. 4 is deliberate. Instead of sticking to Vinsauf's *stylus grandiloquus* in which he had started, Chaucer apparently throws decorum to the winds and suddenly sinks into the *stylus humilis*. Did he know what he was doing? If he did, is this perhaps a new mode of *contentio*, a conscious clash of styles, in which the rhetorical textbooks are first followed with ingenious assiduity and then gaily and impudently abandoned? One would have liked expert guidance here.

A metrical analysis seems certainly to confirm the deliberateness of the stylistic reversal. It will be noticed that the first three lines of the stanza are all end-stopped and with the caesura in exactly the same place each time. They are also all strictly iambic and hendecasyllabic (the last syllable in each line a weak one as in the verse of Chaucer's Italian masters). Thus the five stresses all fall 'correctly' on important words: *lyf, short, craft, longe, lerne, assay, sharp, hard, conquerynge, dredful, joye, alwey, slit, yerne* (six stresses on nouns, five on adjectives, two on verbs, two on adverbs). With l. 4, however, pronounced enjambment sets in, the caesura moves, and the iambic and syllabic regularity breaks down. I have now italicized each final *-e* that is to be pronounced—though presumably they approximated to the mute *-e* of contemporary French verse:

> Al this mene I be Lov*e*, that myn felyng*e*
> Astonyith with his wondyrful werkyng*e*
> So sore iwis, that whan I on hym thynk*e*
> Nat wot I wel wher that I flete or synk*e*.

The first of the four lines begins with two spondees (or perhaps two trochees) and ends, apart from the last weak syllable, with three stresses; and instead of eleven syllables it has twelve (later in the poem whenever *love* is not followed by a vowel it is disyllabic). And the last three lines, though syllabically more or less regular, are equally imperfect as iambics however one juggles with the stresses. Line 6, for example, has only two emphatic syllables (*sore* and *thynke*), and l. 7 can only be scanned as iambic by an unnatural stress on *that* followed by a suppression of the stress on *I*.

In other words, the metre of the first three lines of the stanza demands a slow and incantatory enunciation, with a pause at the caesuras and the end of each line; the last four lines, on the other hand, 'want' to be spoken almost as prose, slowly and emphatically at first and then with a rush which only slows down as it reaches the semi-comic last line.

A possible clue to the variations of style and metre in this stanza may well be the special context of *The Parliament of Fowls*, especially the author-audience relationship implicit in it. As Mr Brewer rightly reminds us in his Introduction, this is a poem that was written to be *heard*. Its original 'publication' must have been a Court occasion similar to that depicted in the now familiar frontispiece of the Corpus (Cambridge) MS of *Troilus and Criseyde*. The poem was written, it appears, to be read aloud by Chaucer himself to an aristocratic, largely royal audience. This is the setting the *Parliament* presupposes. In reading it, then, we must have the Court of the young Richard II at the back of our minds—rather as we have a Globe performance at the back of our minds when we read *Hamlet*.

At the level of communication the crucial difference between Chaucer and Shakespeare is that Chaucer had no Richard Burbage or Chamberlain's Men as intermediaries between his text and his audience; he had to be his own producer and his own performer. *Troilus and Criseyde* shows how skilful he eventually became in exploiting dramatically the limitations of his rôle as Court poet, and there are hints that must not be missed in the earlier poems, including the *Parliament*. It was a heterogeneous audience, almost as heterogeneous as Shakespeare's. We must assume in the first place a sophisticated minority who would welcome the rhetorical bag of tricks; it is likely that Richard himself, an addict of contemporary French poetry, was something of a connoisseur in these things. But it is difficult to believe many of the ladies of the Court shared this taste, and the King's uncles may well have preferred stronger meat. Hence perhaps the dualism of tone in our stanza. The King must be placated, and the highbrows must be shown that Chaucer's poetry was as capable of rhetorical refinement as that written in Latin or French. So we get the first three lines.

But the Wicked Uncles must not be forgotten either; and there

are also the great ladies who, bewildered perhaps by the intricate
enigmas of ll. 1–3, had to be reassured. And so Chaucer's voice
changes. Instead of continuing to pile up the rhetoric to an
appropriate climax ('O Love! O mystic mighty Love!') Chaucer
steps outside his original part with an almost perceptible wink:

> Al this mene I be Love . . .

'Cheer up! What I'm really getting at after all these fine phrases
is our old friend Sex!' Is that to read into the stanza's four last
lines a good deal more than they will bear? Perhaps, but that
there is a change of some sort to a new informality seems clear.
Apart from the absence of rhetoric and metrical regularity, the
writing becomes careless and even slovenly. Thus *myn felynge*
must just mean 'me'; *sore* too is weak (Chaucer's astonishment at
Love's wonder-working powers is not painful but enormous); and
iwis is a mere 'filler', one of those empty phrases the oral poets
used to pad out their lines.

But it is always unwise to accuse Chaucer of incompetence,
even in a comparatively early poem. If the writing in the last four
lines seems slovenly, it is a prudent assumption that it was meant
to seem slovenly. As I see it, Chaucer was preparing the way in
these lines for a return to his favourite rôle in the longer poems of
comic nincompoop. The lines are slovenly only in the sense in
which the Tale of Sir Thopas is 'drasty speche' and 'rym dogerel';
in other words, they are to be judged by their *dramatic* function.
The second stanza of the *Parliament*—in which Chaucer assures
his audience that, unlike the rest of them, *he* has never had any
first-hand experience of love (a joke repeated in *Troilus*)—seems
to clinch this point, though there is really no need to go beyond
the first stanza to settle it. Note, for example, the sudden and
repeated emergence of the first person singular in ll. 4–7—*I* four
times, and one *myn* as well, in the four lines. (The first three
lines are completely impersonal.) It is tempting to guess that
Chaucer had a special tone of voice and cast of countenance
which he reserved for these mock-serious references to himself.
And, secondly, there is the grotesque image of the last line.
Chaucer, we are to understand, is so overcome by the wonder-
workings of love that he cannot be sure if he is on land or on sea
—and if on the latter whether he is floating or sinking. As this
problem of his whereabouts is being raised by the plump poet,
'more fat than bard beseems', one can almost detect a coy peep

from the book to the belly. (Voice of Wicked Uncle: 'Don't worry, Geoffrey, you'll float all right!')

Mr Brewer must forgive me if I am being unnecessarily frivolous. But it is, I take it, a fundamental principle of stylistic analysis that we press the verbal implications *as far as they will go*: to the aesthetic limit on the one hand (the proposed interpretation must not spoil the poem), to the historical limit on the other (the interpretation must not contradict the poem's historical context). A detail of some interest is that many MSS read *wake or wynke* at this point. Was this a revision by Chaucer himself intended to mitigate the comic exuberance of the original image? Or is an early copyist responsible who was more worried by decorum's requirements than the author? Whichever it may be, Mr Brewer is clearly right, on stylistic grounds alone, to prefer *flete or synke*. The contrast between the way the stanza begins and the way it ends ought, one feels, to be maximal—from sublime to ridiculous, from the highest 'highbrow' to the lowest 'lowbrow'.

A general conclusion remains to be drawn, viz.: *there is more than one rhetoric in Chaucer.* By the side of the formal rhetoric of Vendôme and Vinsauf, impersonal, hieratic, Latin, we must also recognize an informal anti-rhetoric, popular, proverbial, English. We are familiar with this antithesis at the level of *genre*, characterization, topoi, audiences—Knight's Tale versus Miller's, romance versus fabliau, eagles and falcons versus geese and ducks, 'gentils' versus 'churls'. But—except occasionally by such scholars as Margaret Schlauch and Charles Muscatine—the opposition has not been worked out systematically at the level of diction or metre. The horse, as usual, has been overlooked in favour of the cart. After all, narrative excellence and brilliance of realistic characterization are only effects; their cause is the style. Take the best words and the best word-order away and nothing is left but plots and character-sketches. It is the style alone that fills out and confers significance on classical legend or folk-motif and their shadowy actors. But Chaucer's style, unlike Spenser's or Milton's, is not 'organic' or 'esemplastic'; its motive force is contrast, irony, parody—a dualism of intention perhaps corresponding to Chaucer's relationship to the ambiguous world in which he lived.

Finally, as a pedantic anticlimax, I want to turn Mr Brewer's principle of *heard* poetry against the reading he has adopted in l. 2 of our stanza. Earlier editors have all read

Th'assay so hard, so sharp the conquerynge.

(Robinson glosses *assay* here 'attempt'.) Mr Brewer, following his
copy-text (the excellent Cambridge MS Gg.IV.27), inverts the
adjectives:

Th'assay so sharp, so hard the conquerynge.

(*assay* has now to be understood as 'assault'; the usual meaning in
Chaucer is 'trial'.) To a modern reader the Brewer reading may
well seem superior, since an assault prepares the way militarily
for a conquest. It completes the metaphor and makes it more
vivid. But then *we* absorb Chaucer's meanings almost entirely
through the eyes, which can usually take in a whole line at a
glance and, if puzzled, can always stop and refer back until the
correct interpretation has been negotiated. The oral audience was
without these advantages. If Chaucer had read out *assay* before
conquerynge, his audience would naturally assume that the word
carried its normal meaning of 'trial', and it would be too late
to make the mental correction at the end of the line after
conquerynge, as by then Chaucer was already presenting them
with the *next* line. Unless Mr Brewer can provide evidence that
the 'assault' meaning of *assay* was more familiar in London than
the *OED* examples suggest (the fourteenth-century ones are all
Scotch or West Midland), he is in effect asserting Chaucer's
incompetence as an oral poet. Simply as oral poetry the pre-
Brewer reading wins hands down. It respects the limitations of
the medium.

It would be a pity all the same to surrender the 'assault' notion
altogether. And the textual critic who enquires how it was that
the early and accurate Cambridge MS came to make his mistake
has still to be answered. Should Mr Brewer perhaps take his
courage in both hands and emend *assay* to *assaut* (a good
Chaucerian form)? The emendation would presuppose an error
in the archetype, since none of the MSS read *assaut*, but arche-
types are not infallible. Chaucer's views on his 'Owne Scriveyn'
Adam are familiar.

But I am not arguing for the emendation so much as for the
principle underlying it. The wisest words I have read on this
question are those of the German classical scholar Paul Maas
(I quote from the English translation of his *Textual Criticism*,
Oxford, 1958, p. 40):

The core of practically every problem in textual criticism is a problem of *style*, and the categories of stylistics are still far less settled than those of textual criticism. . . . [Maas then quotes Bentley's note on Horace, Odes 3.27] *nobis et ratio et res ipsa centum codicibus potiores sunt*. This remark has always tempted some scholars to misuse it, and it will always continue to do so, but it is true.

Mr Brewer will say Amen to that. And we must, he and I now join to suggest, extend Maas's dictum *beyond* textual criticism to the other modes of literary criticism and linguistic study: in all of them, we believe, the core of practically every problem is a problem of style.

Aren't we right?

9

A. E. Housman: The Poetry of Emphasis*

I

The author of *Poems by Terence Hearsay*—a collection now better known as *A Shropshire Lad*, the title suggested by Housman's friend A. W. Pollard of the British Museum—was also the Professor of Latin at University College, London. By the time *Last Poems* came out in 1922 he was the Kennedy Professor of Latin at Cambridge and a Fellow of Trinity College in that university: a man, in short, at the top of the academic tree. It is natural, therefore, for the critic of Housman's poetry to ask what connection there is, if indeed there is any at all, between the pseudo-Salopian Terence, who put down 'Pints and quarts of Ludlow beer' and whose best friend murdered another farm labourer called Maurice (*A Shropshire Lad*, viii)—and the acidulous scholar who freely admitted that he had never actually spent much time in Shropshire. The question is more insistent in Housman's case than in that of such other scholar-poets as Milton or Gray, partly because of the wider gap between the particular poetic *persona* he adopted and the man himself, and partly because of the element of autobiography, usually veiled though often unconcealed, that is present in his best poems.

● From *A. E. Housman: a collection of critical essays* (ed. Christopher Ricks, 1968).

An aspect of the Housman problems to which I shall be returning later in this essay is that he was a homosexual. The lines beginning 'Oh who is that young sinner with the handcuffs on his wrists?' (first published after Housman's death in Laurence Housman's memoir of his brother) can have no other meaning. Another posthumous poem (*More Poems*, xxxi) that seems to be even more directly autobiographical begins:

> Because I liked you better
> Than suits a man to say,
> It irked you, and I promised
> To throw the thought away.

But a critic's first concern is with the poems as poems and not with the neuroses of his poet. At least twenty of Housman's poems are likely to live as long as the language. If these poems continue to tease and fascinate the critical reader today, as I think they do, he will want to define to himself the special *literary* quality that they have. It is a quality almost unprecedented in English poetry that can, I think, be shown to derive from Housman's exceptional sensitivity to both English and Latin considered simply as languages. Looking round for some clue to connect Terence Hearsay with the Cambridge Latinist (whose *magnum opus* was a definitive edition of the almost unreadable *Astronomica* of Manilius), I remembered a book that my own classical tutor had made me read when I was a schoolboy. The book is Sidney T. Irwin's *Clifton School Addresses*, which has a characteristically suggestive dictum in a lecture with the title 'Why We Learn Latin'. Why should the writer who aspires to write good English also learn Latin? 'We learn Latin,' Irwin answers, 'because the merits of this language are not the merits of ours, and its defects not our defects.' If this is indeed true, as I suppose it is, it may help to explain the peculiar flavour of Housman's poetry. The bitter, cynical-sentimental tone of voice is no doubt that of a homosexual rejected both by his friend and by society, but bitterness *per se* is not a recipe for a good poem. As Mallarmé is said to have reminded Degas (who had good ideas but somehow could not make a poem out of them), 'Poetry is made out of words'. (*The best words in the best order*.)

It would be absurd, of course, to suggest that Housman became the foremost Latinist of his generation simply in order to improve his English. What can be said, however, is that his expertness in the Latin language left an indelible imprint on both his English prose style and his poetry. A fact that is often overlooked is that he had proved in a series of articles in the specialist journals his mastery of Latin poetry—and to a lesser extent of Greek poetry too—*before* he had written any of the English poems for which he is remembered, or indeed almost any English poems at all. Of the 105 poems in the two collections that he published himself not one is known to have been written before 1890, though '1887' (*A Shropshire Lad*, i), which is about Queen Victoria's Golden Jubilee, was presumably written in that year. But most of the poems in *A Shropshire Lad* date from 1895, when Housman was already a mature scholar with an international reputation. Any occasional adolescence in these poems is in the subject-matter and not in the treatment or style. 'I did not begin to write poetry in earnest,' Housman explained to a young French admirer towards the end of his life, 'until the really emotional part of my life was over.'[1]

The poetry that was written in earnest was written by the Professor of Latin and most of it in Housman's thirty-sixth or thirty-seventh year. For the rest of his life he continued, more intermittently, to write what are essentially the same poems. Some further implications of this late discovery of himself as a poet are worth underlining. One is that the author of *A Shropshire Lad* was already a virtuoso in English prose. By 1895, in articles, lectures, and reviews, Housman had shown himself a master of that pungent contempt for lesser minds which culminated in the fine art of disrespect later displayed in the prefaces to his editions of Manilius, Juvenal, and Lucan.

The Housman of 1895, then, knew exactly what he was doing. When *A Shropshire Lad* was rejected by the publishing establishment, from Macmillan's downward, and Housman had to pay for the book's publication out of his own pocket, he even made a poem (*A Shropshire Lad*, lxiii) out of his own discomfiture:

> I hoed and trenched and weeded,
>   And took the flowers to fair:
> I brought them home unheeded;
>   The hue was not the wear.

This is not the voice of a poet who has failed. He *knew* that he was writing unfashionable poetry, but he also knew with a self-

[1] The letter is dated 5 February, 1933, and was addressed to Maurice Pollet, who published it in *Études anglaises*, September 1937.

confidence similar to Horace's *Exegi monumentum aere perennius*
that for Housman too

> here and there will flower
> The solitary stars.

Although it may not be immediately clear to the modern
reader, *A Shropshire Lad* bears much the same disrespectful
relation to the poetry of its period that his devastating review of
Schulze's *Catullus* (*Classical Review*, viii, 1884), for example,
bears to its scholarship. This was the 'decadent' phase of English
Romanticism. Yeats and Lionel Johnson had both brought out
their separate *Poems* in 1895; Ernest Dowson's *Verses* came out
in 1896. And Swinburne was still, of course, in full spate
(*Astrophel and Other Poems*, 1894; *A Tale of Balen*, 1896). With
A Shropshire Lad Housman in effect turned his back, ostenta-
tiously and offensively, on all that twaddle. Whereas the typical
Romantic poem, from 'The Ancient Mariner' to 'The Ballad of
Reading Gaol', was diffuse and repetitive, with occasional brilliant details but far too often careless and slovenly, going on and
on and on, a Housman poem is short, precise, and the very reverse
of slovenly in the details of its poetic craftsmanship. It is true that
Housman's poetry is still, in the final analysis, 'Romantic', but the
concentration of style in his best work obscures any underlying
similarity by the exhilarating energy that is the immediate impression the reader obtains from it. This difference is *primarily*
attributable, I believe, to Housman's exceptional susceptibility to
the virtues of Latin.

The proposition has at any rate an *a priori* probability. I agree
that the Latin influence is not always immediately detectable.
Housman himself once gave the chief 'sources' of *A Shropshire
Lad* as 'Shakespeare's songs, the Scottish Border Ballads, and
Heine'.[1] To this list he might have added (i) the Authorized
Version of the Bible (which has contributed more phrases and
idioms to his verse than any other source), and (ii) the poems of
Robert Louis Stevenson, an early idol whose feet of clay he did
not discover until much later. But a literary source is not the same
thing as a linguistic influence. Housman's literary sense was acute
—his undergraduate years had after all been spent in the Oxford
of Matthew Arnold and Walter Pater (though his own tutors at
St John's seem to have been dullards)—and he would not have
needed to be told that both Greek literature and English literature

[1] Letter to Pollet.

were twice as good, considered simply as literature, as Roman literature. Norman Marlow, who has surveyed in some detail in his *A. E. Housman Scholar and Poet* (1958) all the literary sources hitherto reported, has only a few crumbs to record of direct Latin influence. The Mithridates who 'died old' (*A Shropshire Lad,* lxii) is mentioned by both Martial and Juvenal because of the precautions he took to inure himself against poison by taking constant small doses. And there are also a few tags like 'the sum of things' (*summa rerum;* not limited to Lucretius as Marlow states) which turn up from time to time.

The Latin 'influence', by which I mean the influence of the Latin language on Housman's English, operated at a less conscious and much more fundamental level. A few elementary points are all that need to be made here. When Irwin complained in the lecture already referred to that 'superfluity' was the besetting sin of English, he was thinking of Victorian English, of which this was certainly the grossest characteristic defect. More recent English prose and verse, even at its lower levels, has done something to correct the defect. Nevertheless, Irwin's claim that Latin provides a model of 'brevity' that an English writer can benefit from enormously still remains valid. This habit of verbal conciseness is probably Latin's most remarkable quality, and it is one that is inherent in the constitution of the language. It is possible, of course, to be verbose in Latin, but somehow even those Romans who achieved verbosity, as Cicero often did, managed it in fewer words than would be possible in any other European language. And Housman was not verbose. On the contrary, by utilizing a latent reserve of brevity in the Saxon and Old Norse basis of modern English, he was able to forge a style in English that challenges the verbal economy of Horace in Latin.

The critical problem, then, that is posed by Housman's best poems is the apparent union of two apparently incompatible qualities—a classic concision of style and a romantic extremism of temperament. I stress the *appearance* of both the union and the incompatibility, because the reality that lies behind the appearances is, I believe, neither strictly classical nor romantic. I shall call it *emphasis,* a stylistic quality that is inherent in Latin and difficult to attain in English without the artificial aids of italics or capital letters. Now emphasis was also the most prominent characteristic of Housman's personality. Whatever was said or done or suffered by this man surprises us by its excess. How

on earth can so clever a man, the holder of a college scholarship
who had obtained a First in the first part of Oxford's *Lit. Hum.*
course, have failed *completely* in the second part ('Greats')?
What quirk induced the London professor to adopt, not at all
convincingly, the poetic *persona* of a Shropshire agricultural
labourer? Why did Housman, the superbly skilful and sensitive
emender of classical texts, find it necessary to adopt in his prose
the controversial insolence of a Renaissance pedant? I ask these
questions not to attempt to explain them but to illustrate the
quality of personal excess in Housman of which 'emphasis', my
principal concern in this essay, was the stylistic expression in his
writings.

The emphasis of the poems is best approached via the emphasis
of the prose. Here is a characteristic passage from the preface to
Housman's edition of the fifth book of Manilius (1930), which has
the advantage of being detachable from its context and of being
concerned with a modern English poem and not with a Latin one:

> The following stanza of Mr de la Mare's 'Farewell' first
> met my eyes, thus printed, in a newspaper review.
>
>> Oh, when this my dust surrenders
>> Hand, foot, lip, to dust again,
>> May these loved and loving faces
>>   Please other men!
>> May the rustling harvest hedgerow
>> Still the Traveller's Joy entwine,
>> And as happy children gather
>>   Posies once mine.

I knew in a moment that Mr de la Mare had not written
rustling, and in another moment I had found the true word.
But if the book of poems had perished and the verse survived
only in the review, who would have believed me rather than
the compositor? The bulk of the reading public would have
been perfectly content with *rustling*, nay they would sincerely
have preferred it to the epithet which the poet chose. If I
had been so ill-advised as to publish my emendation, I should
have been told that *rustling* was exquisitely apt and poetical,
because hedgerows do rustle, especially in autumn, when the
leaves are dry, and when straws and ears from the passing
harvest-wain (to which 'harvest' is so plain an allusion that
only a pedant like me could miss it) are hanging caught in the
twigs; and I should have been recommended to quit my dusty
(or musty) books and make a belated acquaintance with the
sights and sounds of the English countryside. And the only
possible answer would have been *ugh!*

This, it will be agreed, is emphatic prose. The quantity of contemptuous disgust that Housman managed to pack into its last sentence would have received the admiring approval of Juvenal himself. The sarcasm of the long sentence preceding it is perhaps less effective because the realistic details tend to obscure the conviction Housman wishes to enforce upon us that the bulk of the reading public is an ass. But, of course, he was right. De la Mare wrote *rusting* and not *rustling*. It is typical, however, of this kind of criticism by emphatic assertion that Housman does not actually give 'the true word', or even provide any positive basis for preferring it. What disconcerts one in this case is that Housman relied so exclusively on his own inner literary light that he did not take the trouble to compare his newspaper's text with that in de la Mare's *Motley* (1918), where 'Fare Well' made its first appearance, in book-form, or the *Collected Poems* of 1920, or even with that in such reputable and easily available anthologies as *Georgian Poetry 1918–1919* (1920) or J. C. Squire's *Selections from Modern Poets* (1921), both of which print the poem. If he had done so he would have found that his newspaper had committed a second misprint. De la Mare did not in the end write

> May *these* loved and loving faces . . .

but, in opposition to 'this my dust' of the stanza's first line,

> May *those* loved and loving faces . . .(my italics)[1]

The difference between knowing 'in a moment' that *rustling* was the wrong word and not realizing that *these* was also wrong is the difference between one kind of emphasis and another: that of what might be called the pictorial imagination and that of the logical sense. Housman was more adept, in other words, at making his opponent *look* a fool than at making him *prove* himself a fool.

It is pictorial emphasis too that predominates in Housman's poems. The recognition that de la Mare's 'harvest hedgerows' must be *rusted* is a fellow-feeling for the same broad descriptive brush that he had himself used in the famous 'coloured counties' of 'In summertime on Bredon'; an even closer example of the same habit of generalized description is the later

[1] The assertion raises a textual problem in itself. *Motley* and the 1920 *Poems* both read 'these'; 'those' only appears in Marsh's and Squire's anthologies. But de la Mare must have been sent proofs by Marsh and Squire, and I assume that 'those' was de la Mare's revision in their proofs.

> On acres of the seeded grasses
> The changing burnish heaves.

On the other hand, the introduction of 'traveller's joy' in this poem (*Last Poems*, xl) is untypically detailed and the image may even have been lifted by him from de la Mare's 'Fare Well'.

Pictorial emphasis is common in the poems. The first stanza of 'Reveille' (*A Shropshire Lad*, iv) is thoroughly Latin in its rhetorical elimination of realistic paraphernalia:

> Wake: the silver dusk returning
> Up the beach of darkness brims,
> And the ship of sunrise burning
> Strands upon the eastern rims.[1]

What I have called the illogical strain in Housman is also found in this poem in a transition from these baroque grandiosities (which are continued in the second verse) to the common day of 'Up, lad, up, 'tis late for lying' with which the third verse begins. The indecorum of the transition results in a rather cheap over-emphasis. (The abrupter the descent from magnificence the more the reader sits up, but the descent must also justify itself aesthetically—as Housman's indecorousness often fails to do.)

The problem of Housman's emphatic vulgarities—which have nothing to do with the contemporary vulgarities of Kipling's *Barrack Room Ballads*—cannot be resolved without some further reference to Housman's private life. Indeed, the best poems are almost certainly the most personal ones, though the egotism is sometimes concealed. John Sparrow has already called attention to the special autobiographical significance of one of the poems published after Housman's death by his brother Laurence (*More Poems*, xxxiv):

> May stuck the land with wickets:
> For all the eye could tell,
> The world went well.
>
> Yet well, God knows, it went not,
> God knows, it went awry;
> For me, one flowery Maytime,
> It went so ill that I
> Designed to die.

[1] An even more Latin opening stanza is to be found in *A Shropshire Lad*, x:

> The Sun at noon to higher air,
> Unharnessing the silver Pair
> That late before his chariot swam,
> Rides on the gold wool of the Ram.

> And if so long I carry
>   The lot that reason marred,
> 'Tis that the sons of Adam
>   Are not so evil-starred
>   As they are hard.

Mr Sparrow has pointed out that in 1881, the year when Housman surprised Oxford by failing in Greats, the examination began on 28 May.[1] But the disaster that the poem records must surely have *preceded* the examination, which continued well into June. It seems more probable that the failure in Greats was the symptom or effect of some much more personal tragedy. When he was asked about the examination many years later by a colleague at Cambridge, Housman answered that the examiners had no option: 'he showed up no answers to many of the questions set.'[2] I take this to mean that the failure was a deliberate act, a part of the same mood of depression in which he had 'Designed to die'. Nobody with Housman's command of Latin and Greek could possibly have failed to scrape through Greats in 1881, when standards were decidedly lower than they are today, unless he had *wanted* to be ploughed.

The personal tragedy is usually and probably rightly connected with his feelings for Moses Jackson, his one great Oxford friend in spite of the latter's being 'a scientist and an athlete whose contempt for letters was unconcealed'.[3] It is a reasonable guess that Jackson rejected Housman's homosexual advances with brutal finality that 'flowery Maytime' of 1881:

> It irked you, and I promised
>   To throw the thought away.

But Housman, who later remained on friendly terms with Jackson until the latter's death, then discovered that it was easier to contemplate suicide than to put it into practice. I take this episode to have been 'the really emotional part' of his life. Its recollection in tranquillity more than ten years later was no doubt the efficient cause of *A Shropshire Lad*, though what he remembered was not only the rejection of love but his discovery that his own human heart was 'hard', too hard to have really wanted to end it all by self-murder.

[1] *Independent Essays* (1963), pp. 140–41.
[2] A. S. F. Gow, *A. E. Housman: A Sketch* (1936), p. 7.
[3] Gow, p. 9. A document printed in *Encounter* (Oct. 1967) has converted the probability into a certainty.

These speculations may help the sympathetic reader to get to critical grips with one of the most brilliant as well as one of the shortest poems in *A Shropshire Lad* (no. xvi):

> It nods and curtseys and recovers
> When the wind blows above,
> The nettle on the graves of lovers
> That hanged themselves for love.
>
> The nettle nods, the wind blows over,
> The man, he does not move,
> The lover of the grave, the lover
> That hanged himself for love.

There is not one superfluous word in this exquisite lyric. The last line of the second stanza is not, as a careless reading might suggest, a repetition of the first stanza's last line but a contrast to it; the plurals have become singulars. The lovers of the first stanza may have died together in a suicide pact, but the second stanza presents a solitary suicide, a single rejected or abandoned lover. Housman too had once been a lover of the grave in the sense that he had 'designed' to hang himself when Jackson refused his love. But, in the more literal sense of a dead lover *in* the grave, one who had actually hanged himself for love, Housman can only salute this man who was not as 'hard' as he had found himself to be.

> The man, he does not move.

What does move in the curiously abstract graveyard of Housman's imagination are the stinging nettles on the suicide's grave. In *More Poems*, xxxii, the nettle has become a general symbol of evil:

> It peoples towns, and towers
> About the courts of Kings,
> And touch it and it stings.

But in the *Shropshire Lad* poem the nettle seems to stand too for the gracefulness and resilience of a living object. In the series of verbs with which the poem opens—each verb one syllable longer than its predecessor as the force of the wind increases[1]—the nettle adjusts itself to the pressure of external circumstance by its

[1] The *O.E.D.* cites this line under *recover* 21c to exemplify 'To rise again after bowing or courtseying', but the only other example is from *The Spectator*, 5 December 1711, where the word clearly refers to the movement forward *after* the 'Town-Gentleman' 'made a profound Bow and fell back, then recovered with a soft Air and made a Bow to the next, and so to one or two more. . . .' The interesting discussion of the poem by Randall Jarrell

mobility. Unlike the suicide who 'does not move', who is finished physically, the nettle survives and in due course 'the wind blows over'. The parallel with Housman's own case is difficult to resist (he too was a stinging nettle in his reviews by 1895), though any such an autobiographical interpretation must not be pressed too far. I am only calling attention to what seems to be implicit in the poem's imagery, to a level of personal meaning below the verbal surface.

The theme of suicide, particularly an unhappy lover's suicide, recurs so often in Housman's poems—with its variants of the deserter who is shot or the murderer who is hanged—that the further possibility must be faced that he *exploited* in recollection the 'emotional part' of his life. The insinuation of a degree of insincerity is part of the general thesis I have been presenting of this poetry of emphasis. The general pessimism may also come into the same category. If Housman's letter to his French admirer is to be believed he 'became a deist at 13 and an atheist at 21'. Well, an atheist does not curse 'Whatever brute and blackguard made the world' (*Last Poems*, ix), because he knows that the world was not created supernaturally. And he is not disturbed by the thought that 'high heaven and earth ail from the prime foundation' (*A Shropshire Lad*, xlviii) because he does not believe in either a high heaven or a prime foundation. In these poems Housman seems to be utilizing for merely rhetorical purposes a system of religion that he had abandoned long before he wrote them. Other examples will immediately suggest themselves to anybody familiar with Housman's poems.

An autobiographical core, even if increasing maturity has destroyed its personal relevance—or rather *provided* that some such process has occurred—is a *sine qua non* of this poetry of emphasis. The assumption justifies and excuses Housman's sentimental use of Shropshire place-names, including such errors of detail as the attribution of a steeple to the church at Hughley, because to a boy born and bred in Worcestershire, as Housman was, the Shropshire hills had once really been the western horizon where the sun set. A group of poems that may also have had

Kenyon Review, 1, 1939, 260–71 seems mistaken in saying '*nod* and *curtsey* and *recover* add up to *dance*'. The nettles remain rooted in the ground and so cannot be said to dance even metaphorically. Housman's 'recovers' must be taken with the following line ('When the wind blows above'); the nettle returns to the vertical in a lull of the wind, so giving the appearance of previously nodding or curtseying.

some autobiographical content are those about soldiers. In Housman's London years the regiments quartered there normally provided middle-class homosexuals with their male prostitutes. The suggestion is a guess, but it is a guess that would help to explain his preoccupation with the lower ranks, especially in *A Shropshire Lad*. Indeed, the *persona* of the Shropshire yokel that holds the collection together may well derive from Housman's association with such men, most of whom were at that time country-born. If I am right, the soldier poems and such extensions from them as the pseudo-Pindaric 'To an Athlete Dying Young' would acquire a new dimension from their personal implications.

II

The poetry of emphasis of which Housman was a master can be compared to Latin poetry, but the thesis I have been propounding is not that it is especially like that of a particular Roman poet such as Propertius, his favourite. What I believe he tried to do, with considerable success, was to provide an English parallel to the Roman lyric by using the potentially emphatic elements in English for a somewhat similar purpose. The elements themselves, however, were naturally different, English being an uninflected language without the elaborate system of case-endings 'agreement' of adjective with noun, moods, tenses, and 'persons' of the verb, grammatical genders, etc., that enabled Latin to achieve its special brevity and concentration. In their place Housman substituted three special characteristics of English speech—the monosyllable, internal half-rhyme, and the compound word.

Some statistics may be useful at this point. *A Shropshire Lad* has no five-syllable words at all. Apart from the hyphened compound words there are only seven four-syllable words in it, and with the same exception fifty-five three-syllable words. All the remaining words in the sixty-three poems are monosyllables or disyllables, and no less than twenty of the sixty-three poems have no words at all of more than two syllables. The number of words of Latin origin are therefore inevitably few and far between, though their effect when they do occur is proportionately great. In what is for me the most memorable poem in *A Shropshire Lad* ('Others, I am not the first', no. xxx) the best line is certainly the last,

<blockquote>Beneath the suffocating night.</blockquote>

Here the combination of the four syllables of 'suffocating' and the monosyllabic 'night' clinches with memorable effect a poem made up entirely of emphatic monosyllables and disyllables—with the one exception of line 8, the midpoint of the poem, with its three-syllable latinism,

> Fear contended with desire.

Gerard Manley Hopkins's comment on Dryden ('his style and his rhythms lay the strongest stress of all our literature on the naked thew and sinew of the English language') is equally applicable to Housman. I am thinking now of some of the internal rhymes and half-rhymes, especially in *A Shropshire Lad*, which if it has more failures and vulgarities than *Last Poems* or the posthumous poems also has far more triumphs. Here are a few:

> His folly has not fellow
>   Beneath the blue of day . . .   (xiv)

and

> In the nation that is not
>   Nothing stands that stood before . . .   (xii)

and

> Eyes the shady night has shut
>   Cannot see the record cut . . .   (xix)

and

> A neck God made for other use
>   Than strangling in a string . . .   (ix)

Of the compound words much the most striking are the epithets, notably *sky-pavilioned* (iv), *valley-guarded* (xlii), *twelve-winded* (xxxii), *felon-quarried* (lix), *steeple-shadowed* (lxi)—all from *A Shropshire Lad*. The verbal economy of such compounds is here too a form of emphasis.

The reservation that must always be made with Housman—as with all but two or three of the Roman poets—is whether the stylistic brilliance has not been accompanied by a certain coarseness of human fibre. W. H. Auden's sonnet has made the point in a brilliant image:

> Deliberately he chose the dry-as-dust,
> Kept tears like dirty postcards in a drawer . . .

Since the emotional part of his life ended when he was only twenty-two, did he perhaps have no tears to keep? Were the postcards hoarded because they came in useful for an artist in words who would otherwise have had nothing to write about? Is the emphasis just a little too emphatic?

The questions suggest themselves in Housman's case more insistently than with a Juvenal or a Lucan, two Latin masters of emphasis whom he was to edit, or indeed with any Latin poet, because of the reader's suspicion that Housman exploited in cold blood the emotional experiences of his youth and early manhood. What had been private and intimate has become public, too public; the emphasis is too self-regarding, too egotistical. Such suspicions may, however, be the price that a poet writing in English has to pay who tries to emulate the Roman *gravitas* ('weight') by using a concentration of monosyllables to provide an English equivalent to the verbal density that Latin possessed ready-made in its system of inflections. But these linguistic devices, when elevated from 'language' to 'style', work in opposite directions. When a Horace exploits the compactness of diction implicit in the inflectional system of Latin, the effect is to devulgarize his often commonplace subject-matter and in the process to dignify the poet as a human being. English monosyllables, on the other hand, because of their familiarity and trivial associations, tend to vulgarize and sentimentalize whatever experience they are used to describe.

The point can be illustrated over and over again from Housman's writings. By the side of 'And the only possible answer would have been *ugh!*' from his prose we can set a couplet from 'To an Athlete Dying Young':

> Eyes the shady night has shut
> Cannot see the record cut . . .

To 'cut' or improve upon a record is a modern colloquialism that is not even listed in the *Oxford English Dictionary*; its presence here inevitably lowers the poem's heroic tone. The word is undeniably effective, but almost on the same level as *ugh*—emphatic but decidedly undignified. Unfortunately *A Shropshire Lad* considered as an aesthetic whole 'wants' to achieve a dignified emphasis. It would not be true that Housman never achieves it. I think, for example, of xxxi:

> On Wenlock Edge the wood's in trouble;
> His forest fleece the Wrekin heaves . . .

(But 'in trouble' only just escapes the emphasis of vulgarity.) And there is xl:

> Into my heart an air that kills
> From yon far country blows . . .

Here 'kills' is a superbly emphatic monosyllable; but its effect is
partly mitigated by the artificially archaic 'yon'. The knife-edge
of monosyllables on which Housman's style is poised has on one
side the words felt to be too colloquial (he overdoes *oh*, for
example), and on the other side the words pretending to be rustic
(*lad* is the worst offender, but there is also *lief*). The dilemma in a
sense is one that every poet is in. 'Words too familiar, or too
remote', as Dr Johnson put it in the life of Dryden, 'defeat the
purpose of a poet. From those sounds which we hear on small or
on coarse occasions, we do not easily receive strong impressions or
delightful images; and words to which we are nearly strangers,
whenever they occur, draw that attention on themselves which
they should transmit to things.' For Housman, however, the common problem had become much more acute. Instead of having the
whole of the English language to draw on in his poems he *is*
virtually confined, because of his obsession with emphasis, to
monosyllables occasionally varied with disyllables. And so, if he
has finally to be dismissed as a minor poet of remarkable talent,
the reason is perhaps primarily *technical*. The occasional cheap
sentimentality and affected bitterness are effects rather than
causes of the stylistic ambition to write English poems that would
be *mutatis mutandis* more Latin even than those written by the
Romans themselves. Housman might well have been a much better
poet if he had been less expert in Latin. As it is, the Professor
of Latin had the last word—in the excavations at Wroxeter
(Uriconium):

> The tree of man was never quiet:
> Then 'twas the Roman, now 'tis I.

III

The critical moral of this discussion of Housman's verse has
already been drawn in the essay on Chaucer's *Merchant's Tale*.
It may be summarized as the fallacy of the Intentional Fallacy.
Unless we are encouraged, that is, to ask what the author's
intentions are likely to have been when composing this or that
poem or group of poems, the area of profitable discussion is
apparently reduced to the text; all criticism becomes textual

criticism. The *context* within which even a textual problem must be ultimately considered is either ignored or treated as of minor relevance.

What is 'context', then? The term broadens out almost indefinitely, but a definition of one or two of its senses is worth attempting. Housman's classical triumphs were achieved, for example, almost exclusively in the emendation of corrupt texts. But a context is explicit even in an emendation. Two assumptions governed Housman's practice—*one*, that for each crux there was only one correct reading (the process of composition on wax having destroyed earlier authorial readings), *two*, that the author must have written 'good' Greek or Latin. The assumptions are normally valid within the context of the special conditions of classical literature, but they are not universally valid.

A classical emendation to be acceptable has to make better 'sense' than any alternative usage. The obvious objection to such a principle is that it is equally applicable to non-literature.[1] It works well enough at the level of a misprint in a newspaper, but to understand and respond to literature a merely linguistic sense must be transcended. The successful poem creates via its language an emotionally affecting human situation and once created such a situation can be used as a 'control' on the poem's language. Two words or images may both *per se* be equally 'good', but in the context of the human situation created in the poem one will be preferable to another—even if both are authorial, one the revision of the other.

The Professor of Latin, following the precedent of classical literature, permitted the revision of only one short phrase in the dozens of editions of *A Shropshire Lad* published in Housman's lifetime. In no. lii, 'He hears: long since forgotten/In fields where I was known' becomes sometime in the 1920s 'He hears: no more remembered/In fields where I was known'. Why was this one apparently insignificant change made? The criterion of context provides two possible answers. One is that the date of composition ('1891/2' in Housman's own list printed by his brother) was only preceded by the non-Shropshire 'The Merry Guide', which was written in 1890. No. lii ('Far in a western brookland') may there-

---

[1] Housman himself equates great literature in *The Name and Nature of Poetry* (1933) not with 'sense' but with 'nonsense'; Blake is the most poetical of English poets because sense never intrudes as it sometimes does in Shakespeare! But his own poems present no superficial difficulties.

fore also be outside the Shropshire cycle, its 'I' being Housman himself rather than Terence Hearsay. And if the context is auto-biographical Housman would certainly not have been 'long since forgotten' in his home by 1895.

A second and at least equally relevant context is suggested by an excess of alliteration in 'forgotten' and 'fields'. Here too the Latinist and the English poet were at odds. In the note on p. 8 of *The Name and Nature of Poetry* Housman lists among the prosodic topics he felt able to discuss 'the office of alliteration, and how its definition must be narrowed if it is to be something which can perform that office and not fail of its effect or actually defeat its purpose'. A recently discovered paper on Swinburne that Housman read to the Literary Society of University College, London in 1910 or 1911 amplifies his views. 'The proper function of alliteration', we learn, 'is to add speed and force to the motion of verse.'[1] If Swinburne's temptation was to attempt excessive speed by its use, Housman aimed at and generally achieved force from the use of alliteration. But in no. lii—with its first two stanzas studded with initial consonantal alliterations—the third stanza (in which the revision occurs) may well have seemed on reflection to defeat the purpose of force by overdoing it. And the context in this case would then be a prosodic one, though auto-biography also enters into it. The proportion of vowels to con-sonants is much greater in Latin than in English. The Professor of Latin, knowing this and aware of the resources of emphasis that the fact gave a Latin poet, would consequently be tempted to overdo consonantal alliteration. A comparative ignorance of Latin —say, the 'small Latin' of Shakespeare—would have served him better. This 'no more remembered' is certainly an improvement on 'long since forgotten', but the latter is not the only embar-rassing alliteration in *A Shropshire Lad*. And the two contexts I have chosen to illustrate what may be called the Intentional Necessity might be extended *ad infinitum*. What the author intended is not always fully knowable, but a sympathetic reader who is prepared to take a little trouble and to use his imagination need not be defeated even by an arrogant neurotic like Housman.

[1] *The American Scholar*, 39 (Winter 1969–70), 71.

IO

Second Thoughts: L. C. Knights and Restoration Comedy●

'Restoration Comedy: the Reality and the Myth' is one of Professor Knights's *Explorations* (1946), a collection that is described in its subtitle as 'Essays in Criticism mainly on the Literature of the Seventeenth Century'. Like most of the rest of the volume—one as a whole of great critical and literary distinction—the essay originally appeared in *Scrutiny*, in the number for September 1937, of which Mr Knights was then an active co-editor. In many ways, indeed, it is a characteristic *Scrutiny* product—the revaluation of a conventional assessment concluding in a drastic depreciation. But, unlike some similar critical exercises, this deflation is extraordinarily persuasive. The tone of voice, the selection and presentation of the evidence, the tactful elaboration of the argument, are all—at any rate give the appearance of being—nicely detached, scholarly and conclusive. The essay, not unnaturally, has been acclaimed one of the show-pieces of the Cambridge school. In their useful omnibus anthology *Criticism* (1948) Mark Schorer, Josephine Miles and Gordon McKenzie reprinted it to the exclusion of anything by Dr Leavis—an outrageous preference, of course, but one that is at least comprehensible. And in 1937 certainly, as a

● *Essays in Criticism*, 7 (1957), with minor revisions.

counterblast to the elegant or sophisticated nonsenses represented at their best by Bonamy Dobrée's *Restoration Comedy* (1924) and Kathleen M. Lynch's *Social Mode of Restoration Comedy* (1927), Mr Knights's icy distaste came as a healthy critical shock. His essay ends: 'The criticism that defenders of Restoration comedy need to answer is not that the comedies are "immoral", but that they are trivial, gross and dull.' Even Wycherley and Congreve's most hysterical disparagers, even Jeremy Collier, Macaulay, Thackeray and Meredith (for whom *The Way of the World* is only an exception that proves the barbarous rule) had not gone quite as far as that.

But 1937 is over thirty years ago. The phrase-making and aestheticism and naughtinesses of the 1920s, the whole post-1914–18 philosophy of life for which Lytton Strachey is a convenient symbol, are now as dead as donkeys. The danger today, as I see it, is that because of the brilliance with which its then necessary half-truths were brandished, Mr Knights's essay may come to be mistaken for the definitive judgment on Restoration comedy. I was probably not the only reader of *Essays in Criticism* who was dismayed to read in the October 1956 issue John Wain's almost unqualified acceptance of Mr Knights's general position. The time, it seems, has come when it is necessary to say, politely but firmly, that the Knights line—and *a fortiori* Mr Wain's amusing and ingenious variations on it—misses the essential critical point about Restoration comedy. Etherege, Wycherley, Congreve and Vanbrugh (with Dryden, the only ones that really matter) are not, of course, among the world's great dramatists. At times, even in their best plays, they *are* trivial, gross and dull. But in the best scenes of *The Man of Mode*, *The Country Wife* and *The Way of the World*, the three masterpieces of the *genre*—and perhaps in some scenes of Etherege's *She Would if she Could*, Congreve's *Love for Love*, and two of Vanbrugh's plays—much of the grossness and all the triviality disappear. At their best these dramatists are *serious*—in a way that Goldsmith, Sheridan or Wilde never are—though naturally it is in the paradoxical modes of seriousness appropriate to comedy. Something important is being said by them.

Mr Knights denies any seriousness to the plays. While recognizing that 'there is a place in the educational process for, say, La Rochefoucauld', he cannot detect in Restoration comedy a similar 'tough strength of disillusion' (p. 147). The plays seem to him to be confined to 'a miserably limited set of attitudes' (p. 137). Dorimant's intrigues in *The Man of Mode* are, he asserts, 'of no more human significance than those of a barn-yard cock' (p. 139); and Restoration comedy as a whole lacks 'the essential stuff of human experience' (p. 145). Moreover, the plays have 'no significant relation with the best thought of the time' (p. 133), and the unreal sexual conventions that they appeal to—that constancy is a bore, 'the pleasure of the chase', etc.—contrast unfavourably with 'such modern literature as deals sincerely and realistically with sexual relationships' (pp. 141–3).

Most of these objections seem to me to derive from a misunderstanding of what comedy can or should attempt. There is a concealed premise in Mr Knights's notion of what constitutes non-trivial literature, which comes out when he says, in the essay's first sentence, 'Henry James—whose "social comedy" may be allowed to provide a standard of maturity—once remarked that he found Congreve "insufferable"'. James's judgment, a casual comment apparently in one of his letters, is intended to carry more force than it very well can. Naturally James thought Congreve insufferable. Congreve would have thought James insufferable. And why should James's 'social comedy' provide a standard of the comically serious? How would Shakespeare's or Molière's comedies fare if they were judged by such a criterion? Underlying Mr Knights's more specific objections to Restoration comedy there is always the lurking implication that Wycherley and Congreve *ought* to have written like James or D. H. Lawrence, or at any rate (Mr Knights was writing while the seventeenth-century Dissociation of Consciousness was still booming) like an Elizabethan or Jacobean dramatist.

Ought they? It is the critical issue. Or is literature necessarily limited and directed by the processes of history to different dramatic forms at different times? Now if Eliot's dictum is accepted, as I suppose it must be (it is an unconcealed premise in Mr Knights's own *Drama and Society in the Age of Jonson*), that a 'radical change in poetic form' is almost always the 'symptom of some very much deeper change in society and in the individual' (*The Use of Poetry and the Use of Criticism*), it surely follows that any deep change in society and in the individual's relation to society will be reflected or expressed in a radical change in the dominant literary form. The depth of the social and individual changes brought about by the Civil War

will not be disputed. The first question, then, to be asked of
Restoration comedy, in order to determine a properly relevant
approach to it, is not whether it is like James or Shakespeare,
but in what respects it is the appropriate dramatic expression of
the social revolution of the mid-seventeenth century. Until this
question has been answered the strictly literary issues do not
arise at all. Mr Knights begs it when he contrasts the 'rich
common language' available to an Elizabethan dramatist with the
'mechanical' antitheses of Congreve. Rich in what currency?
And the same fallacy seems to be present in Mr Knights's comparison of Halifax's *Character of Charles II*—and later of some
sentences from Burnet—with passages from *Love for Love* and
The Way of the World. Can dramatic prose *ever* be usefully
compared with that appropriate to historical or political commentary? It is no criticism of chalk that it isn't cheese. The
question is whether it is good or bad chalk.

I have not the learning, nor is this the place, to attempt a
comprehensive critical account of the Restoration comedy of
manners. All that I can hope to do is to suggest a perhaps more
relevant approach to these plays. The sexual impropriety is still,
of course, the real bone of contention. The seventeenth century
distinguished between low comedy, which was merely meant to
make an audience laugh, and high or 'genteel' comedy, which
used the laugh as a form of social comment—*ridendo corrigere
mores*. A defence of Restoration comedy must demonstrate that
its sex jokes have a serious social function. I think it can be shown
that they have and that the plays, at their best, need fear no
comparison even in Mr Knights's eyes, with 'such modern literature as deals sincerely and realistically with sexual relationships'.
But if the demonstration is to be effective it will be necessary to
analyse the Restoration treatment of sex in some detail.

Here, then, as an elementary test case, is part of a seduction
scene between two minor characters in *Love for Love*—Tattle,
who is described in the list of *dramatis personae* as a 'half-witted
beau', and Miss Prue, 'a silly awkward country girl'. Tattle has
just explained to Prue that, if she is to be thought well-bred, she
must learn how to lie; her words must contradict her thoughts,
though her actions should also contradict her words.

> *Prue.* O Lord, I swear this is pure!—I like it better than
> our old-fashioned country way of speaking one's mind;—and
> must you lie too?

Tat. Hum!—Yes; but you must believe I speak truth.

Prue. O Gemini! well, I always had a great mind to tell lies: but they frighted me, and said it was a sin.

Tat. Well, my pretty creature; will you make me happy by giving me a kiss?

Prue. No, indeed; I'm angry at you.

[Runs and kisses him.

Tat. Hold, hold, that's pretty well;—but you should not have given it me, but have suffered me to have taken it.

Prue. Well, we'll do't again.

Tat. With all my heart.—Now then, my little angel!

[Kisses her.

Prue. Pish!

Tat. That's right—again, my charmer!

[Kisses again.

Prue. O fy! nay, now I can't abide you.

Tat. Admirable! that was as well as if you had been born and bred in Covent Garden. And won't you show me, pretty miss, where your bed-chamber is?

Prue. No, indeed, won't I; but I'll run there and hide myself from you behind the curtains.

Tat. I'll follow you.

Prue. Ah, but I'll hold the door with both hands, and be angry;—and you shall push me down before you come in.

Tat. No, I'll come in first, and push you down afterwards.

The episode is not one of Congreve's high spots, but its theatrical potentialities should be obvious. In the hands of a competent actor and actress the scene can be very funny indeed. In what, however, does the fun consist? First of all, I suppose, in the reversal—painless and in a way satisfying—of the auditor's normal rational expectations. On the stage are two human beings —looking, in spite of the beau's oddities and girl's country ways, very much like you and me—and a sort of lesson is apparently in progress. Tattle, the would-be seducer, is instructing Prue in the way a well-bred woman will receive the advances of a young man like himself. Part of the reversal of our expectations is, of course, the unusualness of the subject for a lesson, part of it is the contrast between Prue's uncouth speech and manners with her unerring knowledge of what she wants, but the big surprise, I suppose, is the girl's innocently enthusiastic progress, under her teacher's approving eyes, from kisses to copulation. But Prue is enjoying herself so much that the audience finds itself involuntarily sharing in the sudden topsy-turvy values. Nevertheless the scene is not, as Lamb tried to argue in the Elia essay 'On the Artificial Comedy of the Last Century', an excursion into an amoral fairyland, the land of cuckoldry, a Utopia of gallantry. For the effectiveness of the dramatic paradoxes depends upon the audience's continuous awareness that it is *not* in fairyland. Prue is an adolescent girl, and if she goes on as she seems determined to do she will soon find herself 'in trouble'. As the seduction proceeds to its final physical conclusion the tension between reality and what had at first seemed just a *façon de parler*, a mere make-believe parody of an ordinary lesson, mounts and mounts until the audience's laughter is replaced by an incredulous gasp. Is it all just an elaborate joke, or is Congreve going to take Prue at her word? The Nurse's interruption a moment later comes with the effect of a reprieve. We can laugh now; we are back in the world of the theatre; the realism to which we seemed committed, the ugliness of an actual seduction, has been waived. But it was a near thing, and with the relaxation of the tension the audience giggles happily in nervous relief.

At this point a tentative definition of comedy will have to be attempted. The agreeable reversal of an expectation that will itself be reversed must imply two separated planes of reality which the dramatist can assume in his audience: one that of everyday commonsense, and parallel and contiguous to it the fairyland plane of Lamb's essay, 'where pleasure is duty, and the manners perfect freedom'. It is obviously in the auditor's sudden transition from the objective plane of everyday rational reality, which must always be the point of comic departure, to the subjective plane of dream-fantasy or irrational dream-fulfilment that the ridiculous is born. Its most elementary form is the top-hatted gentleman who skids on a banana-skin. In terms of the dramatic structure of a Restoration comedy it is the continuous collision of the plays' heroes (including the heroines), that is, the 'men of sense', with their grotesque opposites—Sir Fopling Flutter, the Widow Blackacre, Foresight, Lady Wishfort and their like—each of whom is imprisoned in his own fantasy. The refinements all fall within this general pattern. Thus Tattle, who is a grotesque, 'a half-witted beau', in the scenes he shares with Valentine and Scandal, is the realist in the Miss Prue episode. To her the seduction is clearly just a new game, a variant of hide-and-seek ('you shall push me down before you come in'), whereas Tattle means business ('No, I'll come in first and push you down afterwards').

And there is a similar metamorphosis of Prue's own rôle later in the play, when she confronts Ben, the even more fantastic sailor-fiancé.

The possibilities of serious social comment within the comic framework seem to depend upon the degree to which either or both of the opposed planes of meaning are conceptualized. The clash in that case, instead of being between casual examples of human life to which the auditor reacts realistically or fantastically, is now between *representative* examples, that is, figures or attitudes that he recognizes as either typical (on the plane of common sense) or symbolic (on the plane of fantasy).

A historical approach will make it easier to appreciate the 'serious' role of sex in a Restoration comedy of manners. To the Puritans 'immorality' had virtually reduced itself to sexual irregularity, with drunkenness and blasphemy as poor seconds, a man's other sins being considered as a private matter between him and God. (By the 1650 Act 'for suppressing the detestable sins of Incest, Adultery and Fornication' incest and adultery became capital crimes without benefit of clergy, as did fornication on the second offence, first offenders getting three months' imprisonment.) On the other hand, to the restored Royalists by a natural reaction sexual licence—and drunkenness and blasphemous oaths —almost became a political duty. 'Joy ruled the day and love the night', as Dryden summed up Charles II's reign in *The Secular Masque*. The two attitudes were the points of maximum social divergence between the two parties into which England remained divided. As in politics a compromise was eventually worked out, for which Addison and Steele usually get most of the credit. But the relative sexual respectability of *The Tatler* and *The Spectator* was the end-product of a long process that was closely connected with political developments. If the political problem *par excellence* in the second half of the seventeenth century was to avoid the recurrence of a second Civil War, its social parallel, essentially, was to rationalize the sex instinct. Until such a rationalization had been achieved genuine communication between Whigs and Tories was hardly possible. Intermarriage, the final solution, was unthinkable. It is now a matter of history that a kind of sexual rationalization was achieved, perhaps over-achieved (it is a curious fact that hardly any of the eighteenth-century poets married). From one point of view, in the mode of allegory proper to high comedy, the Restoration drama records the strains that accompanied the achievement.

The term 'Restoration comedy' is really a misnomer. The first completely successful comedy of manners, Wycherley's *The Country Wife*, was not written until 1674—fourteen years after the Restoration itself. By that time the rationalization of sex had already made some progress. The two extremes had come to be identified on the stage with (i) younger members of the landed gentry (Tory), who spent their winter months in London applying to the pursuit of love the methods of the chase, which was their principal occupation on their country estates, and (ii) London merchants (Whig), who treated their wives as pieces of property to be even more jealously guarded than their gold. The earlier dramatists were all ex-Cavaliers and inevitably their heroes had been the gentlemanly rakes. In Wycherley's Horner, however, the rake-hero undergoes a sexual transformation, which prepares the way for Dorimant's surrender to Harriet in *The Man of Mode* and the complete rationalization of sex by Mirabel and Millamant in the fourth act of *The Way of the World*.

With these considerations in mind a re-appraisal may now be attempted of the *double entendres* in the notorious 'china scene' in *The Country Wife*. The criterion can now be the specifically literary one on which Mr Knights rightly insists. But an inquiry into the nature of comedy, hurried though it was, and a summary of the play's historical context should ensure that the literary questions which are asked are the relevant questions. It will be remembered that Lady Fidget, the hypocritical urban opposite of the innocently instinctive Country Wife (Mrs Pinchwife), has told her husband that she is going to the China House. In fact, however, she goes to Horner's lodgings, as she has discovered that Horner, who has tricked her friend Mrs Squeamish and the others into believing him impotent, is not really impotent at all. Horner and Lady Fidget disappear, and when they return it is to find Mrs Squeamish, who is just as vicious as Lady Fidget but is not yet in the secret, busily inquiring for him. Lady Fidget has a piece of Horner's china in her hand.

> *Lady Fidget.* . . . I have been toiling and moiling for the prettiest piece of china, my dear.
> *Horner.* Nay, she has been too hard for me, do what I could.
> *Mrs Squeamish.* Oh, lord, I'll have some china too. Good mr Horner, don't think to give other people china and me none; come in with me too.
> *Horner.* Upon my honour, I have none left now.

Mrs Squeamish.   Nay, nay, I have known you deny your china before now, but you shan't put me off so. Come.

Horner.   This lady had the last there.

Lady Fidget.   Yes, indeed, madam, to my knowledge he has none left.

Mrs Squeamish.   Oh, but it may be he may have some you could not find.

Lady Fidget.   What, d'ye think if he had had any left, I would not have had it too? For we women of quality never think we have china enough.

Horner.   Do not take it ill, I cannot make china for you all, but I will have a roll-wagon [=wheel-barrow] for you too another time.

The episode is usually presented as a mere fireworks display of clever *double entendres*. In fact, its insolent power—which no-one has denied, though it has often been deplored—seems to derive from the openness of the innuendoes and the almost equal openness of Mrs Squeamish's apparently innocent complaints. Can Mrs Squeamish have possibly failed to realize what Horner and Lady Fidget had been up to? But such issues of psychological realism should not be allowed to arise. The *double entendres* obtain their shock effects from the fantasy world they create to oppose to and, temporarily, to supersede the world of realistic probabilities. At this fantasy level we approach an allegory of sex. Lady Fidget and Mrs Squeamish, appetite satisfied and appetite still clamorous, are essentially both embodiments of the same possessive feminine lust. And the china—instead of being, as it is at the literal level, either a device to conceal a disreputable act (Lady Fidget) or a precious object desired for its own sake (Mrs Squeamish)—is now a drawing-room phallic symbol. In the general transmutation of values Horner, the would-be aggressively masculine woman-hunter, disappears—displaced by the symbolic china.

Under analysis the scene's sardonic force proves to derive from the insistent repetitions. The word 'china' is used six times. Mrs Squeamish asks what is really the same question twice if not three times. Lady Fidget and Horner keep on repeating the same dirty joke. Wycherley will not let his audience off. The post-Civil War anti-Puritan convention had grown up to think that this sort of thing was funny. Well, they shall have their fun—over and over again. The audience, disgusted but fascinated, is quite unable to break away. The tension—it is a spectacle, within the auditor's

mind, of fellow-human beings persistently reverting into objects
or machines—is disturbing. I may seem to exaggerate if I compare it with that aroused in the reader by Swift's account of the
Yahoos, but a critical parallel can, I think, be worked out. At any
rate it is a measure of the implicit seriousness of *The Country
Wife*—on the whole, I think, in spite of its local imperfections,
the best of all the Restoration plays—that such a comparison can
be suggested.

For the values to which Wycherley appeals are not wholly
negative or satiric. In antithesis to Horner, the professional of the
love-game, and his urban concubines, there is the Country Wife
herself—the 'freehold', as he describes her, of her jealous London
husband—whose innocent amateur escapades put sex into its
proper proportions. Margery Pinchwife is hilariously positive. In
the end, therefore, in terms of the symbolic impression the play
leaves behind, its ultimate 'meaning', it is Horner, the sophisticated Man of Sense, who emerges as a Grotesque or mere
mechanism, and Margery, the primitive country girl, who stands
for the ordinary human decencies. The Tories were, of course, the
Country Party.

No doubt, to carry complete conviction, a defence of Restoration comedy in the terms I have suggested would need to be
greatly elaborated. My sketch is only a sketch. It will have served
its purpose, however, if it has shown that a different and more
sympathetic critical approach is possible, to Wycherley and
Congreve at any rate, from Mr Knights's. And Mr Wain has
already spoken up for Etherege. Critical justice still waits to be
done to the comic scenes in Dryden's tragi-comedies, especially
perhaps *Secret Love*, which prepared the way for the others, and
also, I think, to Vanbrugh, a hit-or-miss dramatist whose best
scenes have to be disentangled from much perfunctory stuff. I
agree with Mr Wain, if with certain reservations, that the
academic commentators have not been very helpful. I have read
a good many more of them than he has, and critically Horace
Walpole's 'Thoughts on Comedy', a most intelligent essay that
everybody (including both Mr Knights and Mr Wain) seems to
have forgotten, is worth all of them put together. As for Mr
Knights's 'Reality and the Myth', well, it takes its place, I suppose, in the roll of sparkling charge and sprightly countercharge
that has constituted hitherto the critical history of Restoration
comedy. Jeremy Collier, John Dennis, Lamb and Hazlitt,

Macaulay and Thackeray, Mr Dobrée, Mr Knights, and now Mr Wain—all of them persuasive and all of them wrong!

For those of us who approach Restoration comedy without the Puritan prejudices of the *Scrutiny* group the final impression is no doubt not of gaiety, though it has its gay moments, but of being unexpectedly disturbed. The detachment that is the usual privilege of an audience viewing a comedy is not maintained. Even Prue and Mr Tattle disturb us; Horner, Lady Fidget and Mrs Squeamish are still more disturbing. To our surprise we find ourselves in immediate, almost physical, contact with these repulsive embodiments of the sexual appetite. Reluctantly we have become imaginatively involved. It is the women who are particularly disturbing through their power over our imaginations. No doubt the introduction of actresses at the Restoration was a stimulus for dramatists as well as for spectators. Here was flesh and blood instead of the make-believe of the Elizabethan boy-actors. And so sex, which was only a spice in the comedies of Shakespeare and Jonson, became the dramatic centre of the Restoration theatre. In Etherege's Mrs Loveit, Dorimant's abandoned mistress, a new pain has entered English literature because of the realism with which she is depicted, but also a new humour—the humour of sympathetic contempt. The scenes between Amanda, Loveless's wife in Vanbrugh's *The Relapse*, and her cousin Berinthia, whom Loveless is trying to seduce, have a similar painful humour; we are amused but we are also involved. In Congreve's Millamant, on the other hand, we find ourselves trying to be involved but continuously thwarted. She has usurped the audience's role of detachment by her own special elusiveness:

> *Millamant*   Mincing, what had I? Why was I so long?
> *Mincing*   O mem, your la'ship stayed to peruse a pecquit of letters.
> *Millamant*   Oh, aye, letters—I had letters—I am persecuted with letters—I hate letters. Nobody knows how to write letters; and yet one has 'em, one does not know why. They serve one to pin up one's hair.

Mr Knights devotes several pages to *The Way of the World*, but he is careful, one notices, not to quote Millamant. If Henry James is to provide a standard of maturity—as in some sense no doubt he may be allowed to—isn't it unfortunate he didn't write better? No one has compared Congreve's prose style to a hippopotamus picking up a pea.

11

Variations on Some Eliot Themes

The Poetry of Pseudo-Learning*

'A little learning is a dangerous thing.' The proposition that seemed so self-evident to Pope and his contemporaries has lost much of its old force. What we now need to know is *how little* the learning has to be to become dangerous. Pope's own knowledge of Homeric Greek, for example, when he began to translate the *Iliad*, could scarcely be described as that of one who had drunk deeply from the Pierian spring. And what is the precise nature of the danger that a little learning entails? The *Essay on Criticism* itself, though not wholly without learning of a sort, is really a very superficial contribution to the theory and practice of literary criticism, as John Dennis, a man of genuine critical learning, hastened to point out at the time. But Pope's poem continues to be read and quoted, whereas Dennis's *Reflections* on it is unknown today except to a few specialists. Perhaps one reason why we still read *An Essay on Criticism* is the 'danger' Pope ran of being exposed as a critical charlatan, the risk of it acting on him as a sort of literary stimulus. The liveliness, then, with which Pope enacted the part of critical mentor may be attributed to his own

● From *Eliot in Perspective: a symposium* (ed. Graham Martin, 1970).

consciousness of a deficiency in critical learning, though the presumption of such a consciousness presupposes his possession of *some* critical learning.

The close parallel between Eliot's poetry and Pope's—as in a different way between that of Auden and Dryden's—has often struck me. The verbal brilliance that Pope and Eliot share is accompanied in both by a similar uncertainty and occasional sheer clumsiness in the structure of their poems. Eliot bluffs his way out generally by an abrupt transition, but to the critical reader this defect is a serious and central one. The poems are all too often fragments only perfunctorily stitched together.[1] It is tempting to connect with this general stylistic characteristic the local stimulus that Pope and Eliot both appear to derive from moments of learning, or rather pseudo-learning, whose shallowness constituted both a challenge and a 'danger'. The thinner the ice the more dazzling the skater's performance becomes. The appearance of sophistication and erudition, not having been honestly earned, has to be maintained in other ways—either by astonishing us momentarily and then hurrying on to something else, or else by sheer verbal wit and the delightful impudence of the whole affair, or finally by an obscurity that suggests more than we are certain it can mean.

Eliot was not an autodidact like Pope, nervously dependent upon the approval of his more scholarly friends, but the quality and range of his learning, in the strict sense of the word, are often exaggerated. As an undergraduate he was, as Irving Babbitt once told me in a long private conversation, 'a vurra poor stoodent'. The comment surprised me at the time. I knew Babbitt had been one of Eliot's early intellectual heroes, and his general anti-romanticism—superficial though it may seem today—clearly derives from Babbitt's celebrated Harvard course on French criticism, which the young Eliot is known to have attended enthusiastically. (I attended it myself, less enthusiastically, some twenty years later.)

Whether Babbitt was right in describing the undergraduate Eliot as a poor student I have no means of knowing. I should add, however, that when I talked to Babbitt—it was in 1928 or 1929—he expressed the highest opinion of Eliot's mature criticism,

---

[1] Thus 'Burnt Norton', the first of *Four Quartets*, grew out of fragments discarded from *Murder in the Cathedral*. See Grover Smith, *T. S. Eliot's Poetry and Plays: a study in sources and meaning* (1956), p. 251.

though this admiration naturally did not extend to the poetry. (I seem to remember that when I tried to point out to him that the poetry at its best was the creative compliment of the criticism I got nowhere at all.)

The clever if lazy 'poor student' grew up, largely under Ezra Pound's influence, into the clever if irresponsible pseudo-scholar of the early poems and essays. I shall not attempt a cataolgue here of the errors of fact committed by the young Eliot in some of the essays, but it is necessary to illustrate briefly what tends to happen in them regarded as scholarship so that the air of authority and expertise can be seen in its true colours. An amusing example will be found at the beginning of 'Shakespeare and the Stoicism of Seneca'. This brilliant critical firework—which Eliot inexplicably omitted from the paperback edition of *Elizabethan Essays* (1963) as unduly 'callow'—originated as an address to the Shakespeare Association who had it published by the Oxford University Press in 1927 as an 18-page booklet. In this decorous format a preliminary apologetic paragraph opens the proceedings, which may be worth quoting since it is not to be found in the essay as reprinted in *Selected Essays* (1932) or elsewhere:

> Desiring to make the most of the opportunity which had been given me of addressing the inmost circle of Shakespeare experts, I cast about, as any other mere journalist would do in the circumstances, for some subject in treating which I could best display my agility and conceal my ignorance of all the knowledge of which everyone present is master. I abandoned several interesting topics on which I might hope to impress almost any other audience—such as the development of dramatic blank verse or the relation of Shakespeare to Marlowe —in favour of one which, if I am in disagreement with anybody, I shall be in disagreement with persons whose opinions will be regarded as suspiciously by the Shakespeare Association as are my own. I am a timid person, easily overawed by authority; in what I have to say I hope that authority is at least as likely to be of my opinion as not.

The cancelled paragraph shows Eliot nicely conscious below the irony of what a dangerous thing a little learning may be— though it also shows how intimidating this 'mere journalist' could be in the use of what learning he had. Between the defensive irony of 'I am a timid person, easily overawed by authority' and Pope's 'Tim'rous by Nature, of the Rich in Awe' (*Imitations of Horace,* First Satire of the Second Book, line 7) the parallel is clearly more than accidental. But the consciousness of a necessity to conceal ignorance comes to grief in the next paragraph—that is, in the paragraph with which the essay opens in *Selected Essays* and *Elizabethan Essays.*

Eliot begins by contrasting three modern Shakespearians (Lytton Strachey, Middleton Murry, and Wyndham Lewis) with a nineteenth-century critical trio (Coleridge, Swinburne, Dowden) and an eighteenth-century quartet who are presented as likely to be 'more sympathetic' to us than their nineteenth-century successors. The quartet is made up of three familar names— Rymer (of *A Short View of Tragedy*, 1693), Morgann (of *An Essay on the Dramatic Character of Falstaff*, 1777), and Dr Johnson. But the fourth eighteenth-century Shakespearian is a certain 'Webster', whoever he may be ('Whether Mr Strachy, or Mr Murry, or Mr Lewis, is any nearer to the truth of Shakespeare than Rymer, or Morgann, or Webster, or Johnson, is uncertain . . .'). After its appearance as a booklet in 1927 the essay was revised before its incorporation in *Selected Essays* in 1932, but though it has been frequently reprinted in one collection or another, the mysterious 'Webster' has remained in the text. Unfortunately there *was* no eighteenth-century Shakespearian scholar or writer called Webster. He is what bibliographers call a 'ghost', Eliot's 'Webster' is apparently just a slip for 'Whiter'. In 1927 Walter Whiter, the clever if eccentric clergyman who wrote *A Specimen of a Commentary on Shakespeare* (1794), would have been just the man to dangle briefly before an admiring Shakespeare Association as a guarantee that the speaker was something more than an agile journalist. But what was dangled should, of course, have been correct. The fact that 'Webster' persists through all the various printings of 'Shakespeare and the Stoicism of Seneca' strongly suggests to me that Eliot had never even skimmed through Whiter's treatise.

Similar errors can be found in most of Eliot's earlier critical essays. The 'sense of fact'—which is made the final *sine qua non* of the critic in 'The Function of Criticism' of 1923—was one that he only acquired if at all in middle age. A phrase that he applies in that essay to Remy de Gourmont, whose influence dominates the early criticism as that of Laforgue dominates the early poetry, can be applied against Eliot himself: Gourmont (we are told) was 'sometimes, I am afraid . . . a master illusionist of fact'. Eliot too, in the early essays, is often a masterly illusionist of literary scholarship. I do not wish to suggest that this mastery of scholarly patter detracts in any serious way from the value of the early criticism. Eliot is to me the best critic who has written in English since Matthew Arnold. Taken in the proper spirit—as a smokescreen behind which a young critic can display his agility and conceal his ignorance—the illusionism adds considerably to the liveliness of the early essays. But the factual fallibility cannot very well be denied. The Marlowe essay is full of errors, false analogies, and ingenious hypotheses that have no real bases in literary history at all. In the Middleton essay it is at least unfortunate that Middleton's occasional poetic brilliance has to be demonstrated by the quotation of a passage from *The Changeling* which is normally assigned to Rowley. Somewhat similar is the use in the Massinger essay of a passage from *Henry VIII* often—and, I think, correctly —believed to be by Fletcher to show that *Shakespeare* is better than Massinger. In the Dryden essay some lines from *MacFlecknoe* are said to be 'plagiarized' from Cowley in what is clearly not a plagiarism at all but a deliberate parody. The mistakes are not gross ones, but a scholar—as distinct from a critic who has dressed himself up to look like a scholar—would not have made them.

The lapses from scholarly precision become noticeably fewer in the later essays; on the other hand, the critical interest of the literary essays decreases in an almost exact proportion to the absence of factual error. It is clear that, so far from a 'sense of fact' being the basic qualification of criticism, in Eliot's own case at any rate dogmatism and recklessness of assertion, underlying and feeding on the master illusionism of fact, were the indispensable prerequisites. Eliot had an important and original critical message to deliver, but he seems to have required the masquerade of scholarship, partly to get the message heard at all but principally as a personal stimulus, as an aid to his own critical self-confidence. Remy de Gourmont was no doubt the model—a better model than the more scholarly Babbitt for two simple reasons: his prose style was a much better one, and his wide if superficial learning was used in the cause of contemporary poetry (Gourmont was a minor Symbolist), not in the cause of conventional ethics (which Babbitt had renamed Humanism). The special fascination of Gourmont, a minor critic, for Eliot, a major critic, was (I believe) the spectacle he presented of learning used as a polemical device which was also a kind of charade. The impudence of such a comment of Eliot's as that in the Jonson

essay—'It is a world like Lobatchevsky's; the worlds created by
artists like Jonson are like systems of non-Euclidean geometry'[1]
—is its critical *raison d'être*. We suspect that Eliot knows no more
about Lobatchevsky than we do, but we know that the old fogeys
he is attacking will *think* he does. It was an effective way in 1920
of silencing the George Saintsburys and Edmund Gosses if they
objected to this new interpretation of Jonsonian comedy. Who
were they to protest if they did not know who Lobatchevsky was?

In the poems the learning is less detachable from the obscurity.
I accept at its face value a statement in 'The Metaphysical Poets'
that obscurity is a necessary consequence of the complexity of
modern life:

> We only say that it appears likely that poets in our civiliza-
> tion, as it exists at present, must be *difficult*. Our civilization
> comprehends great variety and complexity, and this variety
> and complexity must produce various and complex results.
> The poet must become more and more comprehensive, more
> allusive, more indirect, in order to force, to dislocate if neces-
> sary, language into his meaning.

As an example of such linguistic dislocation Eliot quotes ten
lines from the 'Légende' of Laforgue which represent Laforgue's
poetry at its obscurest and most chaotic. Laforgue's formula was
to use the learned or unexpected allusion in an ironic context, but
the formula is grossly overworked by him and soon becomes
monotonous. Eliot's early verse is often reminiscent of Laforgue's,
but unlike Laforgue he provided for each poem a solid and self-
sufficient dramatic structure. 'Mr Eliot's Sunday Morning Service'
is typical of this development.

This poem is, or might be, Laforgue in English. But there are
two immediately obvious differences. One is that whereas
Laforgue would have got the learned words right the 'vurra poor
stoodent' has made two mistakes; the second Greek word (in the
second stanza) should begin with a rough not a smooth breathing,
and 'mensual' should presumably be 'menstrual' (the form
'mensual' is not recorded in the *O.E.D.*). The second difference is
that Eliot has so obviously enjoyed the exercise in theological
sarcasm, whereas the prevailing mood in Laforgue is a self-pitying
ennui. Eliot's enjoyment in this poem communicates itself to the
sympathetic reader, whether he is or is not aware of the errors of

---

[1] The sentence will be found in *The Sacred Wood* (1920), p. 100; it has been
omitted in the reprint of the essay included in *Selected Essays* (1932).

scholarship. In 'Gerontion', on the other hand, a slightly later poem, the learning or pseudo-learning is likely to be missed or misunderstood entirely by the reader. 'Gerontion' begins splendidly with two lines of excellent blank verse:

> Here I am, an old man in a dry month,
> Being read to by a boy, waiting for rain.

It is therefore disconcerting to learn that the two lines come almost word for word, from a sentence in A. C. Benson's undistinguished life of Edward FitzGerald (1905): 'Here he sits, in a dry month, old and blind, being read to by a country boy, longing for rain.' Some twenty years later Eliot admitted that the passage had been 'lifted bodily from a Life of Edward Fitzgerald [*sic*]—I think the one in the "English Men of Letters" series'.[1] By that time he had apparently even forgotten the name of the author plagiarized, though he is correct in saying the life is in the 'English Men of Letters' series.[2]

An even more barefaced act of plagiarism occurs in the short third paragraph of 'Gerontion', this time from a Nativity sermon by Lancelot Andrewes, the relevant passage being:

> Signs are taken for wonders. 'Master, we would fain see a sign' (Mat. xii. 38), that is a miracle. And in this sense it is a sign to wonder at. Indeed, every word here is a wonder. . . . *Verbum infans*, the Word without a word; the eternal Word not able to speak a word. . . . And . . . swaddled. . . .[3]

Eliot has here only abbreviated the passage in Andrewes without verbal change, though the sarcastic tone is, of course, his own contribution. He continues:

> In the juvescence of the year
> Came Christ the tiger
> In depraved May, dogwood and chestnut, flowering
>   judas . . .

There is, as it happens, no such word as *juvescence* in English; it is presumably a happy slip for *juvenescence*. The rest of the passage—apart from the Blakean tiger—is a distillation of some

[1] *Purpose*, 10 (1938), p. 93.
[2] A second echo from A. C. Benson's *Edward FitzGerald*, p. 29, occurs at the end of the first paragraph of 'Gerontion', which reproduces less exactly part of a letter from FitzGerald to Frederick Tennyson that Benson quotes.
[3] *Works of Lancelot Andrewes* (ed J. P. Wilson and J. Bliss, 1841), vol. 1, p. 204.

sentences in *The Education of Henry Adams* (1918), a book Eliot
had reviewed at length in the *Athenaeum* of 23 May 1919. The
relevant passage in Adams is part of a description of Washington,
as it was in his youth, in the spring: 'Here and there a negro cabin
alone disturbed the dogwood and the judas-tree . . . No European
spring had [the] passionate depravity that marked the Maryland
May.'[1]

'Gerontion' made its first appearance in print in the Summer
1919 issue of a short-lived little magazine called *Art and Letters*.
If he had been asked in 1919 to justify the preceding plagiarisms
he would no doubt have replied in similar terms to those he used
in the Massinger essay of the same year:

> Immature poets imitate; mature poets steal; bad poets deface
> what they take, and good poets make it into something better,
> or at least something different. The good poet welds his theft
> into a whole of feeling which is unique, utterly different from
> that from which it was torn; the bad poet throws it into some-
> thing which has no cohesion.

The argument had itself been stolen from Gourmont's *Le Problème du Style*,[2] a book praised by Eliot later in the Massinger
essay, but Eliot's practice had already justified it in the *Prufrock*
collection (1917). As an example, take the brilliant line from 'La
Figlia che Piange' (a poem apparently written in 1911):

> Simple and faithless as a smile and shake of the hand.

The theft, a clear improvement on its original, was from Laforgue's short story 'Hamlet', which has the incidental phrase, in
prose, *Simple et sans foi comme un bonjour*.

The justification of improvement as the excuse for plagiarism
is one with a long history. In English literature the extreme
examples are *The White Devil* and *The Duchess of Malfi*, two
superb plays that are almost wholly fabricated, according to the
latest investigator, from other men's writings.[3] Eliot's special interest in Webster is well known. Perhaps he may have recognized,
without realizing why, that he and Webster belonged to the same
poetical tribe. Pope is another English poet who usually improved
what he stole. Unlike Eliot, however, who scarcely ever revised
his poems after they had achieved print, Pope was continually

---

[1] When F. O. Mathiessen called Eliot's attention to this echo of Adams
years later, Eliot was apparently flabbergasted. Unlike the use of A. C.
Benson and Lancelot Andrewes the reminiscence was an unconscious one.
[2] p. 109.   [3] R. W. Dent, *John Webster's Borrowing* (1960).

improving upon himself either by minor verbal changes or as in the case of *The Rape of the Lock* and *The Dunciad* by completely recasting a poem.

Gourmont's concept of mature poetry as one legitimizing verbal theft—even if the stolen passage *is* improved in the process—raises more questions than it answers. Why is the theft necessary at all? How is the conscientious reader expected to react when the theft is found out? What is the burglar-poet on the lookout for? An alternative and more useful formula is provided by Eliot himself in the section on Donne in 'Shakespeare and the Stoicism of Seneca'. The crucial sentences must be quoted in full:

> In making some very commonplace investigations of the 'thought' of Donne, I found it quite impossible to come to the conclusion that Donne believed anything. It seemed as if, at that time, the world was filled with broken fragments of systems, and that a man like Donne merely picked up, like a magpie, various shining fragments of ideas as they struck his eye, and stuck them about here and there in his verse.

As a comment on Donne I do not find this persuasive: Donne after all *did* believe in a great many things. But applied to Webster, and the extraordinary medley of authors represented in his (hypothetical) 'notebook', the formula is probably correct. And it becomes even more plausible when applied, as so much in the early criticism can be, to Eliot himself. The magpie-instinct—not only for 'fragments of systems' but for all sorts of 'shining fragments' of imagery or phraseology—was unusually highly developed in him. The link between this personal characteristic and the general poetic trend of his generation in Western Europe and America towards 'difficult' poetry is the public use to which Eliot was able to put literary allusion as a mode of symbolism. 'The poet', it will be remembered, 'must become more and more comprehensive, *more allusive*, more indirect, in order to force, to dislocate if necessary, language into his meaning.' The statement dates from 1921, the year of *The Waste Land*'s composition, and the various alternatives listed—comprehensiveness, allusiveness, indirectness, linguistic dislocation—are all present in that poem. But it is the use of literary allusion that is the principal synthesizing devise in it. The difference between the allusions in 'Gerontion' to A. C. Benson, Lancelot Andrewes, and Henry Adams and the learned quotations and references in *The Waste Land* is that the former are private (their function is simply to supply Eliot with poetic

material), while the latter are public (their function is to supply
a poetic commentary on the modern world and they must therefore be more or less immediately recognizable by the modern
reader of poetry).

The rôle of learning—or what looks like learning—in *The Waste
Land* has already received a more than sufficiently detailed treatment elsewhere.[1] An earlier and perhaps less familiar example of
the same technique is Eliot's 'Burbank with a Baedeker: Bleistein
with a Cigar', a poem that has never in my opinion had proper
critical justice done to it. Its technical interest is the dual function,
private as well as public, to which the not inconsiderable learning
packed into it is put. It is also the last and perhaps the best of
Eliot's exercises in semi-comic satire. I will confess to preferring its
verbal concision and poker-face gaiety to the hysterical sublime
of *The Waste Land* and *The Hollow Men*.

'Burbank' was printed with 'Gerontion' and 'Sweeney Erect' in
the same issue of *Art and Letters*. Like its companion-pieces an
epigraph precedes the poem, but instead of the customary extract
from an Elizabethan play we are provided with a passage of almost nonsensical prose which proves on inspection to be a cento of
phrases from Gautier, St Augustine, Henry James's *The Aspern
Papers*, *Othello* ('goats and monkeys'), 'A Toccata of Galuppi's'
('with such hair too') and a masque by John Marston. The method
in the confusion is that most of the extracts are from English
literary classics that are sited in Venice. Burbank, it is clear, has
brought more than a Baedeker with him to Venice.

On the surface the poem is a miniature comic drama describing
Burbank's brief love affair with the Princess Volupine and his
displacement in her favours first of all by his compatriot Bleistein
(a 'Chicago Semite Viennese') and then by Sir Ferdinand Klein,
a knight errant presumably of Lloyd George's creation. But this
simple story of feminine infidelity is narrated in the poetic diction
of ironic scholarship. A member of the Shakespeare Association
would have been delighted to meet in the second verse 'defunctive
music' from 'The Phoenix and the Turtle', which is followed by
two passages from *Antony and Cleopatra*, one diverted to Burbank and the second to the Princess, a scrap from *The Merchant of
Venice* and another from *Hamlet*. There is also, a more recondite

---

[1] Grover Smith's *T. S. Eliot's Poetry and Plays*, pp. 67–98, though heavy-
handed critically, is the most thorough assembly of the quotations, references
and sources. Eliot's own notes are comparatively perfunctory.

allusion, an echo of Chapman's *Bussy D'Ambois* which is itself an imitation of an image in Seneca's *Hercules Furens*. Finally, the poem's fourth line ('They were together, and he fell') is a comic reversal of a line in Tennyson's 'The Sisters': 'They were together, and she fell.' (Burbank's fall is to the sexual charms of the Princess, whereas in Tennyson it is the sight of an earl's corpse that makes a girl faint.)

Eliot's use of familiar, or reasonably familiar, literary allusions in 'Burbank' gives the poem a mock-heroic effect. As in such Augustan mock-heroics as *MacFlecknoe* and *The Rape of the Lock* the reproduction of a sordid or trivial modern incident in the magnificent phraseology of the literature of an early age diminishes the modern participants without in any way degrading the classic models. (Burbank is equated with Shakespeare's Antony and Bleistein with Shylock for the light it throws on *them*, not on their models.) But the total effect of Eliot's poem is very different from that of the Augustan mock-heroics. The learning to which it appeals, for one thing, is not public in the sense in which the conventions of classical epic were public in Pope's time. In spite of occasional suggestions of Pound's *Mauberley* 'Burbank' is very much Eliot's poem and one concerned with Eliot's personal predicament.

Negatively, then, Pound was certainly right when he wrote to William Carlos Williams in 1920: 'Eliot is perfectly conscious of having imitated Laforgue, has worked to get away from it, and there is very little Laforgue in his Sweeney, or his Bleistein Burbank, or his "Gerontion".'[1] 'Burbank' is *not* Laforgue in English. The self-pitying irony of Laforgue is completely absent from it. But Eliot's positive achievement has still to be defined.

A detail that may assist such a definition is a sentence in the *Athenaeum* review of Henry Adams's *Education* already referred to. Eliot wrote in the course of this review that 'Henry Adams in 1858 and Henry James in 1870 . . . land at Liverpool and descend at the same hotel'. 'Burbank', which must have been written within a few weeks of the *Athenaeum* review, begins, it will be remembered:

> Burbank crossed a little bridge
> Descending at a small hotel . . .

To 'descend', in its special nineteenth-century sense, was to step down from a carriage or cab—an impossibility in the Venice of

---

[1] *The Letters of Ezra Pound: 1907–1941* (ed. D. D. Paige, 1951), p. 226.

1919 as a *carrozza* did not ply there. For this moment, however, Burbank has ceased to be an American tourist arriving by gondola in Venice and has become the young Henry Adams, or the young Henry James, who is about to spend his first night in Europe. The allusion here is private to Eliot, but it helps to give the poem a public context. Burbank, who is Adams, James, and Eliot, is also a more representative figure—the young American intellectual with the whole of New England culture symbolized in his name and his guidebook.

The poem, therefore, is a sort of Henry James novel in miniature. Its essential subject is the relationship of American intellectuals to Western Europe. But its date is 1919; Europe is now in ruins after the 1914–18 war, and America has passed from its Burbank phase to a domination by men like Bleistein ('Money in furs'). And so this wry international comedy ends on an almost serious note with the question raised by Burbank in the last verse:

> . . . Who clipped the lion's wings
>   And flea'd his rump and pared his claws?
> Thought Burbank, meditating on
>   Time's ruins, and the seven laws.

If, as seems likely, the seven laws are Ruskin's *Seven Lamps of Architecture*, an element of satire re-enters with them; if so, the pseudo-scholar is again in evidence here, though for the only time in the poem. The work of Ruskin's that a Burbank would have been much more likely to pack with his Baedeker is surely *The Stones of Venice*.

The critical conclusion to which I have been leading up is that the 'learning' in Eliot's earlier poems must be seen as an aspect of his Americanism. As scholarship it is wide-ranging but often superficial and inaccurate. At one level, indeed, the enjoyment that he and Pound found—and successfully communicated to their readers—in exploiting a miscellaneous erudition is the same in kind if not in degree every American pilgrim to British cathedrals, galleries and museums experiences. The appearance of scholarship parallels the tourist's acquisition of 'culture'. When Eliot prefixed to *The Sacred Wood*—facing the title page—the phrase 'I also like to dine on becaficas', he was merely showing off. Why should the reader recognize this line from Byron's *Beppo*? Why should he be expected to know that 'beccaficos'—which both

Byron and Eliot misspell—are Italian birds that make good eating? In any case what is the relevance of this particular line of Byron's on the attractions of Italy as a place to live in to a collection of critical essays?

Such frivolities can be disregarded. Their interest—like that of 'Burbank' (which has other interests too, I have argued)—lies in the evidence they supply of a certain gaiety of spirit Eliot never fully recovered after his nervous breakdown in 1921. For the poetry the significance of the 'learning' is that it was an American supplement to the various attempts made by European poets of the time to escape from the *impasse* of Pure Poetry. In the end the expatriate American intellectuals—with the eccentric exception of Pound—had either to adapt themselves to their European surroundings or to return to America. Eliot gradually merged into the Anglo-French literary establishment, with the poetic consequence that when (in 1927) he had formally become an English citizen the 'learning' had lost most of its aesthetic *raison d'être*. He was no longer an American poet with a revolutionary new technique—as Poe and Whitman had been before him. And so after *The Waste Land* (1922) the learned allusions tend to persist only as a matter of literary habit. In *Four Quartets* (composed 1935–42) in particular it is noticeable how functionless most of the allusions, quotations, and plagiarisms are. The impression one has is of an essayist in the Lamb or Hazlitt manner eking out material that is subjectively and emotionally decidedly 'thin'. The one exception that occurs to me is the half-translation from Mallarmé in the beautiful Dantesque episode in 'Little Gidding'.

The unconscious reminiscences, on the other hand, especially in *Four Quartets*, are not from European literature at all but, as far as I have been able to detect them, from Whitman's *Leaves of Grass*. Pound's curious poem beginning

> I make a pact with you, Walt Whitman—
> I have detested you long enough,

and ending

> We have one sap and one root—
> Let there be commerce between us

might also have been written, whether Eliot was fully aware of it or not, by the author of *Ash-Wednesday* and *Four Quartets*. The anomalies of attitude and subject-matter should not be allowed to obscure the fact that in a final analysis Eliot was an American poet of enormous talent who happened to live in England—as James was a great American novelist who too happened to prefer living in England.

It is in such a context that the 'learning' of Eliot has ultimately to be explained and justified. In the earlier poems the plagiarisms and the façade of erudition are part of the poetry as well as a stimulus to its composition. They are the contributions of an American intellectual—where a great university still has something of the sanctity of a medieval monastery—to the revival of modern English poetry. But now that it has revived English poetry has proved not to require the flowers of learning as its rhetorical premise. Though they persist sporadically in Eliot's later poems their place as stimulus and ornament was taken, less successfully, by the institution caricatured in 'The Hippopotamus' (the earliest of the poems in quatrain form):

> Flesh and blood is weak and frail,
> Susceptible to nervous shock;
> While the True Church can never fail
> For it is based upon a rock.

The scholarship, it is true, was only skin-deep, whereas the Anglo-Catholicism was devoted and sincere, but most of us—English and American—prefer 'The Hippopotamus' and its progeny to *The Rock* and its successors.

12

'Dissociation of Sensibility'•

Hazlitt has described, in the fourth of his *Lectures on the English Poets,* how a critical term sometimes becomes 'a kind of watchword, the shibboleth of a critical party'. The two examples Hazlitt gave of this process were the word *wit* in Pope's time and the word *genius* in 'the present day', i.e. 1818. But the list could, of course, easily be extended. The word *sensibility* is a particularly instructive example of this critical cant, as Hazlitt called it, because it has been the shibboleth of two separate and very different critical parties. It is not proposed to discuss here, however, that eighteenth-century ability to feel 'the *Misery* of others with *Inward Pain*', which was then 'deservedly named *Sensibility*'.[1] The sensibility that is dissociated in the critical writings of T. S. Eliot and his followers seems to have no connection with its sentimental

---

• *Essays in Criticism,* 1 (1951).

[1] The quotation—from *The Prompter,* no. 63, (17 June 1735)—is the earliest use of the word in this specifically 'sentimental' sense that has so far come to light. See R. S. Crane, 'Suggestions towards a Genealogy of the "Man of Feeling",' *ELH* (December 1934), p. 220. *The Prompter* was edited and most of it written by Aaron Hill, the friend of Richardson, and the credit for the introduction of the term should probably go to him. For the later history of the word in this sense, see Edith Birkhead, 'Sentiment and Sensibility in the Eighteenth-Century Novel', *Essays and Studies,* 11 (1925).

predecessor. The modern term is almost certainly French in origin. Though the sense is not recognized by the *Oxford Dictionary* (S–Sh, 1908–14), or its Supplement (1933), the indications are that the term was borrowed by Eliot—who was soon imitated by Middleton Murry and Herbert Read—in or about 1919 from Remy de Gourmont's *Problème du style* (1902), a refreshing but irresponsible work, in which *la sensibilité* makes frequent appearances. Eliot certainly had Gourmont's book open on the table before him when writing several of the essays and reviews collected in *The Sacred Wood* (1920). The word *dissociation* may also derive from Gourmont, with whom it was a favourite, though I have noticed only one example in his writings of the two words in combination. This is in the essay called 'La Sensibilité de Jules Laforgue' in the first series of the *Promenades Littéraires* (1904). Laforgue's intelligence, Gourmont says in this essay, was closely connected (*liée étroitement*) with his sensibility; he adds that Laforgue died before he had acquired the scepticism which would have enabled him to dissociate his intelligence from his sensibility (*dissocier son intelligence de sa sensibilité*). It is at least possible that this passage may have been at the back of Eliot's mind when he coined his phrase.

That phrase enters English critical terminology in the course of a discursive review of Sir Herbert Grierson's *Metaphysical Lyrics and Poems of the Seventeenth Century*, which appeared anonymously in *The Times Literary Supplement* of 20 October 1921, under the heading 'The Metaphysical Poets'. (The article was reprinted by Eliot in 1924 in *Homage to John Dryden*.) The words occur in a passage in which Eliot outlined a new 'theory' of the evolution of English poetry in the seventeenth century. The gist of this theory was that the poetry of the first half of that century was characterized by 'unification of sensibility', but in the second half 'a dissociation of sensibility set in', as a result of which the eighteenth- and nineteenth-century poets 'thought and felt by fits'.

The theory, as Eliot has told us, has had 'a success in the world astonishing to [its] author'.[1] 'The Metaphysical Poets' is certainly —in spite of several brilliant passages—one of Eliot's less finished performances. At one point, for example, in the discussion of Chapman, the grammar breaks down completely. And it is odd, to say the least of it, to be told that Lord Herbert of Cherbury's very

[1] 'Milton' (*Proceedings of the British Academy*, 33, 1947), p. 7.

Platonic 'Ode upon a Question moved' is concerned with 'the perpetuation of love by offspring'. No doubt it would be pedantic to expect precise definitions of the concepts *thinking* and *feeling* in a review that may well have been written against time. Nevertheless the imprecision has resulted in unfortunate misconceptions. Thus it has often been assumed that by *feeling* Eliot meant emotion. This is unmistakably implied in the gloss that Professor Basil Willey provides of *dissociation of sensibility* in *The Seventeenth Century Background* (p. 87):

> The cleavage then began to appear, which has become so troublesomely familiar to us since, between 'values' and 'facts'; between what you *felt* as a human being or as a poet, and what you *thought* as a man of sense, judgment and enlightenment. Instead of being able, like Donne or Browne, to think and feel simultaneously either in verse or in prose, you were now expected to think prosaically and to feel poetically.

By 'to feel poetically' Professor Willey must mean 'to respond emotionally'. This amounts to ascribing to Eliot the conventional nineteenth-century view that the Restoration saw the end of 'a poetry in which emotion always accompanied thought'.[1] Emotion, however, does not come into Eliot's 'theory'. His exemplars of the unified sensibility were able to 'feel their thought as immediately as the odour of a rose'—a sensuous, not an emotional response. It is clear that here—as elsewhere in Eliot's early critical writings[2]— *feeling* means sensation. And the *sensibility* is the faculty which registers sensations. In practice the two words are interchangeable, as is demonstrated by another passage in 'The Metaphysical Poets':

> But while the language became more refined, the feeling became more crude. The feeling, the sensibility, expressed in the 'Country Churchyard' (to say nothing of Tennyson and Browning) is cruder than that in the 'Coy Mistress'.

The word 'sensibility' is obviously being used here to *define* the word 'feeling'; the former is something that can be equated with

---

[1] Stopford A. Brooke, *English Literautre* (3rd edition, 1896), p. 115. What is essentially the same formula—'the emotional apprehension of thought' of Donne breaking down into a 'dualism' in Milton—is to be found in Herbert Read's 'The Nature of Metaphysical Poetry', *The Criterion* (April 1923; reprinted in *Reason and Romanticism*, 1926, pp. 31–58).

[2] Cf. 'Tradition and the Individual Talent' (*The Sacred Wood*, p. 49): 'The experience, you will notice, the elements which enter the presence of the transforming catalyst, are of two kinds: emotions and feelings.'

the latter. And there is another example earlier in the essay of the virtual synonymity of the two words. Jonson and Chapman are commended because they 'incorporated their erudition into their *sensibility*: their mode of *feeling* was directly and freshly altered by their reading and thought' (my italics). (The sentence which follows makes it clear once again that 'feeling' is used in the sense of 'sensation': 'In Chapman especially there is a direct sensuous apprehension of thought, or a recreation of thought into feeling, which is exactly what we find in Donne.')

A paradox, therefore, emerges. Sensibility is feeling, i.e. sensation, but it is also *a synthesis of feeling and thinking* (the two elements that are unified in the undissociated sensibility). This is puzzling. If sensibility is sensation, or a faculty of registering sense-impressions, how can one of the products of its dissociation be 'thought? On the other hand, if the unified sensibility is an intellectual as well as a sensuous faculty, how can it be equated with 'feeling'? But it is not Eliot's habit to use words loosely. The apparent ambiguity of the term in his early writings derives from a doctrine to which he subscribed at the period about the nature of the ratiocinative process. The paradox, if there is a paradox, lies one stage further back. For its elucidation we must return to Remy de Gourmont.

That Gourmont is the *fons et origo* of Eliot's 'sensuous apprehension of thought'—and so of its modern descendant 'thinking in images'—is demonstrated by the Massinger essay in *The Sacred Wood*. This essay, written only some eighteen months earlier, covers much the same ground as 'The Metaphysical Poets'. What is essentially the same theory about the seventeenth century is presented at greater length and in more plausible terms:

> . . . with the end of Chapman, Middleton, Webster, Tourneur, Donne we end a period when the intellect was immediately at the tips of the senses. Sensation became word and the word was sensation. The next period is the period of Milton (though still with a Marvell in it); and this period is initiated by Massinger.

A passage follows on the lucidity of Massinger's style ('the decay of the senses is not inconsistent with a greater sophistication of language') that exactly parallels the eulogy of Collins, Gray, Johnson and Goldsmith in 'The Metaphysical Poets'. But, whereas in that essay the echoes of Gourmont are few and remote, here they are numerous and explicit. For example, the dictum that

'Immature poets imitate' is clearly a condensation of Gourmont's *Pour un adolescent—et il y a des adolescences prolongées—admirer, c'est imiter.*[1] And towards the end of the Massinger essay there are two actual quotations from 'the fine pages' that 'the great critic' devoted to Flaubert in *Le Problème du Style*. The second quotation is particularly significant because it is from a passage where Gourmont defines the sense that *la sensibilité* bears in his writings, though Eliot has omitted the definition in his quotation. What Gourmont wrote was (p. 107):

> Flaubert incorporait toute sa sensibilité à ses œuvres; *et, par sensibilité, j'entends, ici comme partout, le pouvoir général de sentir tel qu'il est inégalement développé en chaque être humain. La sensibilité comprend la raison elle-même, qui n'est que de la sensibilité cristallisée.* Hors de ses livres, où il se transvasait goutte à goutte, jusqu'à la lie, Flaubert est fort peu intéressant.

I have italicized the sentences omitted by Eliot. In the special context of his argument in the Massinger essay there was, of course, no reason why he should have quoted these sentences, but for an understanding of the general critical position that he takes up in *The Sacred Wood* they are of the greatest interest. For here, it is clear, is the clue to the paradox of sensibility. Like Eliot's, Gourmont's *sensibilité* does and does not include the element of thought. This is because for Gourmont thinking was only a kind of sensation. The reduction of thinking to a crystallized sensibility had, as a matter of fact, been effected earlier on in *Le Problème du Style*. According to Gourmont, who quotes Hobbes here and refers to Locke, the cycle of our mental activities can be divided into three separate segments or stages. The first stage is from sensations to images (*mots-images*). The second stage is from images to ideas (*mots-idées*). The third stage is from ideas to emotions (*mots-sentiments*). The cycle then closes in action. The literary sensibility, therefore, straddles the first two of Gourmont's stages. Not only does it build up the sensation into an image, but it at least begins the process by which the image is crystallized into the idea. It is at this point, according to Gourmont, that the best thinking is done (p. 70):

> Le raisonnement au moyen d'images sensorielles est beaucoup plus facile et beaucoup plus sûr que le raisonnement par idées. La sensation est utiliseé dans toute sa verdeur, l'image

[1] *Le Probleme du Style*, p. 109.

dans toute sa vivacité. La logique de l'oeil et la logique de
chacun des autres sens suffisent à guider l'esprit; le sentiment
inutile est rejeté comme une cause de trouble et l'on obtient
ces merveilleuses constructions qui semblent de pures œuvres
intellectuelles et qui, en réalité, sont l'œuvre materielle des
sens et de leurs organes comme les cellules des abeilles avec
leur cire et leur miel.

As examples of the superiority of the logic of the senses Gourmont produces the works of Schopenhauer, Taine and Nietzsche.
Their thinking is apparently 'surer' than that of such abstract
philosophers as Aristotle, Hume or Hegel! Gourmont was never
afraid to follow a bright idea to a nonsensical conclusion.

Eliot's 'theory' can now be seen in perspective. What he has
done, essentially, in 'The Metaphysical Poets' and the Massinger
essay, has been to transfer to the nation Gourmont's analysis of
the mental process of the individual. The unified sensibility that
Gourmont found in Laforgue, Eliot finds in the England of the
early seventeeth century. The scepticism that would have led, if
Laforgue had lived longer, to a dissociation between his sensibility
and his intelligence receives its national parallel in Eliot's 'something which . . . happened to the mind of England between the
time of Donne or Lord Herbert of Cherbury and the time of
Tennyson and Browning'. In Gourmont's terminology, English
poetry proceeded from a period of *mots-images* (Donne, Lord
Herbert, Marvell) to one of *mots-idées* (Milton and Dryden). And
with the coming of 'the sentimental age'—the second effect,
according to Eliot, of the seventeenth-century dissociation of
sensibility—it reached the period of *mots-sentiments* (Collins to
Tennyson). Eliot does not use Gourmont's terms, but a general
debt is sufficiently clear. *Le Problème du Style* did not, I think,
make Eliot a better or a worse critic than he would have been if
he had never come across it. What it did, in several of these early
essays, was to provide him with a *framework* to which his own
critical ideas and intuitions—even then incomparably profounder
and more original than Gourmont's—were able to attach themselves. But Gourmont's psychology is a ramshackle affair, and as
a metaphor from it *dissociation of sensibility* suffers from the
weakness of its 'vehicle'.

It is not unlikely that Eliot soon came to some such conclusion
himself. Echoes of the dissociation of sensibility can, it is true, be
heard in some of the reviews that Eliot contributed to *The Times*

Literary Supplement and the *Nation & the Athenaeum* between 1922 and 1926. On 9 June 1923, for example, writing on a new selection from Donne in the *Nation & the Athenaeum*, Eliot praised the *unity* of Donne's feeling:

> The range of his feeling was great, but no more remarkable than its unity. He was altogether present in every thought and in every feeling. It is the same kind of unity as pervades the work of Chapman, for whom thought is an intense feeling which is one with every other feeling.

And the anonymous notice of a volume of the English Association's *Essays and Studies* in *The Times Literary Supplement* of 31 December 1925, emphasizes the importance of 'the "sensibility" of thought' to Chapman in a way that recalls the 'direct sensuous apprehension of thought' attributed to that dramatist in 'The Metaphysical Poets'.

But these are only passing references. In 1926 Eliot gave some lectures on Donne. (They have not been printed.) In the preliminary reading for them, as he tells us in 'Shakespeare and the Stoicism of Seneca' (1927), he came to the conclusion that Donne did not really do any thinking at all: 'I could not find either any "mediaevalism" or any thinking, but only a vast jumble of incoherent erudition on which he drew for purely poetic effects.' This is a long way from the intellect at the tips of the senses! Even further from it is the statement in the essay Eliot contributed to *A Garland for John Donne* (1931) that 'In Donne, there is a manifest fissure between thought and sensibility.' In 'The Metaphysical Poets' we had been told that 'A thought to Donne was an experience; it modified his sensibility'! Was Eliot's later comment intended as a specific repudiation of the unified sensibility? It reads rather like it.

Eliot's last words on the dissociation of sensibility are in the lecture on Milton that he gave to the British Academy in 1947:

> I believe that the general affirmation represented by the phrase 'dissociation of sensibility' . . . retains some validity; but I now incline to agree with Dr Tillyard that to lay the burden on the shoulders of Milton and Dryden was a mistake. If such a dissociation did take place, I suspect that the causes are too complex and too profound to justify our accounting for the change in terms of literary criticism. All we can say is, that something like this did happen; that it had something to do with the Civil War; that it would even be unwise to say it was caused by the Civil War, but that it is a consequence of

the same causes which brought about the Civil War; that we must seek the causes in Europe, not in England alone; and for what these causes were, we may dig and dig until we get to a depth at which words and concepts fail us.

If this is not repudiation, neither is it endorsement. The change of emphasis is particularly significant. Eliot is less interested now in the nature of the change that English poetry underwent in the seventeenth century than in its origins. As a critical watchword, a propagandist device to exalt the kind of poetry he and Pound were writing and to depreciate those of Milton and the Romantics, the phrase had presumably done its work.

Of course, something like this *did* happen. The relationship between the sensuous and the intellectual elements in poetry did change in or about 1650. And the trend towards their coalescence or confusion in Metaphysical poetry can be called 'unification', though some of the poets themselves, as a matter of fact, preferred to emphasize the 'double sense and meaning' of their style.[1] Dissociation, however, is a misleading term to apply either to Augustan poetry or to its social sources. The poetry of Dryden and Pope is characterized by the *tension* between its constituent elements. If from one aspect the image and the concept can be said to be dissociated, from another they appear almost to collide. *The Dunciad*, for example, is vivid *and* abstract. It is surely these opposite 'pulls' of centrifugal and centripetal forces that is the crucial fact about the Augustan poet.

With the exception of Eliot himself *dissociation of sensibility* and its attendant 'theory' have had few critics until recently. The first even faintly hostile comment of which I am aware is on the first page of Sir Herbert Grierson's *Milton & Wordsworth* (1937):

> The favourite phrase is 'unified sensibility'. We are told, a little pontifically, that this unified sensibility was disturbed by the great influence of Milton, so that the natural medium for the expression of our thought has become exclusively prose, while poetry, I suppose it is contended, became the expression of feeling, of thought only in so far as this had become crystallized as the representative of some mood of feeling . . . I am stating the contention as I understood it, not ratifying it.

The imputed identification of thought with crystallized feeling is interesting; it suggests an acquaintance with the definition of *sensibilité* in *Le Problème du Style*. A more explicit criticism is to

[1] See Richard Fleckno, *Miscellania* (1653), p. 102.

be found in the short *Studies in Metaphysical Poetry* (1939) of Theodore Spencer and Mark Van Doren. Van Doren doubted, for example, whether Eliot had 'thoroughly examined the value in his mind of the words "sensibility" and "experience"' (p. 22), when he wrote 'The Metaphysical Poets'. Professor Bonamy Dobrée's 'The Claims of Sensibility', a review of L. C. Knights's *Explorations* in *Humanitas* (Autumn 1946, pp. 55–8), was apparently the first outright attack upon the new doctrine (which had, of course, been swallowed whole by Professor Knights). The key passage runs as follows:

> The theory is that in the good old days before the Great Rebellion, before Bacon, before the Renaissance (the evil spreads its roots ever further down), man was whole. Everything was thought of together by a process in which thought and emotion danced together, when 'imagination' and 'reason' were one, so that man lived more fully and completely ... Are we quite sure, however, that the old 'integration' was not really just being muddle-headed? And is it not possible that this new analysis may be simply part of the Anglo-Catholic movement seeking arguments to justify its attitude, or merely seeing the course of history through its own spectacles? And was not the change in language far more the answer to purely social demands and the growth of a large new reading public than to an incipient schizophrenia? And finally, is it really better to write like Sir Thomas Browne than to write like Swift? or to write like Nashe than to write like Defoe?

Professor Dobrée's questions have not, to my knowledge, been answered. Some of them at any rate would seem to be unanswerable.

The associated concept 'thinking in images' has not been challenged hitherto. It is doubtful, however, if this is not also essentially a metaphor. There is an obvious analogy between the poetic statement and the statements of philosophers and scientists. Both involve the use of words; both are meaningful; both require the intervention of the intellegence for their appropriate effects to be attained. It is natural, therefore, to applaud the 'beauty' of a philosophical argument, or the 'logic' of a poem's structure. But such flowers of speech must not be taken too seriously. If we do, we are likely to find ourselves talking the same sort of nonsense as Gourmont, when he finds a greater certainty in Taine's reasoning than in Hegel's, because Taine's diction is more concrete. The fact is, surely, that propositional thinking is *different* from poetic thinking, and it only causes confusion to use the same word for both processes. In so far as there *is* thinking in images in poetry, it is not 'thinking' in the ordinary sense. And if there was more 'thinking in images' in the first half of the seventeenth century than in the second half, perhaps it was not because people like Dryden did less thinking than people like Donne, but because they used fewer images.

For *sensibility* divorced from *dissociation*, unless it is restricted to the faculty of sensation (Eliot's 'feeling'), there is little to be said. In the 1920s the word was the shibboleth of a vigorous critical party. At that time its imprecision was useful because *sensibility* appeared to unite the whole of the Anglo-American *avant-garde*—those for whom the senses stood for the concrete objective fact (the Imagists) and those for whom they meant the instincts (like Joyce and D. H. Lawrence). Its use today as a loose honorific synonym for 'taste' or 'personality' can only be deprecated.[1]

[1] Chapter viii of Frank Kermode's *Romantic Image* (1957) is entirely devoted to 'Dissociation of Sensibility', but his approach is very different from mine.

13

'Impersonality' Fifty Years After[*]

I have been rereading—for at least the tenth time, and with an increasing admiration—T. S. Eliot's 'Tradition and the Individual Talent'. The essay, as is not always remembered now, was originally published in two instalments, the first redefining the concept of tradition in literature, the second primarily concerned with the nature of literary creation. The two parts appeared in consecutive months (September, October, 1919) in that strange hodgepodge of Ezra-Poundism and feminism which called itself *The Egoist: An Individual Review*. Whether Eliot obtained a perverse private pleasure in deflating the claims of egoism and individualism under the banner of the review that proclaimed itself dedicated to them—and of which he was an assistant editor —I do not know. But the private joke would have been typical of that irreverent young man. (It was the period of his 'Bolo', Eliot's Rabelaisian mock-epic, which has still to be published.)

When the essay was reprinted in *The Sacred Wood* the text was left unchanged, the third sentence of the second part still beginning *'In the last article* I have tried to point out' (my italics). The words I have italicized were omitted in *Selected Essays*

● *The Southern Review*, 5 (1969).

(1932), where one or two trivial verbal changes were also made, but the essay as we read it today remains otherwise exactly what the reader of the *Egoist* would have had in front of him in 1919. I stress the textual history of 'Tradition and the Individual Talent' because it explains, even if it does not excuse, the notorious episode of the 'finely filiated platinum'. The essay has been criticized recently more than once[1] because of this episode, which is, I agree, annoying and embarrassing. But it must be remembered that—for reasons of space presumably—Eliot's essay had originally to appear in two parts, and it was therefore necessary for him, as for any other writer of a 'serial', to end the first instalment with a statement that would whet the reader's appetite for its sequal a month later. Dipping desperately into his memory Eliot bethought him of the stinks class at school:

> I shall therefore invite you to consider, as a suggestive ana-
> logy, the action which takes place when a bit of finely filiated
> platinum is introduced into a chamber containing oxygen and
> sulpher dioxide.

The sentence does make an effective surprise ending. In what respect can there *possibly* be an analogy between the 'deperson-alization' of the writer and the behaviour of the platinum wire? And if there is one what *can* it suggest?

The puzzles are resolved at the beginning of the second instal-ment. It is, of course, the stinks master's *catalysis* (defined in the *Concise Oxford Dictionary* as the 'effect produced by a substance

---

[1] See the long and complimentary review of Leavis's '*Anna Karenina*' and *Other Essays* in the *TLS*, 30 November 1967 (which is largely concerned with this essay). A critic of a very different stamp from Leavis has also used some of the same terms to characterize the essay. According to W. K. Wimsatt, 'Tradition and the Individual Talent', in spite of 'its forceful suggestiveness, the masterly aplomb and smoothness and fulness of its definition of the poet's impersonality, was a highly ambiguous statement'. While praising the essay as a whole Wimsatt complains that Eliot is saying two things about three ideas (man, poet, and poem) and saying them simultaneously. A poet ought to depersonalize his raw experience, but the reader ought also to read the poem impersonally. And Eliot sometimes uses the term 'poet' in his argu-ment as the antithesis of 'man' and sometimes of 'poem'. Wimsatt's con-clusion is that the two meanings, though 'inextricably interwoven' by Eliot, 'are not one meaning, nor does either entail the other'. (Wimsatt's comments will be found in the *Massachusetts Review*, 7 (1966), 584–90.) I do not find the objection convincing. At the point in his argument that Eliot had reached, the poem's reader was an irrelevance, and a 'poet' is necessarily both non-man (different from other human beings) and non-poem (as the child is different from its parents).

that without undergoing change itself aids a chemical change in other bodies'). 'The mind of the poet', Eliot blandly explains, 'is the shred of platinum.' And he goes on to rub the analogy in with remorseless thoroughness.

Nowadays, when the essay can be read as an uninterrupted whole, the platinum episode is best skipped. As I have said, it can be justified as a sophisticated 'To be continued in our next' device under the conditions of its original publication, but it adds nothing of interest to the theoretical argument. If it is ignored or excised, on the other hand, the essay will be immediately recognized as probably the most original single critical essay that Eliot ever wrote. It is now, I suppose, a classic of our criticism, one comparable to Chapter xiv of the *Biographia Literaria* or to Arnold's 'The Function of Criticism at the Present Time'. What makes 'Tradition and the Individual Talent' especially intriguing is that it was the first substantial piece of criticism Eliot had attempted. In spite of the abstract terms in which it is phrased I regard the essay as essentially the distillation of a critical system Eliot had been gradually forming as he wrote the poems in his first two collections (*Prufrock*, 1917, includes the poems written between 1909 and 1915; *Ara Vos Prec*, 1919, has the poems written in 1917, 1918, and 1919). Since I prefer these earlier poems to *The Waste Land* and *Four Quartets*—for reasons I need not go into here—the coincidence of its date with their culmination in some of the Sweeney pieces, 'Burbank with a Baedeker', 'A Cooking Egg', and 'Gerontion', is significant, at least to me.

I was disconcerted, therefore, to read F. R. Leavis's recent attack on 'Tradition and the Individual Talent' in his collection *'Anna Karenina' and Other Essays*. Whereas, according to Leavis, Eliot's reputation for 'vigorous, penetrating and sustained thought' had been based primarily on this essay:

> Actually the trenchancy and vigour are illusory and the essay is notable for its ambiguities, its logical inconsequences, its pseudo-precisions, its fallaciousness, and the aplomb of its equivocations and its specious cogency. Its offered compression and its technique in general for generating awed confusion help to explain why it should not have been found easy to deal with. Yet the falsity and gratuitousness of its doctrine of impersonality are surely plain enough. 'And I hinted by an analogy,' says Eliot (referring to the famous platinum shred), 'that the mind of the mature poet differs from that of the immature one not precisely in any valuation of "personality",

nor in being necessarily more interesting, or having "more to say", but rather in being a more finely perfected medium in which special, or very varied, feelings are at liberty at enter into new combinations.' But one can be as free as D. H. Lawrence was from any romantic inclination to say that the artist's business is 'to express his personality'—one can see a truism in Lawrence's diagnostic placings of the 'personality', in relation to vital intelligence, as the associate of 'will' and 'idea'—and at the same time believe as intensely as Lawrence did that without the distinguished individual, distinguished by reason of his potency as a conduit of urgent life and by the profound and sensitive responsibility he gives proof of towards his living experience, there is no art that matters.

Leavis's rhetoric is enjoyable—he continues for several pages to deplore Eliot's conception of the Individual and omits altogether the counterbalancing claims of Tradition—but he takes the platinum shred much too seriously, and he ignores the historical context in which Eliot was writing. 1919 was not 1969. In 1919 the 'distinguished individual' could almost be taken for granted in any account of the artistic process. Criticism was still, in spite of Arnold's efforts, at its Romantic stage—with 'inspiration' *à la* Shelley the concept resolving all problems of literary creation, and the distinguished individual (or 'genius') and his 'potency as a conduit of urgent life' had been critical commonplaces ever since the Preface to *Lyrical Ballads*. The crucial problem, as Eliot was almost the first to realize, was the nature of the relationship between the individual genius and the medium he inevitably employed. To be a poet or a novelist implies the preexistence of such literary modes as the poem or the novel. Leavis's metaphor ('a conduit of urgent life') is intended, I suppose, to emphasize the writer's personality as the self-sufficient medium for the communication of 'life'. But after all Lawrence wrote in English; he had had to learn the English language before he could write in it. And before he wrote a novel he had had to learn —from Hardy, Dostoyevsky and the rest of them—what a novel was. The individual writer needs a tradition to work in, to elaborate and to refine; the personality equally needs the impersonal 'conduit' provided for him by his society.

If these propositions seem self-evident to us today, it is partly because we have read Eliot's essay. The key passage in it is the exposition of the *simultaneity* of all European literature, past and present, with its conclusion that 'what happens when a new work of art is created is something that happens simultaneously to all the works of art which preceded it'. I do not suppose Eliot had read Saussure, but the similarity to Saussure's *synchronic* approach in linguistics, which dates from about the same period, is striking. In both, the old *diachronic* method is repudiated. 'We dwell with satisfaction', as Eliot puts it, mimicking here the typical critic of the time, 'upon the poet's difference from his predecessors, especially his immediate predecessors', whereas in reality not only the best, but 'the most individual parts of his work may be those in which the dead poets, his ancestors, assert their immortality most vigorously'.

The diachronic premise was what Leavis calls the 'distinguished individual', a genius who demonstrates his genius by his idiosyncratic originality. The synchronic critic, on the other hand, is concerned with the artifact and not with the artificer; 'the progress of an artist', as Eliot puts it, is therefore 'a continual self-sacrifice, a continual extinction of personality', though he adds that 'of course, only those who have personality . . . know what it means to want to escape' from it. Another way of putting it would be to say that the aesthetic state, because it is accessible to all of us, requires something like anonymity in the artist aiming to make it available. Eliot's explanation that 'the poet has not a "personality" to express, but a particular medium, which is only a medium, in which impressions and experiences combine in peculiar and unexpected ways' becomes immediately intelligible if it is translated out of psychology into aesthetics and if we substitute *'persona'* for 'medium'. A personality, however much 'a conduit of urgent life', will tend only to express itself; a *persona*, on the other hand, is essentially non-autobiographical, non-egocentric. The Chaucer, to take a familiar example, who is one of the pilgrims in the *Canterbury Tales*, is only *pretending* to be the historical Geoffrey Chaucer.

The term *persona* was not in general use in 1919. In its absence Eliot found himself compelled to accept and adapt such Romantic diehards as 'intensity' (which makes several appearances in 'Tradition and the Individual Talent') and 'taste'. A review of his in the *Athenaeum*, 27 June 1919, headed 'The Education of Taste', contains a passage of great interest because it supplements the account of the creative process in 'Tradition and the Individual Talent' from the point of view of the reader. It has not, I believe, been reprinted:

Taste begins and ends in feeling. Sometimes it is thought that taste is a weak derivative of enthusiasm. What taste is, I suppose, is an organization of immediate experiences obtained in literature, which is individually modified in its shape by the points of concentration of our strongest feelings, the author who has affected us most strongly and deeply. It cannot be had without effort, and without it our likings remain insignificant accidents. To be immediately and without effort pleased by Donne is easy for some people, to be in the same way moved by Shelley is easy for others; the difficulty lies in that process which is not of abstract thought, but which is an organization of feeling, making possible, not only to appreciate Shelley in one mood and Donne in another, but the inclusion of even greater diversity into a system of perception and feeling. The *Apperzeptionsmass* thus acquired is something of a test for anything new that appears.

The passage here quoted is the conclusion reached at the end of a long review of J. W. Cunliffe's *English Literature during the Last Half-Century*, a now forgotten American textbook, and it overlaps in some places the more autobiographical 'On the Development of Taste in Poetry' that is appended to the first chapter of *The Use of Poetry and the Use of Criticism.* Taken together with 'Tradition and the Individual Talent' the passage is perhaps Eliot's clearest statement of the nature of the critical faculty.

What 'The Education of Taste' did not make clear is how the acquisition of a good taste differs from the acquisition of a bad taste. The process is not controlled, apparently, by any external or objective criterion or discipline. The ability to appreciate Shelley in one mood and Donne in another is self-acquired, a matter of a private 'organization of feeling'. And no doubt such confident subjectivism was still possible in 1919, especially if one happened to have been born an American. What I find odd is that Leavis in repudiating Eliot today is still appealing to a similar system of values. Particular instances are indeed quoted, to demonstrate Eliot's 'radical conventionality of judgment', but they are really no more than assertions and no serious attempt at all is made to analyse what is defective in Eliot's criticism *within the historical context that it reflects.*

It is not as if Leavis did not himself grow up within that context. He tells us now that he bought a copy of *The Sacred Wood* in 1920, the year in which it was published. A passage in *Scrutiny* (December 1947, p. 58) had already informed us that 'for the next few years I read it through several times a year, pencil in hand'. At what point Leavis discovered Eliot's poetry he has not told us, but he has no doubt now that 'it was the poetry that won attention for the criticism, rather than the other way round'. The quality of the poetry *guaranteed* the quality of the criticism. Good poet and *therefore* good critic.

The presumption had of course been a commonplace of classical and neoclassic poetics. 'To judge of poets,' according to Ben Jonson, 'is only the faculty of poets; and not of all poets, but the best.' What is of special interest, however, is that the process or criterion that the young Leavis unconsciously applied to Eliot's earlier criticism finds no confirmation in any of Eliot's own essays until the first Milton essay (1936), in which he announces that for him 'the only jury of judgment is that of the ablest practitioners of my own time'. But this 'practitoner' test, which appears several times in Eliot's later essays, will not be found either in 'Tradition and the Individual Talent' or in 'The Education of Taste'. Its first appearance—to be canvassed and then rejected—is in 'The Function of Criticism' (originally published in the *Criterion*, October 1923).

> At one time I was inclined to take the extreme position that the *only* critics worth reading were the critics who practised, and practised well, the art of which they wrote. But I had to stretch this frame to make some important inclusions; and I have since been in search of a formula which should cover everything I wished to include, even if it included more than I wanted.

The formula Eliot had to satisfy himself with ultimately in 1923 was 'a very highly developed sense of fact', which is no improvement really on Arnold's 'object as in itself it really is'. And it comes as an anticlimax to an essay largely devoted to depreciating Arnold, who is, we had been told earlier, 'one whose place, on the whole, is with the weaker brethren'.

Had Eliot originally intended to end 'The Function of Criticism' with an enunciation of the 'practioner' principle? I ask the question because I was myself involved in an incident which has a direct bearing on his 'stretching the frame'. According to Leavis, *The Sacred Wood* had very little influence or attention before the Hogarth Press brought out *Homage to John Dryden,* the pamphlet in which the title essay was accompanied by 'The Metaphysical Poets' and 'Andrew Marvell'. It was with the publication in this form of those essays (the Hogarth Press had recently published *The Waste Land*) that Eliot became the important contemporary critic.

Well, it may have been so at Cambridge. At Oxford, where I was an undergraduate from 1920 to 1924, the situation was very different. Until the publication of *The Waste Land* in the *Criterion* (October 1922) we were hardly aware of Eliot the poet, whereas we were very much aware of Eliot the critic. *The Sacred Wood* was almost our sacred book. It was Eliot the critic who prepared us to welcome Eliot the poet, and not vice versa as apparently at Cambridge. My friends and I were very much aware of Eliot's articles and reviews then appearing in the *Athenaeum, Art and Letters,* the *Nation,* the Poetry Bookshop's Chapbooks, the *Dial* (New York), and *The Times Literary Supplement,* and it was Eliot's growing reputation *as a critic* that persuaded us to invite him to address the university literary society of the time (absurdly called the Ordinary). I cannot remember his poetry being mentioned once in the animated discussion that followed his paper.

The occasion itself is still vivid to me, though I am not certain of the exact date (it was either late 1922 or early 1923). Eliot was still in the Foreign Branch of Lloyd's Bank at the time, and he wore the black suit that is considered suitable in the City. The trousers, I remember, were impeccably creased (a foible that Virgina Woolf refers to in her diary); the hair too had been heavily greased and perfectly parted, not a hair out of place, and the refined and handsome face was almost chalk-white. I suppose he was desperately overworked at the time. Robert Graves had come along to the meeting and the contrast between the two poets, who sat next to each other, added to the memorability of the occasion —Graves tousle-haired, fresh-coloured, in an old jersey and with unpolished shoes. Eliot read us, without a trace of an American accent, a beautifully precise and elegantly phrased paper. Balliol, the college where the society met that night, received a lesson on how English should be written and on how it should be enunciated.

But Eliot did not print that essay, and in the hindsight of

history one can see why. The thesis that he advanced in his paper was in fact exactly that described in 'The Function of Criticism' as 'the extreme position that the *only* critics worth reading were critics who practised, and practised well, the art of which they wrote'. That the position was extreme *was* made clear that evening by one dissatisfied undergraduate after another. What about Aristotle? And Quintilian? And Scaliger? And Hazlitt, De Quincey, or Leslie Stephen?

My own contribution to the refutation of the 'practioner' thesis was to ask Eliot whether he was not, as I had heard, an admirer of the criticism of Remy de Gourmont. When he agreed that this was so, I asked him bluntly whether he *really* thought Gourmont had practised well the poetry of which he often wrote. I had not in fact read much Gourmont at the time, but by a fortunate accident I had recently bought the excellent anthology of Symbolist verse edited by Ad. van Bever and Paul Léautard called *Poètes d'Aujourd'hui*, which actually devotes twenty-four pages to Gourmont's now forgotten poetry. I seem to remember that Eliot hesitated for a moment before agreeing that Gourmont's verse would not do. To include Gourmont as practitioner-critic, the frame would indeed have required a lot of stretching. But, though I am not sure that I realized it then, Gourmont was at that time to Eliot the critic what Laforgue was to Eliot the poet—at once the model and the stimulus for his own criticism. Gourmont was 'The Perfect Critic' of *The Sacred Wood*, and a tribute to him appears in 'The Function of Criticism', where we are told that 'Comparison and analysis, I have said before, and Rémy de Gourmont has said before me (a real master of fact—sometimes, when he moved outside of literature, a master illusionist of fact), are the chief tools of the critic.' Apart from a footnote in 'Shakespeare and the Stoicism of Seneca' I have not noticed a single reference to Gourmont in Eliot's later criticism; instead, the doctrine of impersonality takes a semi-Marxist turn, and the Coleridgean version, which had no doubt been nourished by his Ph.D. thesis on F. H. Bradley, disappears. It has been left to others, notably I. A. Richards, to develop the concepts sketched in 'Tradition and the Individual Talent'.

To Lawrence, on the other hand, at least as he is interpreted by Leavis, the writer's personality is crucial: 'Without the distinguished individual . . . and the profound and sensitive responsibility he gives proof of towards his living experience, there is no art that matters.' Agreed—but responsibility to whom and on what terms? Leavis cannot tell us; Eliot's quality as a critic is proved to me above all by his awareness of the artist's social responsibility—even if his attempts to define it were at best tentative.

English Literature in the University

14

Democracy and the Study of English[*]

If compromise inevitably has the last word, whether it is liked or
not, in the *active* social life of a son or father, a lover or husband,
a neighbour or citizen, the individual's *intellectual* life is as
necessarily—or at least desirably—extremist. Unless the argument
is pursued whithersoever it will lead, the arguer proclaims himself guilty either of intellectual incompetence or of intellectual
dishonesty. Good educational practice can never, therefore, *coincide* with educational theory. Utopia is by etymological definition
non-existent. But though it is silly to use a Platonic idea to beat
its imperfect human copy with, it is worse than silly—a Sin
against the Holy Ghost—to deny that our day-to-day realities of
tutorials, lectures and examinations must somehow distinctly
reflect, within reasonable limits of practicability, the exigencies
of philosophic truth. Too little thinking has been done about the
teaching of English literature to undergraduates. In its absence, in
the surrender to muddle and irresponsibility that often characterizes university Departments of English on both sides of the
Atlantic, corruption creeps in.

● *Essays in Criticism*, 9 (1959).

In this essay my progress is to be from a more general to a more particular educational theory, sheltering myself against objection under Oxford's traditional privilege of extremism. The abstractions come down to earth as it proceeds.

I

The award of a university degree is the most explicit admission a democratic society has so far consented to make that some of its citizens are superior to their fellows. The nature of this superiority, in so far as it is one, deserves a closer analysis than it usually receives. It is significant, for example, that in most universities the degree is still always a B.A., whatever the course of studies the particular undergraduate may have pursued. Symbolically, in effect, the universities are claiming that the superiority their degree confers is something over and above a technical or professional qualification. And, surprisingly, extra-university opinion has been willing hitherto to accept the universities' claim. In the eyes of the external world a graduate does not leave the university today a historian, a theologian, a classicist, or a chemist; he is just one more 'educated person'. The degree is taken to be a qualified authority's guarantee, not of a functional aptitude, but of a general mental or spiritual superiority in its recipient. Although a trained intelligence has obvious practical uses in the modern world, the graduate's superiority does not derive from this so much as from a recognition on the part of the uneducated of something approaching a difference of kind, something ultimate and absolute, which separates them from the educated.

The presence in an equalitarian society of this alien element represented by an educated élite is a political paradox. Logically, it does not make sense. And what makes it peculiarly paradoxical is the coolness with which the anomaly is taken by everybody. The inferior majority, implacably hostile to superiorities or birth or wealth, appears to find it in the nature of things that a certain number of its sons and daughters shall rise, via the universities, to a superiority of status not so very different, considered objectively, from that of a feudal aristocracy or a capitalist ruling class. And the élite, though conscious of their superiority, do not feel it as something precarious or artificial, for which an apology is called for.

The paradox is clearly the expresion of something basic to the idea of democracy. Somehow, instead of there being a contradiction between democracy, considered as a political concept, and the principles of university education, a connection has established itself between them. The nature of the connection and its educational consequences are the theme of this essay. It will be agreed, I imagine, that to be educated is not primarily a matter of being well-informed, or intellectually agile, or emotionally sophisticated, although these qualities (one or more of them) do usually characterize the educated person. The essential *differentia* is rather, I suggest, that educated men and women have a higher degree of self-consciousness than the uneducated or half-educated. If they are better informed, it is because they know what they know—and *a fortiori* what they don't know. If they think more quickly and more clearly, it is because they are able to think about their own thoughts. If some of them are also emotionally more mature, that may be because they can, in a sense, feel their own feelings. What it amounts to, I think, is that the educated person, in addition to being able to experience things like other people, directly and spontaneously, can also detach himself from his own experiences and contemplate them at a distance, as though they were somebody else's experiences. In other words, the self-consciousness of the educated man or woman is dual, a consciousness *with* the self (self-regarding, self-assertive) and a consciousness *of* the self (which can include criticism and even condemnation of the self).

A similar dualism is also implicit, within a democratic society, in the relationship between a political majority and a political minority. Indeed, if pushed to its logical conclusion, this relationship is quite as paradoxical as that between an élite and the democratic rank and file. To a minority the majority must necessarily be 'wrong', but the fact that the majority *is* the majority makes it, under a democratic constitution, 'right' in a certain sense even to the minority. An vice versa the right conceded to the minority to go on earning its living and expressing its opinions, in spite of being a minority, points to a similar ambivalence in the majority's position. It is true most democrats would not put it like that. Most of us are not aware of the logical implications of the political and social institutions among which we have grown up. But a democracy, because its mode of political action is government by mutual discussion, has an inner impulsion to know its own nature. A democracy 'wants' to become conscious of its own dualism, as the student discovers in the course of his university studies a similar necessity to become conscious of the embryonic dualism within his own personality. And the parallel is more than an analogy, just as the ideal of an educated democracy is more than a slogan. It is at least possible—the hypothesis is worth considering—that the democratic masses have already realized, dimly and at the back of their minds, that to be 'educated', in the full sense of the word, is in fact to achieve on the individual plane the conscious interplay within the ego of self and non-self that is represented on the political plane by a common Government and Opposition. I commend the hypothesis to the universities, if only on precautionary grounds. It has an important practical corollary. The privileged position of the universities can only be defended, logically and morally, so long as they continue to fulfil a democratic function. The superior status the graduate claims for himself can, however, be justified if it can be shown to be based upon the psychological reflection within himself of the tensions and compromises characteristic of a genuinely democratic political system. In so far as the universities produce graduates of this type, their alibi is complete. But, as each subject develops and new subjects are added to the syllabus, they must be careful, in their own interests, to see that the teaching continues to be directed to this end. If the superiority arrogated should ever prove to be a non-democratic superiority, the anomaly would soon be found to be intolerable. And then our equalitarian society would eat the universities up, as it is already eating up the feudal mansions and the millionaires' fortunes.

There is a moral case, of course, for higher education as there is for equalitarian democracy. In order to love one's neighbour as oneself, it is necessary to understand him as oneself—which calls for the detachment of an educated self-consciousness. And a respect for one's opponents' point of view is the political beginning of charity. But I prefer to rest the case for a democratic university education on its pragmatic advantages. As Mill pointed out, in his essay on Coleridge, we simply cannot manage, 'in the present imperfect state of mental and social science', to do without 'antagonist modes of thought, which, it will one day be felt, are as necessary to one another in speculation, as mutually checking powers are in a political constitution'. There is a similar passage in the second chapter of *On Liberty*: 'Truth, in the great practical concerns of life, is so much a question of the reconciling and combining of opposites, that very few have minds sufficiently capacious and impartial to make the adjustment with an approach to correctness, and it has to be made by the rough process of a struggle between combatants fighting under hostile banners',[1] which points to the Coleridgean source of the principle. His key formula of a 'balance or reconcilement of opposite or discordant qualities' is preferable to Mill's because it brings out the essential creative nature of the mutually reflected dualisms in democracy and the edcated mind. The opposites and discordances are not just forces that keep the political and psychic machines turning. There is always the prospect of something new emerging from their interactions.

The fact that Coleridge was talking about poets is also encouraging to one who believes, as I am now inclined to do, that the English School is destined in time to become the educational centre of the university in the English-speaking democracies. The poet is the educated person *par excellence*. I do not mean, of course, that a university is to be rated by the number of poets it produces per decade, though a correlation will probably be found, but rather that the way a poet's mind works when he is being most a poet may be taken as the model of the process that operates as democracy in the political field and as education in the psychological field.

II

What is the process by which the universities inculcate the special self-consciousness that distinguishes, according to the preceding analysis, the fully educated graduate? An answer, if one can be found to the question, should make it easier to discriminate between the more and the less essential elements in the university system as it exists today. As a point of departure I propose to appeal to a familiar educational distinction: between learning by Imitation and learning by what can be called Self-projection. Up to the age of puberty, if not later, the two educational modes proceed side by side. The more formal lessons are based on Imitation, the information accumulating in the

[1] The first edition of Arnold's *Essays in Criticism* (1865) has as epigraph a quotation from Burke's *Reflections on the Revolution in France:* 'Our antagonist is our helper. This amicable conflict with difficulty obliges us to an intimate acquaintance with our object, and compels us to consider it in all its relations. It will not suffer us to be superficial.' The quotation was dropped in later editions.

child's head being (generally speaking) a *copy* of what a parent, a teacher or a textbook has transmitted; that is, right or wrong according to the closeness of the mental imitation. In the more informal work, on the other hand, or in reading done outside school hours, the ruling principle seems to be self-projection, the incentive being the primitive pleasure every child takes in identifying himself with some figure of history, myth or fiction (the three categories are almost indistinguishable at this stage). The point I wish to emphasize is the way the two modes persist in maintaining their separate, parallel courses in spite of all the efforts of educational reformers. The explanation seems to be that imitation only reaches the child's emotional nature externally, through the prospect of applause, the fear of punishment, or the competitive urge to remember more than the others in the class. Similarly, Self-projection only becomes effective if the child's fantasy, the non-reality principle, is engaged. Thus the *Odyssey*, *Pilgrim's Progress*, *Robinson Crusoe* and *Gulliver's Travels* all have to be reduced, if they are to be assimilated, to what is essentially the same adventure story, with the various protagonists becoming, in spite of their inherent differences, identical fantasy-substitutes for the child. The distinction, therefore, as far as the child's inner nature is concerned, is between a passive acceptance via the memory of the public world's values (facts, words, dates, events, names, etc.) and their metamorphosis via the fantasy into a private, imaginary world.

In the mental life of an adult, who is in the fullest sense an educated person, the same elements are involved, but the two parallel but mutually irrelevant processes are now two stages in a single thought-process. Self-projection is no longer dominated by fantasy, at any rate at the conscious level, and the reader is now able to submit himself provisionally to the demands made on his sympathy by a neighbour or an author without betraying his own inner integrity. The procedure has lost its imperiously subjective character (the need to translate reality into a drama of which the ego is the hero) and is now simply the ability to see a situation from somebody else's point of view. We may say that Self-projection has become Self-identification. And just as Self-projection is no longer wholly active and subjective, so Imitation is no longer wholly passive and objective. The adult has dispensed with the schoolmaster-intermediary between the self and the ordered body of knowledge and attitudes that constitutes a culture or civilization. In an adult situation the ultimate reference is not to what a teacher once required the child to remember, but to an external reality that is recognized to be, up to a point, knowable. In other words, the memory has ceased to be the principal mental agent by which knowledge is acquired and has itself become an intermediary, a guide for the mind's questions to the methods and authorities by which the answers can be obtained. ('Cromwell died in 1658; I learnt it at school' becomes 'I believe Cromwell died in 1658, but I'd better look it up in the *D.N.B.*') We may add, Imitation has become Verification.

I do not propose to apologize for this simplified sketch. The reader can make whatever reservations and corrections he or she wishes. Its excuse is that it provides some sort of context in which to ask what the essential difference is between the education provided by a school and the education provided by a university?

In the terminology that I have been using, the answer is clear enough. The university's general function is to complete in each individual student the transition from the thought-processes of the child to the thought-processes of the adult that have only been initiated in the school. The principal differences between the two stages are that Imitation, which survives even in a sixth form, should virtually disappear at the university, and Self-identification, which the exceptional schoolboy may cultivate in himself out of school hours during his last year or two, is one of the unspoken premises of the university curriculum. It is possible, of course, to blur or even deny these distinctions. They should, on the contrary, be made the most of by an alert university, so that the stimulus which mere arrival there generates in the freshman may not be wasted educationally. A university is not just another school; its ethos and modes of social organization are wholly different. A school is a communal institution, in which the boys' relations with each other tend to be as conformist as the knowledge and attitudes that they are expected to acquire from their masters. At a university, on the other hand, an undergraduate's difference from his fellows is one that tends to earn a measure of reward *per se*, whatever the form may be that the difference takes. A good tutor is one who exploits and encourages this latent individualism. It follows that, just as the class is the appropriate educational medium at school, so university education at its best seems to *demand* the tutorial or its equivalent. Ideally, a tutorial is not a meeting of the one who teaches and the one who is taught, two abstract educational units, but of two human beings of differing ages, experience and background, who meet as co-operating individuals. (Too often, alas, what the don and under-graduate are cooperating in is a private conspiracy to defeat an obsolete examination system!)

The individualism of the university provides the undergraduate with the incentive to 'think for himself'. What the cliché means, in the terms I have been using, is that Self-projection is now able to come out of its hiding-places and make a more regular contact with external reality. The first step towards Self-identification, i.e. the power to enter into another mind without egotistic distortion, is generally marked by the birth of intellectual curiosity. 'I like pretending to be Robinson Crusoe' becomes 'I would like to know more about Robinson Crusoe, so that my reading of Defoe may give me a more varied and mature pleasure than the pretence-Crusoe of my schooldays can now give me.' At this stage a primitive form of Verification is being summoned to the assistance of a primitive form of Self-identification. The central problem of university education, from the psychological point of view, is how to supervise a continuous and balanced interplay between the two faculties, so that they may eventually develop into the dual but coherent mental vision of adult self-consciousness.

The exercises, inevitably, are exercises in Verification. The tutor's function is not to provide his pupils with the answers to questions that may be expected in the final examination, nor even to questions that are the spontaneous product of their own intellectual curiosity. It is intellectual machinery with which the tutorial is preoccupied—analytical devices, techniques of com-parison, organizational procedures, fact-finding aids. Essays and examinations become, from this point of view, tests in working out right solutions rather than in knowing what the right solutions are. The emphasis, quite rightly, is on technical expertise. It is desirable that the right answers should be reached, but it is much more important that the students should learn how to work out their own answers themselves.

But, if Verification must supply the answers, the questions should come from Self-identification. A good tutor will allow his pupils a measure of choice in the topics to be treated in their weekly essays. The point of view from which the topic is approached and the selection of the aspects and evidence to emphasize must always be left to them. Unless an undergraduate can identify himself in some sense with the subject that he is studying, he is either reading the wrong School, or he has no business to be at university at all. One assumes, therefore, a certain personal interest and sense of vocation. The problem, however, is to achieve, for each student and in each course of studies, a balance of Self-identification and Verification. In fact, owing largely to the prestige of science in the modern world, the universities often exalt Verification unduly and allow Self-identification to look after itself. An instructive example of this trend is the fate of Classics. Until recently a student of Latin and Greek was encouraged to consider himself the heir of the ages, a repository of traditional wisdom in a barbarous world. Under such circumstances the Self was able to raise a glow of enthusiasm which might even carry him through the private speeches of Demosthenes and Cicero. But today the Classics are in retreat, and there is more than a suggestion in some universities of a policy in the Classical Departments of Verification for its own sake.

Another and related difficultiy is to achieve the proper balance within the course. The sense of personal involvement in which Self-identification consists has often to be imported from outside the course—an overflow perhaps from an undergraduate's extra-curricular student activities, or his family background, or his private reading. The danger in this case is not only that the exercises in Verification will tend to become too intellectual and too abstract, but that the creative interplay between the two faculties will be lost. The self-consciousness of the fully-educated person is not a two-compartment affair, but a matter of continuous action and reaction, question and answer, inward-looking and outward-looking. The university that is not encouraging such a dualism in its students might be accused—I will accuse it—of not preparing them to take their proper place in a democratic society.

III

I now turn from the generalities of educational theory to the special case of the English School. The alliance between Verification and Self-identification can be negotiated more easily in the study of English literature than in any other form of university education. There are several obvious reasons for this. (i) Unlike every other course of study, it calls for little or no special pre-

paration at school, the only essential prerequisite being an ability
to speak, read and write the English language. (For this reason
Imitation, which tends to seep into all university work unless
special precautions are taken against it, can easily be excluded.)
(ii) Self-identification, which can often be an embarrassment by
its absence in other fields of study, has full scope here and
provides a special incentive to the intelligent and sensitive undergraduate. (iii) As few English Departments are more than fifty or
sixty years old, many of the techniques are new and the student
who uses them often has the stimulating sensation of partaking in
a minor cultural revolution. The list could be extended. It is also,
for example, an undoubted fact that every year a number of able
young men and women emerge from the English Schools, who
are in every sense of the word educated people. In their cases the
proper balance has been triumphantly achieved. Unfortunately
the favourable impression that they create is often diminished
when it turns out, after a cross-examination, that their education
has been obtained in spite of, rather than because of, the curriculum that they nominally pursued. Moreover, in addition to the
few who emerge fully educated, there are many, a higher proportion perhaps than any other university course sends into the
world, who are only half-educated. The contradiction between
theory and practice is glaring and puzzling.

To counterbalance its special advantages, the English School
is faced with a peculiar difficulty that it has not proved easy to
resolve. This is the invitation that its study offers to emotional
Self-projection terminating only in itself. To the adolescent a
poem's or novel's importance derives from the feelings that it
liberates within himself. But feelings, as feelings, are incom-
municable. The undergraduate, who is asked to parade his feelings before the tutor, analyse them, justify them, or argue about
them, is naturally tongue-tied and resentful. On the other hand
the tutor who misunderstands or is unaware of the pupil's feelings
and confines the tutorial to facts and dates, defeats communication just as effectively. The dilemma was apparently at the back
of T. S. Eliot's mind in the note 'On the Development of Taste in
Poetry' (in *The Use of Poetry and the Use of Criticism*), which
ends by wondering 'whether the attempt to teach students to
appreciate English literature should be made at all; and with
what restrictions the teaching of English literature can rightly be
included in any academic curriculum, if at all'.

Eliot's scepticism was based on the intense but entirely un-critical pleasure that poetry gave him between his fourteenth and his twenty-second year. Generalizing from his own experience, he describes how 'At this period, the poem, or the poetry of a single poet, invades the youthful consciousness and assumes complete possession for a time. We do not really see it as something with an existence outside ourselves; much as in our youthful experiences of love, we do not so much see the person as infer the existence of some outside object which sets in motion these new and delightful feelings in which we are absorbed.' No doubt, when the Self-projection is as complete as this, a balance between Self-identification and Verification must be a very distant prospect. But the private ecstasies that Eliot described are more characteristic of the literary schoolboy than the literary undergraduate. It is difficult to believe that there was no important change between what poetry meant to him at fourteen, when FitzGerald's *Omar Khayyám* opened 'a new world of feeling' for him, and his reactions to it at twenty-one, when he wrote his 'Conversational Galante'. In the years between, according to his own account, he had taken 'the usual adolescent course with Byron, Shelley, Keats, Rossetti, Swinburne'. In most adolescents, however, as one favourite writer succeeds another, a body of comparative literary experience is gradually being built up, so that, though it may still not be possible to criticize the enthusiasm of the moment, the outgrown enthusiasms become susceptible to criticism by the mere fact of their supersession.[1] By the time the young Eliot was imitating Laforgue, a good tutor should surely have been able to interest him in the technical devices—of tone, diction and metrics—that make FitzGerald so irresistible to the inexperienced reader. And from FitzGerald it would not have been difficult to advance to the more delicate and complex technical problems raised by the great Romantics and the Pre-Raphaelites.

Eliot's misfortune was that, when he was an undergraduate at Harvard, the attempt was still being made 'to teach students to appreciate English literature'. I take it that by 'appreciation' he means what I have called Self-identification. As an educational method 'appreciation' has the disadvantage of inserting the

[1] The point is made by Eliot himself in the review headed 'The Education of Taste' in the *Athenaeum*, 27 June 1919. The final sentences of this extremely interesting review are quoted on p. 158 above.

teacher between the work of literature and the undergraduate reader. A professor recounts as eloquently as he can how he himself reacts to a particular work, and the student is then expected to identify himself with the professor's Self-identifications. This is a variant of childish learning by Imitation. The only literary response that can be made to a poem, play or novel is a personal response, a spontaneous act in which the whole of the reader's being concurs. In so far as the self is not being identified with the actions, emotions or reflections in the particular text and a pseudo-self, a secondhand copy of the teacher, is substituted for it, no genuine appreciation is taking place. This is one reason why a dominant or magnetic personality can be so dangerous a gift in a university teacher. The teaching of technique, on the other hand, has an antiseptic virtue. The sentimental interpretation and the insincere acclamation have a way of disappearing in its disinfectant neighbourhood.

The answer, then, to Eliot's doubts is that the teaching of English literature can rightly be included in an academic curriculum, but that certain restrictions do need to be imposed. As in other branches of university study the objective must be (i) to encourage the undergraduate to ask his own questions, and (ii) to train him in the techniques that will enable him to answer his questions himself. The problem of balance, however, is the opposite of that raised in other courses. In the study of literature there should normally be no difficulty about Self-identification or the stimulation of intellectual curiosity. The danger is that Verification may not receive enough emphasis. In terms of a syllabus this means that lectures, tutorials and examinations need to concern themselves, to an exceptional degree, with the closer *understanding* of literature, in the most literal sense of the word. At the lowest level a degree in English should be a guarantee of the ability to read English (of any period) at least as closely and accurately as the Classics man is expected to read Greek (from Homer to Lucian) and Latin (from Ennius to Ausonius). There is a natural inclination, on the part of teachers as well as students, to take such an ability for granted, which is responsible for the bad name—for irresponsibility and intellectual slovenliness—that the English School has in certain quarters. Exercises in 'translation' (the rendering of passages from the English classics, prose as well as verse, into idiomatic modern prose) should be an important part of the curriculum, especially in the student's first year. Implied in the ability to 'translate' an author correctly is a knowledge of his meaning that can be explained to others and even justified objectively. Of the various senses that a word can bear, one will have to be selected rather than another, and although the choice of the correct or most appropriate meaning is often almost automatic, the crucial word or arrangement of words sometimes requires a reference *inter alia* to the general theme or argument, the linguistic usage of the period, the conventions of a genre, the author's verbal habits or recorded intentions, or to a combination of one or more of these factors. The *raison d'être* of an English School lies in these wider areas of interpretation, but the more abstract forms of Verification can only operate if the verbal foundations are secure. The logical order is to follow up exercises in 'translation' with practical criticism, not of an arbitrarily detached passage or extract but of a whole work, preferably a poem, story or essay short enough for the whole of it to be carried in the memory at the same time. The Self-identification that will accompany a first reading, if it is a careful one, will normally result in a number of questions on the student's part, and the tutor's function is to suggest the techniques that may be used to answer such questions. There are a great many potentially useful forms of knowledge. They include, for example, the history of the English language in all its aspects, English literary history (the sequence of 'schools' and 'kinds'), the influence of foreign literatures (especially Greek and Latin), literary biography, 'rhetoric' (style) and general critical theory, prosody, social history and sociology, semantics, psychology and philosophy. No doubt some of the techniques are more useful than others, but none of them can be dispensed with altogether. All that can be expected, therefore, of the student is some knowledge of the principles of these sciences, and perhaps of the uses and limitations of some of the standard treatises and works of reference. As a student of English literature, he should not be expected to have a detailed knowledge of English sound-changes, for example, so much as an awareness of the constant possibility of sound-change (with its effects on rhymes, puns, etc.). Before reading *The Winter's Tale* he need not know that Shakespeare and his contemporaries pronounced the first syllable of Hermione's name like the first syllable of 'harmony'. But after he has read the play and Hermione's harmonizing rôle has become clear, he should be able to suspect that the two words might have been pronounced in the same way, and he should perhaps know that Helge Kökeritz has written a book on Shakespeare's pronunciation in which such probabilities are assessed authoritatively.

It follows, as I see it, that English studies at the university must be organized round the texts of English classics rather than the sciences and special studies from which techniques of interpretation can be borrowed. The weekly essay, which experience has found the best basis of the tutorial, should not be on Middle English syntax, the Romantic Movement, Shelley's poetics, allegory, the heroic couplet, *et hoc genus omne*. Its topics, on the contrary, should be *particular* literary works (preferably one work per essay), and in each essay the student should try to utilize, as expertly as possible, *all* the techniques relevant to the principal problem of meaning the work raises for him.

It remains to relate these recommendations to the final examination, which inevitably determines the actual emphases in a syllabus. In a modern democracy examinations are an important part of the competitive structure within which equality of educational opportunity functions. The case for an English School falls to the ground if it is not possible to devise objective and reliable tests to determine whether, after his three or four years' study of English literature at the university, the undergraduate has or has not become an educated person. The demand for class-lists within those who have satisfied the examiners, instead of a simple pass or fail (as in the Middle Ages and down to the nineteenth century), is also comprehensible if unfortunate. It must be admitted that a satisfactory examination-system has not yet been evolved. The margin of error in the order of merit implied in 'Firsts', 'Seconds' and 'Thirds' is notoriously larger in English Finals than in any other university examination.

A special difficulty of an examination in English is that the better the examinee is the more he tends, in effect, to answer a different question on each occasion from any of his competitors, even when the subject-matter of the question is the same. (Unless he has something new to contribute, something individual in the way he looks at literature, he has not been making the best of his time at the university.) An examiner therefore, who is almost always working against time and without any personal knowledge of the candidates to help him, is faced with an extraordinarily difficult task. No wonder he tends to allow factual detail, especially verbal quotations, to count for more than they should.

Facts are right or wrong, and are therefore easily markable; quotations are at least a guarantee of industrious reading. But the decisive test in a university examination should be the relevance of the facts in a particular act of Verification and the degree of Self-identification which has been achieved shown by the selection of the passages quoted. And the assessment of logical relevance and critical discrimination is a delicate business, calling for careful consideration and perhaps a second or even a third reading of the script—luxuries that the tired and harried examiner, much of whose attention is taken up in the mere deciphering of the scrawls of the equally tired and harried examinees, can only occasionally afford.

In most English examinations the papers and questions conform to two types: (i) the request for information ('Write brief descriptive notes, in the manner of an entry in a dictionary, on each of the following . . . '); (ii) the request for a critical estimate ('Illustrate the range and discuss what you consider to be the finest achievement of ONE of the following . . . '). Type (i) tests the examinee's industry and powers of memory and very little else. Though suitable in a school, it is wholly inappropriate at university level, because it attempts to assess the candidate's powers of Imitation rather than the level of balance achieved of Self-identification and Verification. Type (ii) amounts to an invitation to the examinee to reproduce what he can remember of the essay he has already written on this topic for his tutor. In so far as questions of Type (ii) provide, even though it is at second-hand, an objective test of the quality of the essays written during the preceding years, they do no doubt serve a useful purpose. The objection to this type of question is that it presupposes an equally good verbal memory and an equally fluent pen in all those who are taking the examination. In fact, however, there are wide differences between individuals in these qualities (which have little value in themselves, except perhaps in journalism). Many able undergraduates are not at all fluent and find that the memorizing of quotations does not come easily or naturally; in their cases the examiners are not in fact getting a reproduction of the earlier essay but fragments of it eked out with whatever supplementary matter can be thought up on the spur of the moment (another skill useless in after-life, except for journalists). The test would be more equitable, clearly, if the examiners were presented with the original essays instead of the more or less imperfect reproductions of them that are served up under the present system.

Such a proposal would be unworkable administratively. The sensible thing might be to substitute for the Type (ii) questions a short dissertation on some literary topic selected by the candidate himself, with his tutor's help, and approved in advance by the examiners. A dissertation is only a glorified essay, and it would have the advantage, as a test of the student's quality, of being written under exactly the same conditions as the ordinary weekly essay, on a similar topic, and treated in a similar style. As the essay is the basis of English work at the university, it is only logical to base an undergraduate's final class, at any rate in part, on his essay-writing ability. The dissertation would have the great advantage of excluding the artificial and accidental elements in the conventional examination. (No race against the clock, no ban on the use of notes or works of reference, no premium on phenomenal memories, no dependence on luck with the questions set, no penalty on temporary ill-health.) Moreover, the fact that a dissertation would eventually be required should have a healthy influence on the ordinary essays. More attention would have to be paid to presentation and organization. One of the most important lessons that essay-writing can teach is the ability to conduct a coherent argument that is supported by relevant, reliable and convincing evidence. In the typescript of a dissertation the absence of these qualities is immediately evident, but it can easily be concealed in a confidently read essay or a half-legible examination script. If the dissertation was limited to *c.* 5,000 words, typed in double spacing and submitted at the end of the candidate's penultimate term, its correction would not impose a serious burden on the examiners.

The dissertation will, of course, have to be supplemented by more conventional examinations at the end of the last undergraduate term. Otherwise there would be an obvious risk of premature specialization. In reality, of course, a dissertation of the kind I have in mind—in which a literary work, or group of works, is interpreted, by the balanced exercise of Self-identification and Verification, in terms both of its text and its context—is not possible without a thorough preliminary training in the whole range of English studies. And unfortunately the one way to ensure that the preliminaries are not skimped is to insist on a final examination in them.

If there are to be several papers, as I think there must be, the principle of differentiation can only be chronological. Division by 'kinds' (the lyric, drama, the novel, etc.) is almost impossible in our untidy literature, and to allot a separate paper to each of the interpretative techniques (philology, prosody, social background, etc.) would be to sin against the principle of the primacy of the text. There are bound to be differences of opinion as to the kind of question that should be set in a period paper. In order to avoid the question that is really only a memory test, I myself would demand one 'translation' question (twenty lines or so to be rendered into modern prose, but with the freak words or forms glossed by the examiner in footnotes) and one practical criticism question ('What is the central theme, and how is it worked out?'). There should, I think, be several passages or poems to choose from in both these questions, and the pieces set for practical criticism should include the authors' names and the dates of composition. In a three-hour paper I should not myself ask for answers to more than two questions of this type. To be a fair test of the examinee's ability, neither question ought to be rushed. A translation, to be done properly, has to be worked over in rough first of all and then copied out, and a competent piece of practical criticism requires a preliminary hour or so of note-making and experimental interpretation before a beginning can be made with the exposition in writing. The written papers should perhaps be followed by an oral examination, in which the dissertation would also figure. In determining a student's class equal weight might be given, as is now the practice at Nottingham University, to the dissertation and the other papers. A tutor's report on each candidate should also be available to the examiners. The great advantage of an internal examination over an external examination, such as the General Certificate—an advantage often thrown away—is that the imponderables can be given some weight. An examinee is not just a code-number on the examination list; he is also, and more significantly, a human being who is different, in one way or another, from any other human being. In an ideal world his performance in the examination would be related not only to an abstract concept of intelligence and efficiency, but also to the personal conditions of temperament and background which characterize and determine his performance of a concrete act of intelligence and efficiency. No doubt an exact correlation is not possible in this imperfect world, but an examiner who refuses the

help that a tutor's report might give is making it so much more
difficult for him to be a just judge. Circumstances alter cases, and
it is reasonable to require from an examiner some knowledge of
the circumstances of those whom he is examining—particularly as
his verdict may affect the whole of their after-careers. Even in an
examiner some degree of Self-identification is needed to balance
the severities of Verification.

IV

A closer alliance between literary criticism and the historical study
of language seems to me one of the principle *desiderata* of an
English School. At present there is too much rigidity on both
sides. The literary critic's interest in the best words and the best
word-orders does not often extend to the words themselves and
the connections between words outside literature. To the philologist, on the other hand, all words tend to be equally interesting, irrespective of the human uses to which they may or may not
have been put. It is sufficient that they exist, or can be demonstrated to have once existed. The philologist's point of view may
be called Darwinian. Ideally, for him, a word's meanings, forms
and sounds are traceable back in uninterrupted succession to its
earliest ancestors. Provided the changes are tabulated in an
orderly way, in strict adherence to etymology, analogy and
phonetic law, he is satisfied. But the critic is a Lamarckian. It is
not enough for him that a word has survived, though with a
gradual change of meaning. He must know why it survived
whereas its rival synonyms didn't, and why it changed its meaning
at this date or that. Language only becomes intelligible, for him,
as the human reaction to a changing environment, and he is
generally in so much of a hurry to refer changes of meaning back
to the psychology of the speaker or the pressure of society that
strictly linguistic considerations are apt to be overlooked.

The strained relations between 'Language' and 'Literature' in
the typical English School—which my proposals for a final examination limited (apart from the dissertation) to 'translation' and
practical criticism should help to improve, since both disciplines
require a Darwinian–Lamarckian attitude to language—are part
of the old quarrel between Criticism (= Self-identification) and
Scholarship (=Verification). No doubt, in the last resort, each
must resist and deny the other's claims—just as in the last resort

a democratic minority must retain a moral right to secede from the majority. But if a democracy is to survive such crises must not occur too often. The danger in an English School, as I see it, is that what is mistaken for a last resort is often a failure, on one side or the other, to take the analysis far enough.

What W. W. Robson has aptly called our Terror of the Cognitive—it afflicts linguistic studies as well as literary 'appreciation'—may explain why the public impact of verbal analysis *à la* Wittgenstein has been so much greater than that of our books. But the philosophers, acute though they have proved to be in the abstract discussion of analysis, have had curiously little to say about verbal synthesis. Indeed, the theory of metaphor (which must also cover such other modes of multiple speech as irony and paradox, antithesis and symmetrical balance) has not advanced much since Coleridge. In spite of the useful excursions of I. A. Richards, Empson, Donald Davie and Christine Brooke-Rose, the one classic of the century is Saussure's *Cours de Linguistique générale*. Saussure was a linguist who was unterrified by cognitive criticism, and the relevance of his distinction between *la parole* and *la langue* to literature as well as speech has still not been fully appreciated. It is clear, however, that *parole*, the particular speech-act, must extend to such recorded and memorable speech-acts as a particular poem, play or novel, just as *langue* cannot be confined to what is to be found in a dictionary or grammar but must also include poetic diction, figures of speech, 'topoi' (in Ernst Robert Curtius's sense), and the *genres*. And the most useful approach to *parole*, a region left unexplored by Saussure, is likely to be by way of a sound theory of practical criticism or 'explication'.

Of the political desirability of a less superficial and more widely diffused understanding of the synthetic or multiple nature of language there can, I suppose, be no doubt at all. Many of the strains and pressures of the modern world are due, primarily, to a lag in the mental processes of international communication. Language has not caught up with the techniques of physical communication, long-distance transport and long-distance artillery. A collaborative survey by linguists and literary critics of some eminent contemporary hypostatizations or reifications might well prove a minor contribution to world-peace. As things are, extremists in both the U.S.S.R. and the U.S.A. are able to exploit unscrupulously innocent metaphors like *capitalism*, *people*, *atheism* and *freedom*. Even this blessed isle, the home of the modern concept of democracy, is only precariously committed in a process of self-democratization towards the conscious linguistic awareness of its necessary complementary antinomies. An English School cannot afford the moral luxury of complacency. Whether we like it or not—to judge by our respective proclivities towards the triviality of literary journalism or the escapism of research most of us do *not* like it—we are the citizens of no mean city.

I will try and summarize my argument in a final paragraph:

1. A balance or reconciliation of opposite or discordant qualities is the operative principle (*a*) on the public plane in the twofold relationship between majorities and minorities in a democratic state, (*b*) on the private plane in the twofold self-consciousness that characterizes the fully educated person. The two dualisms reflect and complement each other. Hence the special importance of the university in a democracy.

2. The child learns by Imitation and Self-projection, but these two opposites remain unreconciled. At the university a gradual reconciliation is effected by substituting a Self-identification for Self-projection and Verification for Imitation. Exercises in various intellectual techniques provides the training in Verification, and the answers that are being verified are to questions suggested in the practice of Self-identification.

3. The English School's special advantage is that a proper balance of Verification and Self-identification naturally obtains within the course of its studies. An intimate discussion of the student's weekly essay with the tutor is the best medium for the achievement of such a balance. A short dissertation should therefore make up half the final examination. The other half might well be tests in the techniques of reading ('translation' and practical criticism, in contexts as well as texts) appropriate to the different periods and kinds of English literature.

4. The cooperation of Self-identification with Verification within the field of English literature, which is the special function of the English School, requires a similar cooperation among its teaching staff, especially between philologists and critics. The ideals of democracy provide a criterion to which reference can always be made.

15

*The Indispensable Weekly Essay**

When I began teaching at Oxford in the autumn of 1945 I was
disconcerted to find the School of English Language and Literature still in almost as chaotic a condition as it had been when I
was an undergraduate in the early 1920s. The 'Language' had, it
is true, been tightened up, but the 'Literature' side of the School
was still as engagingly amateurish as ever, with tutorials, lectures
and examinations (particularly the *viva*) conforming to no
coherent discipline whatever. We muddled through and hoped
against hope for the best. A tutorial was supposed to occur once
a week, to be limited to one or at most two students at a time,
and to go on for about an hour, but what should properly occupy
the weekly hour beyond the fact that the pupil(s) read the tutor
an essay was anybody's guess. I started to ask questions. Should
the tutor take notes while the essay was being read to him? It
seemed that nobody did, though the practice is surely essential if
an essay is to be criticized seriously. (I always do now.) Should the
essay be restricted to one of the hoary topics guaranteed to turn
up as a question in the Final Examination? That, it appeared, was
up to the individual tutor. Were there any models about that a

* *The Critical Survey!* (1962).

pupil could be referred to when preparing his essays? Nobody knew of any. Were there simple bibliographies the student could consult if he wanted guidance on the plays, poems, etc., that he must read (apart from the actual set texts), the editions in which to read them, and the critical commentaries he ought to know about? Apparently there weren't. The general impression I got was that the undergraduate could—and indeed should—read as much or as little as he liked in any edition he fancied without any critical assistance whatsoever. *Fay ce que vouldras* seemed to be the motto for tutors, lecturers, examiners and undergraduates alike. (No wonder the dose of compulsory Anglo-Saxon had been stiffened.)

It wasn't perhaps quite as chaotic as it seemed to be, but I found my earnest and conscientious ex-Forces students genuinely puzzled, and so in my first Long Vacation I had a hundred copies printed of a leaflet for them that I called *Notes for My Pupils*. In addition to a longish bibliography and some pages of detailed advice about critical and historical method the leaflet had a section on 'The Weekly Essay' which is perhaps worth reprinting here, if only because no other Oxbridge English tutor, as far as I know, has actually put on to paper what he expects his tutorials to be. Here, then, with some omissions is what I wrote in 1946:

'In the Oxford English School the principal point of contact between the tutor and the undergraduate is the weekly essay. Although the essay should certainly be supplemented by occasional papers written under examination conditions and by a weekly seminar, it is potentially, in my opinion, much the most effective educational tool that the English universities have so far developed. Unfortunately there are no textbooks on essay-writing. Or rather, it is a different kind of English essay for which the textbooks cater. When writing a university essay you should forget all about Charles Lamb, newspaper "middles" and the School Certificate essay paper. We do not want fine writing or whimsical humour or the personal note. A university essay is primarily a report of your findings in a particular investigation. The analogy is with a Royal Commission reporting or the exposition of a piece of scientific research.

Although there can be no hard and fast rules in these things, the procedure I have found most useful myself is to divide the period of preparation for each essay into five consecutive stages:

1. A subject is agreed with the tutor, who will indicate in a general way both the *primary* reading required (e.g. Keats's *Endymion*) and some *secondary* works (e.g. Keats's letters, ed. M. Buxton Forman, Miss Spurgeon's *Keats's Shakespeare* and Robert Bridges's essay). The title of the essay and the approach to be adopted will be left to the student.

2. The student will begin by reading the whole of the primary work or works assigned to him. The object is to read one's author as if one were a member of his original reading public. In other words, one should read quickly and without *arrières pensées*, only stopping to look up unfamiliar words or allusions that the original readers would have taken in their stride. Too much looking up notes is to be deprecated, and the temptation to take elaborate excerpts or to score too many margins should be resisted.

3. When the process of assimilation has been completed, the student will find it useful to compare his own impressions, which at this stage will still be vague and general, with those of readers with superior qualifications to his own. The order of priority should generally be: (i) comments by authors upon their own writings (prefaces, letters, table talk, etc), (ii) comments and reviews by an author's friends, contemporaries or immediate successors, (iii) formal criticism by a later *outstanding* literary critic (a Matthew Arnold or an A. C. Bradley), (iv) background material assembled by a modern scholar (the specialist journals, such as the *Review of English Studies*, provide the best general quarry), (v) modern biographies and critical discussions. Much of this material will generally be found in the standard edition of your author, which you should always consult first.

4. The comparison of his own impressions of his author with those of others will have made the student's awareness of his own reactions when reading more precise. It will now be worth his while to go back to those passages in the primary works that impressed him most at the time of reading—or that on re-collection now seem the most significant. This rereading must be done slowly and with the greatest care. The object is to try and put one's finger on the technical devices or personal idio-syncrasies that seem to be responsible for—or at any rate clues towards the definition of—the special impression that the best passages leave. On the whole verbal clues will be found the most profitable. Any word that is repeated more often than might be expected is a potential clue. Epithets, metaphors, and similes, and

the *range* of a writer's vocabulary (does it include colloquialisms *and* technical terms *and* poetic diction?) are always particularly worth examination.

5. So far the student has only been assembling the materials from which a critical judgment can emerge. On the one hand, he has a general diffused impression of his author's characteristics. On the other hand, he has collected a number of peculiarities— favourite words, tricks of style, recurring themes, and perhaps certain obscurities and contradictions. Criticism proper begins with the relation of these significant details to the original general impressions. And, although earlier criticism may sometimes provide the scaffolding for the student's own critical structure, in the main he must now depend on his own wits. A process of trial and error in the form of rough notes is all that one can recommend. The *direction* in which the final analysis terminates will depend to some extent upon the student's own interests and predilections. Until recently biographical interpretations were the rule, but there is no reason why other links between the work of literature and the world out of which it grew should not be explored.

In practice there will, no doubt, be some overlapping in the five preparatory stages. Eventually, however, the period of preparation will be completed and a beginning will have to be made on the actual writing of the essay. One or two suggestions on this final stage may also be of some help.

What is pre-eminently lacking in undergraduate essays is orderly exposition. The essential thing is to make up your mind what the principal critical point is that you wish to make. The essay will then resolve itself, *ceteris paribus*, into (i) a statement of your thesis, (ii) a recapitulation of the evidence upon which the thesis is based, and (iii) a conclusion in which the thesis is related to current critical theory or the conventional estimate of your author's importance. If possible the title of the essay should summarize your thesis, and each of its subdivisions should be given a subheading.'

I have not made any drastic changes in my tutorial methods since 1946. The weekly essay still seems to me, potentially, a supremely valuable educational tool in the teaching of English literature. But *why* is it so valuable? Is it really the literature tutor's job, as I think I assumed in 1946, to turn his pupils into more or less good literary critics—or at worst into competent readers, who would generally be able to tell a good book from a bad one? Or is the literary criticism, as I am now inclined to suspect, really something of a *façade,* a means rather than an end.

The end is a trained mind. The young graduate should have begun, as we say, to 'think for himself'—by which we mean, I suppose, that he should be beginning to think *relevantly* for himself. The bright ideas, no longer mere irresponsible squibs, emerge logically now from premises which have also come to include the contexts—historical, intellectual and social—of the immediate problem. Life, as it were, has come in to supplement and complicate Art. That something like this does tend to happen with one's abler pupils will, I suppose, be generally agreed. The question that is not usually asked is '*How* does it happen?' Obviously growing up, the mere passage of years from eighteen or so to twenty-one or so, is an important part of the answer, and much of an undergraduate's education is, of course, supplied unofficially by his contemporaries. But the tutor and the tutorial make their contribution too. In my own case, to be candid, it was the tutorial rather than the tutor (who happened to be ignorant and lazy). The weekly essay is, however, an ideal instrument of self-education, because it has to be prepared, organized and written up by the pupil himself without any immediate help from anybody or anything except his topic. And when the essay is a failure nobody can be more agonizingly conscious of it than its undergraduate author. A special advantage of the Oxbridge essay—which is lacking in the American term-paper and its Redbrick equivalents—is that it is not too ambitious. The preliminary reading, for example, need not normally take more than six to eight hours, and another six to eight hours should be enough for the remaining processes, including the actual writing of the essay. (The optimum length is 1,500 to 2,000 words.) An even more important consideration—one not shared to the same extent by any of the other Arts Faculties—is that in the discussion of one's native literature mechanical and stereotyped responses are difficult to fall into. The undergraduate is trying to recognize and define *his own* reactions to a classic written in his own language. If the written essay performs the function successfully it will necessarily be a good essay, however many incidental errors it may embody. (In this combination of the subjective and the objective—but with the last word always remaining the subjective one—the undergraduate essay is a nice mirror of adult realities.)

But the ultimate case for the weekly essay is more abstract. Since thought, the essential human activity, is verbal (when we 'think', i.e. organize percepts into concepts, we are mostly talking to ourselves), the thought-process is not complete until verbalization is complete—which means, until it is communicated (either in speech or translated into written words). The tutor, then, if only as an audience, is the indispensable correlative of the essay. Moreover, the fact that he expects a weekly essay provides the stimulus which turns what might be aimless conceptual improvisations, the common reader's common responses, into a coherent and discussable whole. In itself, however, the essay is only the first act in the drama of the ideal tutorial. Apart from the briefest occasional interruptions by the tutor the pupil at this stage is addressing a captive audience; it is soliloquy overheard. But for the remainder of the tutorial the drama is in dialogue form, with tutor and pupil alternately asking questions and providing answers, though for the latter it is now the pupil's turn to take notes. The kind of tutorial which consists of a lecture by the tutor on the topic of the essay represents, at least for me, a failure of communication almost as gross as my own old tutor's silences. Nevertheless, such is the inherent virtue of the weekly essay *per se*, even a bad tutor cannot altogether spoil a tutorial. The pupil does at least carry away his essay.

One related advantage (it is perhaps the most important asset of the system) is often overlooked. A common objection to the weekly essay is that, since it must be written fast, it inevitably encourages stylistic slovenliness. This is nonsense. The assumption that what is written slowly must be better than what is written rapidly is contradicted by all the evidence of literary history. Pope is reported to have said that 'what he wrote fastest, always pleased most', and he instanced *The Rape of the Lock* and the *Epistle to a Lady* (Moral Essay ii), whereas the greatly inferior *Epistle to Bathurst* (Moral Essay iii) was 'laboured into ease' over several years. And it will be remembered that Shakespeare's 'mind and hand went together' (Jonson's regret that he hadn't 'blotted a thousand' referred to the final tidying-up, not to the rapidity of the original composition). I need not continue the catalogue. The theoretical justification of rapid writing is adumbrated in Shelley's symbol of the fading coal: 'When composition begins, inspiration is already on the decline.' Put in common-sense terms the principle reduces itself to the inevitable interval, but the shorter the better, between verbal conception and verbal communication. The longer the delay the greater the temptation will be to embellish rhetorically the original mental verbalizations. As Keats put it to Woodhouse, when explaining his dislike of revision ('unless perhaps a word here or there'): 'Shall I afterwards, when my imagination is idle, and the heat in which I wrote has gone off, sit down coldly to criticize, when in possession of only one faculty, what I have written when almost inspired?' (*The Keats Circle*, 1948, i, 128–9.) Stripped of its inspirational trappings the principle is one that every writer, however humble, will have experienced in his own work. Spontaneity, naturalness, a fidelity of the final expression to the original conception—these are clearly intellectual virtues, however we may define them, of supreme value wherever they are found. Overelaboration, whether it takes the form of too many or too few words, is the complementary defect. If the weekly essay does indeed encourage the one and discourage the other it needs no further defence.

And if it is asked by a tutorially-minded new university how many words the undergraduate essay-writer should be capable of in an hour I answer boldly: 500 *words*.

16

Eng. Lit. as it Could Be•

'Chatter about Harriet', an anonymous improvement on a Regius Professor's 'chatter about Shelley', summed up trenchantly Oxford's attitude to the new Honours School of English Language and Literature, when it was finally founded in 1896. Poor Harriet, Shelley's abandoned first wife, typified the washing of poets' dirty linen in public that seemed to be the likeliest product of the new discipline.

Apparently the poems, plays and novels of such writers as Shelley were supposed to 'read themselves', without any tutorial assistance, simply because they were in English. 'English literature' was the books that are read out of school or college hours to oneself, for the subjective emotional excitements that they provide. They could not possibly be *studied*—as Latin and Greek, mathematics or the sciences are studied. And so they had no natural place in the curriculum of a university. One does not study lollipops; one sucks them.

The Victorians' attitude may seem naïve today, but they were right at least in recognizing that English literature is different in kind from all other university subjects. Its social implications, for one thing, are drastically equalitarian; even its best teacher

• *The Times Educational Supplement*, 28 November 1969.

cannot be *necessarily* right (his superior knowledge may sometimes be matched by the pupil's superior perceptiveness). And
the fact that English literature of the highest quality came into
being before it was publicly studied at all suggests that university
departments of English are not at least needed by creative writers.
I believe that Aldous Huxley was the first writer of importance to
obtain a B.A. in English, but it is difficult to believe that his novels
and essays would have been very different if he had spent his
three years at Balliol reading another subject. Evelyn Waugh,
whose prose style was perhaps the best of his generation, read
Modern History.

It is true that most undergraduates will not become professional
writers, but the process of intimate re-creation that the reading of
imaginative literature demands—especially if the literature is
poetry—is at least quasi-creative. The words to which the reader
submits himself become things, and the things become symbols
or personifications or fictional characters by his 'willing suspension of disbelief'. And when this illusion is translated back again
into words or paraphrase, analysis or judgment, a condition is
reached that is close to literary creation. It is not an accident that
our critics who most bear rereading—notably Dryden, Johnson,
Arnold and Eliot—all wrote such excellent English.

The submission to literary illusion is a mental habit that we
acquire in childhood. The psychological processes of self-identification with the hero or heroine, or of detachment from the comic
butt, are at this stage almost entirely unconscious. At the university, however, the aesthetic experience—with its sources in special uses of the language and literary tradition; its centre in patterns
of structural progress; and its sequel in the critical judgment—is
increasingly conscious. The adolescent subjective excitement
becomes an object of knowledge.

An English syllabus should not deny to an undergraduate the
right to enjoy great literature. Indeed, the capacity for such enjoyment is an ultimate *sine qua non* as confirming the structural or
symbolic analysis. But the university's essential function is to
guide and encourage the literary undergraduate's new reading
habits—from unconscious to conscious, from emotional to critical,
from a slipshod rapidity of reading to an alert and leisurely
response that may require a return to an earlier passage to confirm or refute the plausibility of a freshly realized potential interpretation.

The Victorian opponents of Eng. Lit. were right, then, it may be agreed, in insisting on its difference from other subjects in the university curriculum. The corollary of that difference is to liberate English from the methods of teaching and examination that other subjects employ. If I am asked what is the special proficiency that an English department may be expected to instil and to test, I answer: 'An exceptional perceptiveness into some aspect of great literature expressed in unusually good English'.

An equal weight should be given in any test or examination to the literary perceptiveness and to the excellence of the English, a term including effective organization of the commentary as well as vividness and *le mot juste* in phrase or sentence. Since the corpus of English literature runs to many billion words, the undergraduate will have to select—under sympathetic guidance—the particular works on which he proposes to comment, as well as the kind of commentary—historical, bibliographical, theoretical, stylistic, practical criticism—he will specialize in.

I prefer a historical framework myself, but the only rational criterion here is the individual undergraduate's particular interest and talent. The present examination system must go. English literature is the supreme achievement of our race. No system that does not make it possible to assess the achievement of each undergraduate by what Arnold called a Real Estimate—judging it, that is, as literature—or at least would-be literature—in providing conditions free from such irrelevances as arbitrary time limits and compulsory questions can be considered equitable. A compromise might be for each candidate to submit to the examiners a list, with dates, of all his essays, vacation papers and dissertations, with an asterisk attached to two or three items that he wished to submit for his degree, the examiners retaining the right to call for other essays in addition to the asterisked ones.

My conclusion is simple, almost self-evident: Eng. Lit. has been the product of a vicious examination system. To expel it from a university syllabus we need only require our undergraduates to read some of the English classics more seriously, using whatever critical technique they find congenial; to comment carefully on their reading—preferably in weekly essays because of the exercise in unselfconscious writing they provide, but in any case in their own time and with the texts and works of reference open in front of them.

17

Literature and Atheism*

The Necessity of Atheism, for whose promulgation in print Shelley was promptly sent down from Oxford in 1811, has turned out (paradoxically) to be the one solid argument for *litterae humaniores*. What I mean is that since the commonest intellectual honesty increasingly requires us to surrender the Christian afterlife and its Triple Custodian, suitably de-supernaturalized, to cultural anthropology, we are now proportionately compelled to objectify our ethical ideals in some non-religious mode. The educational corollary follows. Since great literature, Christian and non-Christian, seems to embody such an objectification in a generally accessible form, the literary classics necessarily become more 'serious' for us than for our pre-scientific ancestors. And literary instruction takes the place of religious instruction. They had their John Knox and we have our Dr Leavis.

The crucial issue in our culture is, I suppose, the adult individual's attitude to his own death. Because—in spite of psychical research and ESP—the evidence at present available to us answers Hamlet's question with the blankest of negatives ('not to be'), tragedy, which has always been the supreme literary form, pre-

* *The New Statesman*, 17 Dec. 1965.

sents itself today as also the supremely representative objectification of the whole human condition. The Necessity of Atheism has made all the difference. To a Racine, according to Jacques Rivière as quoted by T. S. Eliot, a tragedy was just *pour distraire les honnêtes gens* ('for the entertainment of decent people'). To us, however, who are only too aware of the precarious life-span of the individual consciousness, a great tragedy is inevitably much more than an elegant entertainment. (The *utile* exceeds the *dulce*.) Hamlet's mimic death is able to fortify us to some degree and even to reassure us in the face of our own physical destruction, imminent and total though that may be, since it demonstrates somehow that it can nevertheless be *right* to die. Indeed, in so far as the Stratford-on-Avon theatregoer's illusion of a higher reality has been made possible or been intensified by a literary education, the modern equivalent of a Jesuit's High Mass may perhaps be achieved. It is significant at any rate that three of the most influential prophets of 'culture' in this country—Coleridge, Arnold and Middleton Murry—have been distinguished literary critics.

T. S. Eliot, it is true, reserved one of his most biting apophthegms for Arnold's 'conjuring trick' which turned religion into poetry. 'Nothing', Eliot said, 'in this world or the next is a substitute for anything else; and if you find that you must do without something, such as religious faith or philosophic belief, then you must just do without it.' To which, I suppose, the simple answer is that we are continually having to do without things, but that gains can sometimes be balanced against losses. If orthodox Christianity can only be maintained by what amounts to a lie in the particular Christian's soul, ought it to be preserved by that particular Christian? And again, if a non-supernatural substitute is available, such as literature (or the other arts), ought it not to be pursued with all the vigour—and rigour—one can muster? Eliot is the best possible witness against himself. Was *The Sacred Wood* written *pour distraire les honnêtes gens*?

These exalted considerations may seem an inappropriate prologue to a review of this soberly factual account of the progress of English literature to academic respectability.[1] But it is only in such wider contexts that Mr Palmer's patient accumulation of details becomes significant. The book began its life as an Oxford thesis under the supervision of F. P. Wilson, at that time the Merton Professor of English, and though better written and more

[1] D. J. Palmer, *The Rise of English Studies*, Oxford 1965.

thoughtful than most B.Litt. theses, the limitations of the genre do restrict its interest. I suspect that it will be mainly read within the profession. Mr Palmer covers much of the same ground as *The Muse in Chains*, though with little of Stephen Potter's zest and wit. A curious omission, one of the very few I have been able to detect, is the failure to make any reference to Mr Potter at all, though the Palmer Chapter Five is called 'The Muse in Chains'. Mr Palmer gives us more dates and quotations, but he has not the fire in his belly that his predecessor had. A little more indignation would have made this a far better book. The disinclination of our universities to recognize their obligations to the most distinguished literature the world has ever known is one of the major scandals of English educational history. The Scottish record—to which Mr Palmer devotes an interesting appendix—is much more creditable.

As might be expected, London University was the first to organize regular lectures and examinations on English literature. The 'Godless institution of Gower Street' appointed a Professor of English Language and Literature as early as 1828, and its Anglican rival in the Strand retaliated with a Professor of English Literature and History in 1835. It is typical of Eng. Lit.'s sordid origins that the same man, a clerical nonentity called Thomas Dale, was the first holder of both chairs, one after the other. Mr Palmer tells us that what Dale demanded in the annual examinations was the ability to repeat parrotwise the information that the Professor had dispensed in his lectures. Ruskin was one of Dale's pupils at King's College, and it is not exactly reassuring to learn from Ruskin, in a letter to his father, that one of Dale's lectures was devoted to the 'birth, parentage, education, etc.' of the nonexistent Sir John Mandeville.

Oxford gets four of Mr Palmer's nine chapters. A Final Honour School was established there in 1894, which combined in theoretically equal proportions the study of English as language and as literature, though the syllabus was in fact grotesquely overweighted linguistically. Gothic, for example, was a compulsory subject, whereas 'about six plays' was considered a proper ration of Shakespeare. Oxford had been a centre of Anglo-Saxon research since the seventeenth century, and in Victorian times German philology added a new severity to the linguistic discipline. Literature, on the other hand, then in its Paterian phase of 'appreciation' (how gem-like is your flame?), had all the appearance of being the softest of options. 'Every idle young man,' the President of Corpus thundered in the crucial debate in Congregation, 'thinks he has a literary taste.' And if he hadn't, what would the London type of lecture teach him? Chatter about Harriet! (The *mot* is often attributed to Freeman, the Regius Professor of Modern History, but what Freeman actually said was 'chatter about Shelley'.)

Mr Palmer's hero is Walter Raleigh, who became Oxford's first Professor of English Literature in 1904 and did a lot to readjust the balance. But Raleigh was a brilliant phrasemaker and a first-rate critical journalist rather than the farsighted literary scholar-critic that the crisis demanded. I remember him as a superlative talker, but it was the gaiety of the talk and the distinction of the man that one remembered rather than anything that he actually said. It was his ambition, as it has been that of his more pedestrian successors in the Merton chair, to build a bridge between 'language' and 'literature'. But the bridge is still unbuilt; it is by no means certain that there can ever be such a bridge at the university level.

It has been Oxford's misfortune, which it shares with the older provincial universities who have modelled their English departments on Oxford's, that it has had no one who was willing or able to think the academic problem of English literature through to a coherent and viable conclusion. Nor are the immediate omens especially encouraging. The recent correspondence in *The Times* about *Beowulf* revealed some strange abysses of muddled thinking. The case against Anglo-Saxon as a compulsory subject for the B.A. in English is simply its irrelevance. The language of the author of *Beowulf*, King Alfred and the others is not strictly speaking English but a language that was the precursor to English. Old English, as it is now tendentiously denominated, bears precisely the same relationship to Middle and Modern English that Latin bears to Italian, French and Spanish. Like Latin an inflected language, it has the same elaborate apparatus of genders, declensions and conjugations; like Latin, too, its principles of word-order are flexible and not rigid like ours today. Because of these fundamental differences of linguistic type and the additional fact that so much of the old vocabulary became obsolete after the Norman Conquest, the editors of the *Oxford English Dictionary* sensibly decided to make the middle of the twelfth century their point of departure. English, if we are to abide by this expert and authoritative ruling, is the language spoken in England from about 1150 onwards.

The discontinuity between Anglo-Saxon literature and later English literature is even greater. Chaucer and his contemporaries had not read a word of it; our reading of it (I speak from many years' experience) will add nothing whatsoever to our understanding of Middle English and later English literature as literature. This is not to deny the melancholy charm of much Old English literature, especially the poetry, but it is a charm similar to that of a palaeolithic cave-painting—an art that comes out of the unknowable and leads, it seems, nowhere.

Language is an especially slippery and ambiguous term. The professional linguist's primary concern is with the verbal sign (including the structure of signs that constitutes syntax); the literary scholar's primary concern, on the other hand, is with verbal meaning (including ultimately the meaning of human existence, with tragedy providing its directest aesthetic correlative). At the graduate level Oxford has recognized this bifurcation; Cambridge, however, is the only one of the older universities to recognize the undergraduate's right to choose between the two approaches to English. Mr Palmer's last chapter is called 'From Cambridge to Brighton' (he is himself a lecturer in the Department of English at Hull), and it is clear that in spite of his Oxford training he believes the younger universities have been right to follow the Cambridge lead. I too sympathize with their aspiration 'to make the study of English literature the central ideal of modern humane education'. After all English is not only the medium with which one Englishman communicates with another, it is also the medium in which an Englishman does most, perhaps all, of his thinking. Latin and Greek cannot compete with it—for us—in delicacy and precision of utterance. But the Cambridge system is vitiated by its unhistorical bias. The Cambridge fallacy has been the failure to recognize that English literature from 'The Owl and the Nightingale' of *circa* 1200 and the lyrics contemporary with it to the present day is a continuum. The undergraduate does not have to read all the English literary classics from 1200 to 1965, but he must have read enough to be aware of what he has not read. The typical Cambridge critic—even a Leavis, an Empson, a Donald Davie—is fatally apt to misread his favourite authors, because he does not read them in the context of the continuum which constitutes English literature.

The Necessity of Atheism derives its force for us, whatever it meant to Shelley (or Harriet), from its respect for the fact of death simply as a fact. It follows that if the true poets must be truthful, so must the true readers of poetry. That is perhaps the literary-educational moral to be drawn from Mr Palmer's instructive book.

Oh God!
Oh Montreal!
Oh Oxford!

Preliminary note

England's Senior University has its incidental or accidental advantages—some good medieval and Renaissance architecture (but also, as Gerard Manley Hopkins complained, the 'bricky skirt' of its suburbs), a first-class library (the Bodleian), and many, but not too many, exceptionally intelligent or pleasantly eccentric undergraduates. There are also the dons, some of whom certainly serve a useful purpose. But the examination-dominated system around which both the junior and senior members of the University rotate is inexcusable. The following essays from *The Oxford Magazine* are principally concerned with the inefficiency and inequity of Oxford's Final Examination. Since other universities have opted for the same routine the irrationality of the traditional hierarchy of classes (First, Second, Third, etc.) has a more than local interest. What has shocked me most about modern Oxford is the unwillingness or inability of the dons to submit the system to objective statistical tests. Does it *work*—even on its own philistine assumptions? Or is such education as Oxford supplies only obtainable in the interstices of the system—in the private arguments and reading that are already available to undergraduates, in their innumerable meetings in clubs or specialized societies, or in their discussions with dons off duty? In my twenty-five years as a tutor I have had pupils of almost impenetrable stupidity acquiring Seconds and Thirds. Only two of my pupils failed completely; unfortunately, they were two of the cleverest men I have had the privilege of teaching.

The solution that Stephen Potter reached in *The Muse in Chains* was to leave examinations to schoolboys and to abandon the whole horrid business, at any rate for those reading English, once the university has been reached. But, though I deplore the competitive incentive provided by classes, some standard framework is, alas, necessary and inevitable. The framework will need to be carefully distinguished from the *raison d'être* of university education—which is simply to produce an educated man or woman. But if the schoolboy duress of a long series of three-hour invigilated papers is avoided such a framework should not be difficult to devise. Flexibility is the *unum et necessarium*. That a rational flexibility is in fact possible is now being demonstrated by York University. (See the illuminating article by Philip Brockbank, 'Examining Exams', *The Times Literary Supplement*, 25 July 1968.) The one essential is to defeat the crammer, who often lives on in Oxford disguised as a tutor.

I have included, for those interested in a lesser Oxford scandal, some notes on the battle between 'Eng. Lang.' and 'Eng. Lit.', which seems at last to be going the right way. Anglo-Saxon has a certain interest as one of the etymological sources of the English language. But Latin and French, its two other most important linguistic sources, offer far richer literatures that have had an infinitely greater influence on English culture. For too long the undergraduate reading English literature at Oxford has asked for bread and been compelled to put up with a philological stone.

18

The Fallibility of Finals*

I am not sure that, in the event, the gaining of a First Class [in Modern History] was sufficient justification for the pressure I was under. Nobody ought to write feverish essays in his sleep for weeks and months on end. And learning got by cramming is soon forgotten. I took as 'Special Subject' the Crusades. I received 'alpha plus' for my papers in that subject, and was congratulated by the examiners. Within a couple of years of going down, all that I knew of the Crusades were a few vague memories of *The Talisman*, which I read as a child. (Sir Lawrence Jones, *An Edwardian Youth*, 1956, pp. 145–6.)

Plus ça change . . . If anything, because a good class is so much more important now, the sum of undergraduate misery that Finals can inflict has probably increased; Jones of Balliol's nightmares may become suicidal depressions today. The irony of it is that all the grind of memorizing, all the nervous agony of the *viva*, and the depths of despair that 'missing' a First or finding oneself mysteriously relegated to a Third can induce, are reserved in their full horror precisely for undergraduates who have *responded* to the ideals of which Oxford likes to think itself the guardian. That grim race in the Schools is not to the sensitive or the subtle but, other things being equal, to the tough and the slick.

* *The Oxford Magazine*, 7 May 1964.

Our paradox might be excusable if our Finals were (i) techni-
cally efficient, or (ii) educationally rewarding. But are they? Such
questions are seldom put in plain, blunt English, but unless at
least one of them can be answered with a confident 'Yes' our
paper mansions—the forthcoming reports of the Kneale Committee and the Franks Commission, for example—will be built on
sand. Some preliminary investigations that I have been conducting are not exactly reassuring.

I. Technical defects

Two or three years ago I asked a number of my colleagues to
predict the class each of their finalists would obtain. (The ques-
tionnaire was distributed and returned a week or two before the
examination began.) The answers that I got were so flatly contradicted by the classes actually obtained that I repeated the
process with rather more tutors the following year as well as at
the intervening Prelim. (which I thought might be useful as a
sort of control). Reduced to percentages the returns worked out as
follows:

Finals I (10 tutors, 83 results forecast)
                   Pupils' results incorrectly forecast 36·1 per cent
Prelim. (14 tutors, 85 results forecast)
                   Pupils' results incorrectly forecast 14·5 per cent
Finals II (15 tutors, 116 results forecast)
                   Pupils' results incorrectly forecast 46·6 per cent

These samples represented between a third and a half of those
sitting each examination, and as forecasts could not very well be
requested from tutors who were actually examining they were of
from a half to two thirds of the *available* candidates. The reason
why tutors were more successful in predicting their pupils' classes
in Finals I was probably because the numbers in each class that
year conformed closely to those of the immediately preceding
years. Finals II however had fewer Firsts and Seconds and more
Thirds and Fourths than usual, the former decreasing by 12·6 per
cent and the latter increasing by 10·1 per cent (the 'Groups' and
Fails also increased). The 'true' discrepancy therefore between
tutors' expectations and the actual results was in fact almost
exactly the same in both years, that is, about 35 per cent. Inciden-

tally, the instances in which tutors were more optimistic than the results warranted cancelled out almost exactly those in which they were too pessimistic.

Why were the tutors so much better at predicting the Prelim. results than the Finals results? After all they would have had seven more terms in which to get to know their pupils' capabilities. Is it more difficult to assess a man's proper class in Finals than his chance of passing the Prelim.? There is no obvious reason why it should be. Assuming an equal fallibility as between tutor and examiner in the Prelim. the discrepancy of 14.5 per cent means that the average tutor has misjudged the quality of every seven candidates in the hundred. But if he also misjudges the potentialities of about seven candidates in every hundred in Finals we must presume a margin of error on the *examiners'* part of 28 per cent there.

I would not stress this figure if it did not happen to be confirmed by other evidence. Some years ago I analysed in some detail the whole of four Finals mark-books, two from my own Faculty and two from another Faculty where double marking is also the rule, and one striking fact that emerged was the similarity with which the two examiners' original marks for the same script differed by a class or more.

The disagreement between tutors and examiners, and one examiner and another examiner, seems to derive from three defects in the Finals system as it operates in our larger Schools. They are (i) examiner-exhaustion (no examiner should be expected to mark more than fifteen scripts a day); (ii) unresolved incompatibilities within the particular board of examiners (my 'originality' is your 'silliness', your 'accuracy' is my 'pedantry'); (iii) the narrow and almost meaningless dividing lines between the four classes. Something could no doubt be done about (i), and (ii), given enough good will, can often be compromised, but (iii) is built into the whole structure of a Classified Honours system. I cannot see that (iii) is ultimately either morally tolerable or intellectually defensible. No doubt the Prelim. has its borderline too between the passes and the fails, but the Prelim. can at least be taken again and its one notional borderline is three better than the four of Finals.

At some arbitrary point—determined primarily by the proportions of each class in the preceding two or three years—the Finals examiners have to draw a line between A, who is at the bottom of

the Firsts, and B, who is at the top of the Seconds. And so on
with the other classes, etc. But in a large School A's superiority to
B, however conscientious and consistent their examiners, is so
microscopic as to be almost non-existent, whereas A's inferiority
to those at the top of the First Class is real, demonstrably visible
even on the crude tape-measure of our pluses, minuses and queries.
But A will go out into the world in all the panoply of an Oxford
First, and poor B's *siccum lumen* will be officially undistinguished
from the dim candle of C, who has scraped a Second by the skin
of his teeth—which however will start C off £120 richer per
annum on the Burnham Scale than the equally dim D (who just
failed to get out of the Thirds and is consequently ineligible even
for the B.Phil. or B.Litt. course). It would not be so bad if these
hair's-breadth segregations did not have to be made on less than
all the relevant evidence. But who is to tell the examiners about
A's sleepless night before the first paper, or B's bout of hay-fever,
or C's menstruation period? And there may well be psychological
or intellectual factors too of which they should ideally be aware
—and which the tutor will often know about. Inevitably the
examiners play for safety in what they suspect to be such cases,
which tend to pile up in the no-man's-lands between the classes
(which also include the straightforward marginal cases of A and
B, men clearly too good for a Second and yet not really good
enough for a First). For Finals II I asked my tutors to distinguish
between the pupils whose proper class they were reasonably
certain about and the borderline cases (for which they had to be
content with predicting the *probably* correct class), and as many
as 39 per cent of them proved to be these borderliners. Moreover
in the mark-books that I analysed the borderline marks—e.g. beta
double minus and beta gamma for the Seconds/Third border—
accounted for just about half of all the original marks recorded.

An unhappy awareness of such borderline anomalies must be
presumed to explain Oxford's retention, almost alone in the
academic world, of a *viva* for undergraduates. I have no statistics
to offer at this point, but educationalists seem to agree that *in
general* written papers provide a far better test of ability than
any form of interview. (See, for example, W. D. Furneaux, *The
Chosen Few*, 1961, pp. 85–8.) The two tests in any case are not
strictly *in pari materia*. Thus that mental alertness, the immediate
seizing of an examiner's point, which makes such a good impression at a *viva*, is often the product of social self-confidence rather

than of any intellectual quality, and *per contra* when self-confidence is lacking nothing may be communicated at all. A college report would, I believe, usually be far more helpful. Finals falls at present between the two stools of external and internal examination. Since it is not in fact a fully external examination (the candidates' names are disclosed and tutors mark their own pupils' papers), it is surely illogical not to make use of such internal resources as are readily available; a board of examiners will always know which of their colleagues' reports must be taken with a grain or two of salt. An increase in the number of classes might also help; the borderliners already constitute, in fact if not in name, separate classes.

II. Educational consequences

Powell's undergraduate record, on the official side, is soon told. He worked with concentration and easily won that honour, a first class, which doubtless gives more satisfaction to an educated English youth than any other thinkable. So highly does our custom rate the average work of fifty (*sic*) short and hasty essays, done under cruel pressure of time by a man just of age, as the first fruit of a year's training. It is indeed not strictly a training for any occupation except journalism, where the conditions of the School are nightly more or less reproduced. However enlightened the tutor, of the Schools he has to think. The real discipline in the craft of research comes later, if at all, and its first step is to unlearn undergraduate method (Oliver Elton, *Frederick York Powell: a life and a selection from his letters and occasional writings*, vol. i (1906), pp. 16–17).

York Powell's First, in 1872, had been in the then combined Law and History School; Elton got his own First (in Greats) in 1884. A lot has happened since that Victorian heyday, but Elton's short scathing aside has lost none of its force and relevance. In one respect indeed Finals is perhaps even less educationally respectable today: generally speaking, Elton's 'man just of age' (who is now also a woman) seems to be more adult, more responsible, more professional than his Victorian and Edwardian counterparts were. If this is not an illusion, the reversion to schoolboy values and machinery that the three-hour papers and compulsory questions epitomize is even more anachronistic than it was when Elton wrote. It is not as if 'the craft of research' has now to be totally postponed to the post-graduate stage. In a tentative way even unenlightened tutors will now encourage at least some of their pupils to examine some of the evidence on which their essays will be based at first hand. When they quote they will be instructed to quote with accuracy and not to depend upon their memories. How different the conditions in Finals! Then you *must* quote from memory, and you may not even consult your own notes. What is 'scholarship' outside the Schools is 'cheating' in them. It is the one place where you will not find it a very good practice always to verify your references.

In an extremely interesting note to *The Use of Poetry and the Use of Criticism* T. S. Eliot has described his own early mental development. At about the age of twenty-one his earlier subjective and egocentric response to poetry changed, he tells us, into what he calls the 'mature stage of enjoyment of poetry' when the 'critical faculties remain awake'. 'The poem has its own existence, apart from us; it was there before us and will endure after us.' *Mutatis mutandis* what Eliot is saying here of the reading of poetry is true, I believe, of all the subjects—except perhaps mathematics and the sciences—that are taught at a university. The undergraduate comes up an adolescent, who is prepared to swallow whole almost everything that his teachers and his text-books tell him; when he has completed his undergraduate career he is, ideally, an adult, who is beginning to see intellectually through his own eyes and can even distinguish up to a point between what is subjectively attractive (or perhaps, as in his relations with 'knowledge', what is the line of least resistance) from what is objectively valid. He has been taught, as we say, to learn to think for himself. Hence the crucial difference between the relationship of undergraduate to tutor and that of schoolboy to schoolmaster. As R. W. Chambers once put it, in a long-forgotten English Association pamphlet:

> What we all wish is that the student, equally with his teacher, be trying to find out things: taking in the post-graduate stage his actual share in research, but in the pre-graduate stage equally sharing in spirit. Such sharing is even more helpful to the teacher than to the student.

What is not helpful to either, as Chambers went on to rub in, is mere memorization, the mugging-up euphemistically described as revision that spoils for most of us the last term or two before Finals.

Soon after I began tutoring, some twenty years ago, I set myself as an experiment an old Finals paper which I proceeded to answer 'under examination conditions'. The experiment taught me two things. One was the irrational demands the system makes on one's verbal memory; the other was the total impossibility of answering the prescribed number of questions in the time available. Now, if tutor and pupil are essentially cooperating in 'trying to find out things' in a manner appropriate to the intellectually adult, it *must* be unfair to construct as a final test of the pupil's success in the joint enterprise a situation so artificial that the tutor himself could not succeed in it. What must be tested is not mnemonic or verbal facility so much as the ability the examiner himself is presumed to have to work things out for oneself—within the limits of course of one's own subject. And to do this properly 'cheating' consists in *not* using the original source, *not* writing with notes and texts open on the table, *not* trying to 'beat the clock'.

Elton eventually became the first Professor of English Literature at the University of Liverpool. In his new Chair he was able to put into practice in the English Finals at Liverpool what his undergraduate experience at Oxford had taught him. Some of the three-hour papers did survive at Liverpool, but the special emphasis in the new English School there was on a short dissertation which every Honours student was expected to submit. I can see no reason why a very short dissertation, or perhaps more than one, should not be required in our Finals too, at any rate in the non-science Schools. The weekly essay is after all the backbone of the tutorial system, and since our undergraduates spend so much of their time learning how to write essays it would seem only reasonable to demand a super-essay or two by which to estimate at the end of their time the degree of competence they have reached in essay-writing. Certain safeguards would no doubt be required, such as an approval of the topic, a limitation on the number of words, an insistence on the essay being typed, and a guarantee from the tutor that it was the candidate's unaided work. But in principle I think the case for an essay or two in Finals is cast-iron. If three-hour papers are to survive the examinee should be *encouraged* to bring in his own notes and texts if he wishes to, a concession that would partly remove from Finals the stigma of the schoolroom.

I have a second, a more revolutionary, suggestion to offer. It is that Honours—in Finals, if not in Mods—should cease to be classified. The technical impossibility of allotting the correct class to more than perhaps three out of every four of those sitting for Finals seems to be an ineradicable defect. However the system is reformed, whether by increasing the number of classes or by getting the assistance and advice of tutors, the intellectual borderline problems and the physical or psychological hazards can never be eliminated altogether. The basic difficulty is simply that there are too many incommensurates in adult processes of thought and expression. An essay may be brilliantly written and yet wholly mistaken, when it will presumably have to be marked 'alpha delta'. But there is no alpha delta class and to split the difference at beta gamma (a top Third) is to misclassify, because top Thirds cannot write brilliantly and are too conventional even to be able to achieve a total mistake. But remove the classes and Honours (Oxford) will then be an umbrella under which all the intellectual virtues can congregate, and the examiners will be spared the invidious stratifications now demanded. The four classes descend historically from the four degrees of merit in composition traditional in the old grammar school—*bene, satis bene, satis* and *vix satis*; to try and compress into this primitive schoolboy hierarchy the full range and complexity of mature modern thought is surely absurd.

It is true there will always be undergraduates who are not happy unless they can compete for public glory. But they will still have University Prizes, now often unpatronized for years, to try their luck with. And the rest of us, dons and pupils alike, can at last proceed in our several ways with our mutual education to the end of the third year (think of it!) in a joint exploration of the culture to which we are both committed. I am tired of apologizing to my students for the senseless cruelty of Finals; I resent even more having to tell my graduate supervisees that their first step must be 'to unlearn undergraduate method'.

19

Finals Results: Tutors' Expectations[*]

Towards the end of last term tutors in English, Geography, Law, Mathematics and Modern Languages (French and German only) received through the college messenger service a form headed 'Strictly Confidential'. This was accompanied by a stamped envelope addressed to the Editor of the *Magazine*, also marked 'Confidential', and a letter signed by the Editor and myself, which invited the recipient to predict the classes that his or her pupils would receive in the Final Examination that they were then about to take. Borderline cases could be met, we suggested, by a formula I/II, II/I, II/III, III/II, etc., the first figure to indicate in the tutor's opinion the marginal probability of a First rather than a Second (or a Second rather than a First, and so on). The unpredictable case could be marked with a query. Examiners were asked to return a blank with the words 'Tutor examining' entered on it.

  The object of this exercise, as we explained, was to discover how wide—or how narrow—the gap tends to be, at least in some of the humanities and social sciences, between the classes a tutor expects his pupils to get in Finals and those that the examiners actually award. Our concern was with probability rather than

● *The Oxford Magazine*, 8 November 1968.

with justice, and tutors were therefore asked to ignore their candidates' intrinsic worth 'in the mind of God', as we put it. An undertaking was given, which has been strictly observed, that no colleges' or tutors' names would be disclosed to anybody except to our 'scrutineer', Mr E. F. Jackson of the Institute of Economics and Statistics, who kindly promised to keep the presentation and conclusions upon the paths of statistical rectitude.

Fifty-two tutors completed the forms, the total number of candidates whose class was predicted being 362. Only four queries were returned. The names of seven candidates do not appear, however, on the class-lists, and they presumably either failed or withdrew. These have all been omitted from the following tables. Occasional duplications, with two tutors predicting the performance of the same candidate, have been resolved by splitting the difference in the rare cases when the tutors disagreed. A complete coverage of the five class-lists was ruled out by the decision not to invite predictions from tutors who were also examiners, but for each of the Schools predictions were obtained for at least half of the *available* candidates. Predictions were received from tutors throughout the University, with the unfortunate exception of two women's colleges who seem to have abstained on principle (what principle was not clear).

TABLE I

	No. of tutors predicting	No. of candidates included in predictions	No. of examiners	Total No. on class-lists	Approx. % of available candidates included in predictions
English	21	128	8	238	65
French and German	12	48	10	151	50
Geography	8	33	4	72	65
Jurisprudence	8	71	5	199	50
Mathematics	14	75	6	144	70
TOTALS	63	355	33	804	60%

The final column is admittedly somewhat speculative, since it depends on subtracting from the grand total of candidates in the five subjects those who were being tutored by one or more of the examiners at the time when the forms were completed. Further research would probably correct some of these percentages. Their function, however, is simply to provide some reassurance as to the general adequateness of the sample. It may be added that no predictions were received from the women's colleges for French and German. However, the rest of the University provided a total of 109 candidates for these two subjects (either separately or with one as major and the other as minor), and when the examiners' pupils have been subtracted the proportion of predictions in them rises to some 65 per cent.

But it is with Table II, which is self-explanatory, that the findings acquire a more general significance.

TABLE II

	Class or pass awarded as predicted	Disagreements between tutors' expectations and results
English	88	40 (31%)
French and German	35	13 (27%)
Geography	27	6 (18%)
Jurisprudence	51	20 (28%)
Mathematics	54	21 (28%)
TOTALS	255	100 (28%)

The percentages in the Table appear to discredit completely the old myth that only a tenth of our Finals' results are likely to be 'wrong'. In the humanities at any rate the proportion seems to be a quarter or more. Of course, this is not to say that the 'error' is necessarily the examiners' *fault*. What the statistics measure is simply the degree of disagreement between the tutors as teachers and their colleagues as examiners.

Why should there be this surprising, indeed sensational, difference of opinion? A tutor does not undergo an intellectual metamorphosis when he becomes—temporarily and without any special training—an examiner in Finals. A clue to the discrepant evaluations is provided by the virtual identity of the percentages for English, French and German, Jurisprudence and Mathematics in Table II. Candidates, tutors and examiners in four such very different Schools are not likely to be uniformly fallible as human beings. The identity may therefore be expected to lie in the examination system that is common to all the four Schools (to which Geography can really be added, because its discrepancies are almost as striking).

The mechanics of the allotment of classes is the same in all our

Final Examinations. Approximately the same ratio of Firsts and Seconds and of both to Thirds is maintained year after year in each School. And inevitably with this limited number of classes some of those who appear in the same class are better than others. At their bottom end the Firsts shiver on the brink of the best Seconds, just as the lowest Seconds are practically indistinguishable from top Thirds. *Hinc illae lacrimae.* The intellectual superiority of a brilliant top First over a plodding bottom First, or of a top Second over a bottom Second, is a reality, whereas the hair's breadth that divides the bottom First from the top Second, or the bottom Second from the top Third, is essentially accidental. The point need not be laboured, but it is strikingly confirmed by the tutors' predictions. Of the 355 individual predictions as many as 129 (36 per cent) were 'hedged' by borderline reservations (I/II, II/I, etc.). Moreover, of the 100 discrepancies as many as fifty-eight were among the borderline cases. The uniformity in the tutors' discrepancy presumably reflects a similar deficiency of evidence at the same crucial points, whatever the subject. It is clear, then, that a first reform in Finals must be to narrow the more or less fortuitous borderline area by providing examiners with further evidence that will supplement what they can learn from the scripts. A report from the college, one or more short dissertations, the permission to introduce texts or notes in some of the three-hour papers to reduce the memorizing now necessary—these would all help.

But can Classified Honours ever be made academically respectable? In this sample, in addition to the borderline discrepancies, seven clear Firsts were predicted but not obtained, and five obtained though not even partially predicted. Only eleven clear Firsts were correctly predicted. Similarly, thirty-nine Seconds were awarded though they had not been predicted, and nineteen that had been predicted were not obtained. No doubt the predicting tutors may often have been wrong or over-optimistic, or the candidates may have suffered from such handicaps as hay fever or 'examination nerves', but an efficient system of examination must include the elimination of such false expectations in the teacher, and also a scheme of compensation for the pupil's physical mishaps rather less crude than the Oxford *viva*. To disagree about 28 per cent of the candidates' classes is surely a confession of failure. A car with one tyre permanently flat is not a good buy.

As compared with our post-graduate degrees like the B.Litt. and the D.Phil. the machinery of Finals is clumsy and irrational. An excellent survey of some more humane alternatives will be found in the article 'Towards a Rationalisation of Examination Procedures' (*Universities Quarterly*, 21, June 1967) by Professor Hilde T. Himmelweit of the London School of Economics. It should be internally digested by every member of the General Board.

A comment on Bateson's sample of tutors' forecasts
E. F. Jackson

As Mr Bateson says in his article I have, with the help of my colleague John Odling-Smee, scrutinized the completed questionnaires he collected from college tutors and the relevant Schools lists, and am happy to certify that the tables he has compiled from them contain an accurate account of the discrepancies revealed between tutors' forecasts and examiners' awards.

But, like many an auditor, I have strong reservations about the conventions he has adopted in drawing up his accounts. To be perfectly blunt, I think that his tables, though accurate, are highly misleading.

Bateson obtains his Table II by adopting the rule that a tutor's assessment of I/II is 'accepted' by the examiners if, and only if, they award a First. Similarly, an assessment of II/I is vindicated if the examiners award a Second, made ridiculous if they award a First.

One could adopt another convention. One could argue that a tutor who assessed his pupil as I/II would feel his judgment was vindicated, provided his pupil was awarded either a First or a Second. He would, doubtless, be more disappointed if his I/IIs got Seconds than if his II/Is got Seconds, but not *much* more disappointed.

A table constructed on this assumption shows figures that differ not just marginally (Social Studies word) but dramatically (Eng. Lit. word) from those in Bateson's Table II.

TABLE III

	Class pass awarded in range predicted by tutors	Disagreements between tutors' assessments and results
English	108	20 (16%)
French and German	41	7 (15%)
Geography	32	1 (3%)
Jurisprudence	59	12 (17%)
Mathematics	65	10 (13%)
TOTALS	305	50 (14%)

Judged by this laxer, but surely more realistic, criterion college tutors as a group appear to be far less inefficient as punters than Bateson suggests. Moreover, the mistakes the tutors in the sample made were never great: it can be seen from Table IV that in no case were they more than a class out.

TABLE IV Distribution of discrepancies

	Errors of Optimism				Errors of Pessimism			
	1:2	2:3	3:P	Total	2:1	3:2	P:3	Total
English	2	9	—	11	1	8	—	9
French and German	1	4	—	5	1	1	—	2
Geography	—	—	1	1	—	—	—	—
Jurisprudence	1	4	1	6	—	6	—	6
Mathematics	3	1	3	7	2	1	—	3
TOTALS	7	18	5	30	4	16	—	20

On average they were slightly over-optimistic. They did, however, vary rather a lot—which is hardly surprising, given that some of them are not much older than their pupils whereas others are experienced students of form. In the English School, for example, at the Second-Third border five of the errors of optimism came from one tutor and three of the errors of pessimism from another. If these cases of systematic disagreement between tutors and examiners are eliminated there remain only twelve wrong predictions in English or 11 per cent, not significantly greater than the figure scoffed at as folklore by Bateson.

Bateson's reply to Jackson

Though a statistical red herring Mr E. F. Jackson's Table III does raise an extremely important issue. I am grateful to him for it as well as for the interest and time he has taken over this investigation. The table is a red herring because we must compare like with like, and the class-lists do not have the I/II, II/I, etc. that were available to the predicting tutors. What Mr Jackson's table shows is that the *real* gap between tutors and examiners is more like 14 per cent than 28 per cent. Unfortunately the Oxford class system successfully conceals this crucial information because of the fiction that all Firsts are equally first-class, all Seconds equally second-class and so on. In comparing predictions and results I had therefore no option except to base it on the class the tutor thought more probable, however slight the degree of probability one way or the other. Examiners are faced with exactly the same problem.

My object in allowing tutors to hedge their bets with the I/II kind of thing was to discover how many of their pupils fall into the borderline areas between classes; the answer that the predictions provide is that 36 per cent of them do.

There are therefore, if I may summarize, three built-in defects in Finals (apart from such human elements as nervous pressure, the luck of the question, overworked examiners and the risk of prejudice): (i) the system conceals the wide differences in intellectual quality between those awarded the same class; (ii) it ignores the hair's breadth that divides those at the bottom of one class from those at the top of the next; (iii) by its dependence on the invigilated three-hour paper it encourages superficiality (instead of 'thinking for yourself'), the glib pen and excessive memorization.

And the moral of that 28 per cent discrepancy between the classes obtained and those predicted by the tutors? The fact that the percentage is almost identical in subjects as different as English, French and German, Jurisprudence and Mathematics must point to a common factor that I have still to define. But it really stares us in the face. The candidates we have been concerned with obtained either a First, a Second, a Third or a Pass. There were therefore only four borderlines—that between a First and a Second, that between a Second and a Third, that between a Third and a Pass, and the much rarer borderline between a Pass and a Fail (of which only those who achieved a Pass are recorded in my figures). If the examiners had only been required to distinguish between those who passed and those who failed, the average discrepancy between tutor and examiner would have been under 5 per cent—a margin of disagreement that candidates and dons would both be prepared to live with. And even if just the two lowest borderlines—those between a Third and a Pass and between a Pass and a Fail—were retained the figures would still be under 10 per cent.

The conclusion that these considerations suggest is that if the invigilated three-hour papers are to remain the present class system must be abandoned—leaving only perhaps Honours, Pass and Fail. If on the other hand the class system is retained a much more sophisticated mode of examination will need to be introduced.

20

*Examination versus Education**

'I never wonder to see Men wicked, but I often wonder to see them not ashamed.' The genial dictum, which will be found among Swift's 'Thoughts on Various Subjects', was not directed *specifically* at examiners, though Swift himself is said to have been almost ploughed in the logic at Trinity College, Dublin. But its aptness as a comment on the examination system here—and decreasingly elsewhere—is not likely to be denied. We have got so used to what the Kneale Committee called the 'necessary evil' of examinations that the sense of shame which should surely accompany the deliberate performance of evil has become hardened. An undergraduate comes to a university to be educated; instead he finds himself being 'prepared' for this or that examination. If he acquires some incidental education—generally from his fellow undergraduates or dons off duty—this is secondary to the continuous rehearsal for a series of invigilated three-hour papers that are to be the culmination of his career here.

The wickedness of Finals can easily be demonstrated. Is there any other public test (for adults) from which there can be no appeal, because the evidence is destroyed before a decision is announced that has been reached solely on the basis of that evidence? Even O-level scripts are not destroyed until twelve

● *The Oxford Magazine*, 17 May 1968.

months after the results have been announced, so that a head-master can always appeal against a grotesquely unfair mark. But there is a further area of wickedness in Finals that is perhaps more shame-making because it affects all our examiners, the most conscientious ones as well as the lazy ones. This is the class system —a natural academic product of the abandonment by the nine-teenth century of the stratified society of the eighteenth, but that our more egalitarian age need not have persisted in. Our private use of alpha, beta, gamma and delta instead of percentages is ex-pressed publicly in the four classes awarded in an Honours School. When the results are announced in *The Times* and else-where the innocent reader is expected to think that Tom, who has got a First, must be first-rate intellectually, whereas poor Dick who has just missed his First, must be second-rate, and the miser-able Harry with a Third a thorough third-rater. But, as we who are inside the system all know, even with examiners who are efficient and responsible and the examinees 'do themselves justice', the difference between a good First and a low First is far greater than that between a low First and a high Second. And a similar distinc-tion runs the whole way down the classes and passes. The fact that we qualify our Greek letters with a plus (double or triple), a minus minimized in the same way, a generous sprinkling of queries, and even a strange collocation of letters (beta beta alpha, etc.) gives the whole show away. We are not really thinking in classes but in an order of merit. Even the four letters have now detached themselves from the four classes, a gamma double minus, for example, being generally more likely to get a Fourth or no class at all than a Third.

If we had the moral courage of our convictions the class nonsense would, I suppose, be dropped altogether, and *The Times* would be provided instead with a list of names in their order of merit as determined by the marks, just as the mathemat-ical 'wranglers' used to be at Cambridge. But we find it difficult at Oxford to be intellectually honest and so we defend the charade of Finals by expecting a tutor's testimonial to counterbalance the examiners' errors of judgment. There is also the erring house-maid's excuse: Please, ma'am, it was only a little one. In other words, there is a pious hope that such misclassifications are only occasional. A close analysis of four mark-books in different Schools that I supplemented by twice inviting the tutors in one School to prognosticate a week before Finals the classes their pupils would get has convinced me that our baby is quite a big one. I reported my findings fully in an earlier number of the *Magazine*; some indication of what was revealed may, however, be repeated. The second enquiry covered two-thirds of all the candidates, excluding those actually tutored by any of the examiners themselves, but the tutors' prognostications coincided with the class finally obtained in only 52 per cent of the cases! These fifteen tutors expected five of their pupils to get a First; of the five four in fact got Seconds and one a Third. The examiners, on the other hand, awarded four Firsts to pupils of these tutors, all four of whom had been expected by them to get Seconds. Not a very good advertisement for the system.

A tutor is not infallible, of course, but he is likely to be less fallible than an examiner because the range of evidence at his disposal is so much longer and wider than that available to an examiner. The contrast between the accumulation of different kinds of evidence that determines an undergraduate's acceptance at Oxford and the dependence on memory and mere verbal facility which play so large a part in determining the final handshake is really grotesque—especially as the class awarded in our Finals can often affect the whole of a man's future. I remember the dismay and despair with which I read the list on which my own Second appeared may years ago. Cheerfulness only broke in when my tutor sent me the marks. My worst paper—in which gross factual errors were combined with much journalistic hot air—received an alpha minus and my half dozen or so really good papers wavered between a beta and a beta double plus. I went on to do a B.Litt. without a supervisor, as was then possible, and the thesis was duly published by the Press. My examiners, overloaded with far too many scripts, had blundered; my later analysis of the four mark-books has demonstrated to me that they continue to do so, since the two marks on each script tend to vary by a class at least in 30 to 40 per cent of the separate scripts.

The errors of examiners must be ultimately ascribed to a contradiction between the tutorial system of education and the three-hour paper, the method we have used for the last hundred years for conducting our examinations. The invigilated paper is no doubt appropriate for schoolboys and schoolgirls. It tests the degree of thoroughness with which they have memorized the term's work and the ability to organize and present what has been memorized. Since the undergraduate is usually only a term or two removed from school when he takes it, our First Examination may with some justice also employ the three-hour paper. But when he takes Finals the abler undergraduate is on the threshold of such courses as the B.Litt. and the D.Phil. which are geared to a thesis, and even for those about to enter the Civil Service or commerce some training in the more elementary forms of research, with the ability to present one's findings logically and economically, is infinately more valuable than simply being a good examinee. The tutorial, even under the present system (with Finals always at the back of both tutor's and undergraduate's minds), can perform just such a pedagogic function. The essential immediate reform therefore is to reduce drastically the number of three-hour papers and to introduce into Finals a few semi-scholarly 'super-essays' to supplement and perhaps ultimately supersede the present schoolboy tests.

The mechanism will naturally vary from School to School. A halfway stage might be to award Honours—and classes if the absurd system must be retained—on the basis of (i) three papers of not more than 3,000 words each, preferably originally contributed to classes not given by the tutor, (ii) a tutor's report, (iii) some four or five conventional three-hour papers. To reduce the burden on examiners the 'super-essays' could well be submitted between the end of the Trinity and Hilary Terms preceding the candidate's last term. A necessary and welcome requirement would be that the 'super-essays' are typed, and the *viva* might well be limited to discussing them. The absurd suspicion I often encounter that such miniature dissertations would be sure to be stolen from some out-of-the-way periodical is unfair to our examiners. Fallible though they may be they are not as fallible as all that. I have corrected hundreds of term-papers in American universities and have never had the least difficulty in detecting the unacknowledged plagiarisms.

In any case, *abusus non tollit usum*. Such papers are worth doing in themselves; they are the logical sequel to the ordinary weekly essay because they demand more original thinking and more scholarly factual reinforcement. And once completed something is left, if only the carbon copy, for the mature student to build on later. Above all they would combine something that is itself very much worth while in its preparation, the material for a rational test publicly available when concluded—a Marriage of Heaven and Hell.

21

*Beowulf and All That**

The case for compulsory Anglo-Saxon in the Eng. Lit. course may be said to have been lost by default. When he was consulted, almost exactly a year ago, by the *Oxford Mail* on the proposal to make Old English optional, the Rawlinson and Bosworth Professor of Anglo-Saxon could only object that it would make Oxford like Cambridge ('terrible place Cambridge')—a proposition he clinched by asserting that there has been no literature since 1830 ('only books'). The long and often hilarious correspondence which followed in *The Times* and elsewhere returned again and again to a point that nobody really disputes, viz, that O.E. literature can be well worth studying for its own sake. But so can Persian literature or Chinese—to say nothing of Latin and French, with which the cultural and stylistic links of our literature are much closer than with Anglo-Saxon. By all means let us encourage the undergraduate with an interest in the Grendels to read *Beowulf* in the original if he wants to. What is not clear is that there is a rational justification for compelling *every* undergraduate interested in English literature to do the Anglo-Saxon grind. Shakespeare may have had small Latin and less Greek (and not much

• *The Oxford Magazine*, Michaelmas no. 5, 1966.

French), but he had after all no Anglo-Saxon at all. And I have never discovered that the Anglo-Saxon I learnt when I did the English School here—and which I assimilated sufficiently to be able to tutor in it without disgrace—has ever helped me to understand any of the masterpieces of our literature, except perhaps marginally and to an insignificant degree.

But Beowulf and his ilk is not what the hullabaloo in the English Faculty is really all about. We combine by our founding Statute two incompatible disciplines (each of which, incidentally, would fully occupy an industrious undergraduate for three years) —an Honour School of the English Language *and* an Honour School of English Literature. (As it were, Biology and Biography.) When we came into being some seventy years ago the superimposition of Eng. Lang. on Eng. Lit. (including at that time compulsory Gothic) was tactically necessary to meet the objection that Eng. Lit. *per se* would be a 'soft option'. There was for Victorian Oxford the awful possibility that the undergraduates might actually enjoy their work!

The extraordinary thing is that nobody—apart from a short and cheerful exercise in blatant sophistry by C. S. Lewis in his *Rehabilitations* (1939)—has ever asked if there is some logical necessity that compels a study of the English language and its antecedents for a degree in English literature. For the moment one starts thinking about it it is obvious that there isn't. After all the typical Oxford freshman has no difficulty in *speaking* good English. And I have known plenty of undergraduates who wrote far better English prose than their language tutors—who tend, with honourable exceptions, to a heavy stylistic hand.

In an English-speaking country the undergraduate 'knows' English—with some minor gaps—long before he reaches a university. The parallel therefore with Lit. Hum. or the Modern Languages School, in which some facility with the language must proceed *pari passu* with a reading of its literature, does not apply. A tutor in Eng. Lit. takes it for granted that his pupils will understand the surface sense of Jane Austen or Defoe; if in reading Shakespeare or Chaucer some minor reinforcement may be necessary in the way of notes or a glossary the difference is still only one of degree. The general if unspoken literary assumption is in fact that the English language as used by our greatest writers forms a semantic continuum from *c.* 1200 (the actual *terminus a quo* of the *Oxford English Dictionary* is 1150) down to the present day. There have been minor changes, of course, through the centuries, but 'Sumer is icumen in' *works* for us in basically the same way as a lyric by Yeats or Graves.

For the Oxford linguist, on the other hand, as for any historian, it is the changes that matter. His approach to language is *diachronic*, whereas the literary assumption is that within its limits English is *synchronic*. As against the linguist's emphasis on differences, however minute, between one period and another, a literary critic takes for granted an essential identity between the English of the past and that of today. If you can read Dickens you will be able, with a litle care and good will, to read Chaucer too. The fact that even a language tutor tends when reading Shakespeare and Milton aloud to give them a B.B.C. pronunciation may be seen as his reluctant confirmation of the synchronic approach. And the fact that Anglo-Saxon resists any such modernization is one more item of evidence that it isn't English—even Ye Olde English—but its etymological predecessor (as Latin, for example, preceded Italian).

In some modern universities a School of English Language has hived itself off, as an autonomous and parallel faculty, from the one joint school. It is surely the only sensible solution. Our present habit of forcing all our literary students to spend nearly half their time in the irrelevant intricacies of historical linguistics only ensures that their knowledge of English literature is unnecessarily limited and superficial. (They know their *Beowulf* much better than they do their Shakespeare.) *Quod est absurdum.*

22

Miscellaneous Antipathies

Scandalously Anonymous: The Times Literary Supplement*

TLS, as it is usually abbreviated in print (as against the 'Lit. Sup.' of informal or infuriated conversation), is still, strictly (legally) speaking, a weekly supplement of *The Times*. The Editor (A. P. Pryce-Jones since 1947)[1] and his staff are appointed, and so can presumably be sacked, by the Management of *The Times*. In the last resort, therefore, *TLS* toes a Printing House Square line. But short of such a resort—as when Northcliffe, in 1922, suddenly ordered its termination and was only circumvented by a conspiracy of deliberate misunderstandings—the dependence is now not much more than the technical one that both are printed and published by *The Times* Publishing Company. For day-to-day purposes, as an organ of current critical opinion, *TLS* is a separate periodical entity—as is demonstrated by *The Times*'s page of book-reviews on Thursdays, which are not duplicated but are sometimes actually contradicted by the *TLS*'s notices of the same books on Fridays. In 1902, however, when *TLS* started— exactly one hundred years after the *Edinburgh* had first made anonymous reviewing a form of literary criticism—it was a supplement in the full sense of the word. That is to say, the reader of

● *Essays in Criticism*, 7 (1957).   [1] Arthur C. W. Crook since 1959.

The Times got it thrown in, automatically and for nothing, as he now gets an occasional American, Engineering or Bible Supplement. The first slim number—for Friday, 17 January 1902—carried a succinct announcement, all that was provided by way of introduction, at the foot of the table of Contents: 'During the Parliamentary Session LITERARY SUPPLEMENTS to "THE TIMES" will appear as often as may be necessary in order to keep abreast with the more important publications of the day.' The necessity turned out, and has continued ever since, to be a weekly one, Parliament or no Parliament, though it was not until February 1914 that *TLS* was conceded a measure of economic independence, and subscribers to *The Times* had to order it separately.

But this is not the place to attempt a short history of *TLS*. To 1938 it has already been done in the Fiftieth Anniversary Number (18 January 1952), as 'A Record of its Beginnings', a discreetly informative survey that allows no cats to escape from the official bags. However, the *TLS* tradition of genteel anonymous reviewing—as distinct from the mask-and-dagger anonymity of the Jeffreys and Crokers in the *Edinburgh* and *Quarterly* (which had a *political* origin in the menace of Government prosecution or victimization)—is only comprehensible in the context of its original identity with *The Times*. The anonymity was implicit in the identity. For its first twelve years *TLS* carried the superscription, 'Issued with *The Times*' (it was at first only obtainable with the Friday copy); its readers were primarily readers of *The Times*, who would naturally expect similar practices to obtain in the supplement as in the newspaper. Obviously, for the original reviewers, many of them members of *The Times*'s editorial staff, to have signed their separate reviews would have been the height of irregularity—if indeed the term *review* is applicable at all to the genial, well informed and nicely phrased summaries of new books (Literature) that then preceded shorter sections on Science, Art, the Drama, Music and (how typical of the Edwardian ethos!) Chess. As an alternative to the front-page review—but the modern reader hardly notices the difference —there were sometimes essays in the Lamb–Hazlitt manner on such topics as 'Railway Reading', 'Heroines of Fiction', 'The Decline in French Influence', or 'Ancient Rome in Fiction' (the titles all come from the first volume). A. B. Walkley, who was *The Times*'s dramatic critic at this time, had a particularly neat hand at such things.

The star reviewer in the early volumes was apparently Arthur Clutton-Brock, who combined uplift with a sort of Art-and-Craft culture (Oxford had given him a Double Third). According to the *DNB* article on him, the early *TLS* 'owed much of its steady success and wide reputation' to him, and 'its editor went so far as to say that Clutton-Brock "made it"'. In all, however, there were soon nearly two hundred occasional reviewers, the most frequent being (in addition to Clutton-Brock) J. C. Bailey, Thomas Seccombe, E. V. Lucas, Mme Duclaux (*née* Robinson), H. C. Beeching, Quiller-Couch, de la Mare and G. S. Gordon. It is only necessary to recite these names to show the low critical level at which the pre-1914 *TLS* functioned. (I would not wish to deny 'Q's' and de la Mare's extra-critical distinction.) The period between the death of Arnold and Eliot's beginnings was a nadir of English criticism—A. C. Bradley and Arthur Symons must be excepted, though neither of them, I think, contributed to *TLS* —and it should not be held against it that it reflected the contemporary inanity.

Those, then, were the (often silly) salad days. Recollecting them in satiric tranquillity, Ezra Pound has described what the early *TLS* looked like to a militant younger generation:

> When I arrived in England (A.D. 1908), I found a greater darkness in the British 'serious press' than had obtained on the banks of the Schuylkill. . . . It was incredible that literate men—men literate enough, that is, to write the orderly paragraphs that they did write constantly in their papers—believed the stupidities that appeared there with such regularity. (Later, for two years, we ran fortnightly in the *Egoist* the sort of fool-column that the French call a *sottisier*, needing nothing for it but quotations from the *Times Literary Supplement*. Two issues of the *Supplement* yielding, easily, one page of the *Egoist*.) ('How to Read'.)

The *Egoist sottisier* was called 'Our Contemporaries', and, though not as prolonged as Pound's words would suggest, they often make excellent comic reading. A nice specimen (*Egoist*, May 1918, p. 75, where it is ascribed to *The Times*) comes from the *TLS* of 18 April 1918: 'Mr Gellert's verse is often what the Australian critics have a habit of calling "luminous"—but phosphorescent would be a better epithet.' As so often in a *sottisier* the comment in its original context, an elaborate review of some poems by an Australian on the Gallipoli campaign, is not quite as fatuous as Pound and Eliot have made it look. But the review taken as a whole is certainly a pathetic performance—pompous, dogmatic, sentimental, and completely taken in by Gellert's rubbish. *TLS* was particularly unfortunate in its poetry reviewing in those days. The short notice of *Prufrock* (21 June 1917), tucked away in the 'New Books and Reprints' section at the back, has to be read to be believed.

The tide turned in or about 1920. Eliot's now classical 'Ben Jonson' was actually the front-page piece on 13 November 1919, and this very personal reinterpretation was followed by the first part of the equally unorthodox Massinger essay (27 May 1920), and, in 1921, by the three decisive reviews ('The Metaphysical Poets', 'Andrew Marvell', and 'John Dryden') reprinted under his name in *Homage to John Dryden*, where Eliot specifically acknowledges 'the encouragement to write them' he had had from *TLS*'s editor B. L. (later Sir Bruce) Richmond. Richmond, who had taken over the editorship from J. R. Thursfield as long ago as the second half of 1902, was surprisingly sympathetic to the new intelligentsia that emerged at the end of World War I, and he soon recruited as reviewers critics of the calibre of Middleton Murry (who had made a start in 1913), Richard Aldington, F. S. Flint, Herbert Read, W. J. Turner, Edmund Blunden, John Hayward, John Sparrow, James Sutherland and Geoffrey Tillotson, with the result that by 1930, if not earlier, *TLS* had become very much the journal we know today. At its best the reviewing was very good indeed.

The original unsigned review had justified itself so long as the reviewer was content, as he generally was between 1902 and 1919, with producing a readable *précis* or miniature essay round the book he had been assigned. But in the 1920s the longer reviews ceased to be mere summaries embroidered with amiable chit-chat, and considered recommendation or detailed criticism began to take the place of the *précis*. With the new seriousness and assumption of authority—the legacy largely of Middleton Murry's brilliant but too short-lived *Athenaeum* (1918–1921)— the anonymity, instead of remaining a deprecatory gesture of humility, sometimes became, or seemed to become, the voice of a sort of oracle. A striking example is the review of Eliot's *For Lancelot Andrewes* (6 December 1928), which ends, more in sorrow than in anger:

> . . . by accepting a higher spiritual authority based not upon the deepest personal experience . . . but upon the anterior and

exterior authority of revealed religion, he has abdicated from his high position. Specifically he rejects modernism for mediaevalism. But most of us . . . have gone too far to draw back. It is to the country beyond the Waste Land that we are compelled to look, and many will consider it the emptier that they are not likely to find Mr Eliot there. Recently he recorded his conviction that Dante's poetry represents a saner attitude towards 'the mystery of life' than Shakespeare's. Not a saner, we would say, but simply a different attitude, and to the majority, the great majority, to-day no longer a vital one.

Here, instead of the bare summary of the book's contents that an early *TLS* would have provided, is polished, magisterial rebuke. The review—by Middleton Murry perhaps, or possibly by Richard Aldington, who has a critic proclaiming himself a Classicist, a Royalist and an Anglo-Catholic in *Death of a Hero* (1929)—made something of a sensation at the time, and Eliot replies to it in a note somewhere. But it was a review, I feel, that cried out for a signature. Signed, it might well have been fair and responsible comment; unsigned, it is intolerably pompous and pretentious.

The problem of *TLS* anonymity, this power of critical invisibility corrupting (I suspect) to its possessor and terrifying (I know) to its object, has become more pressing since the end of World War II. To prepare myself for this survey I renewed a long-lapsed subscription in 1955, and for the last two years I have been industriously reading all the reviews included in the Contents under the headings Art, Biography, Classical Studies, Literature and Literary Criticism, Philosophy, Poetry and Theatre, as well as many of the others. First impressions were decidedly favourable. Two things particularly struck me about the more specifically literary reviews—to which I propose to confine myself here—as compared with their equivalents in the 1920s and 1930s, when I was an avid *TLS* reader: the higher level of scholarship maintained, and the improved quality of the actual writing. Both are, of course, in a sense negative virtues. It is something, I mean, to have a weekly in which one is *not* irritated by the elementary errors of fact that keep on turning up in reviews in *The Spectator*, *The Listener*, *The Observer* and *The Sunday Times*. (I don't say that *TLS* is impeccable. The description *tout court* of the scene in progress in De Witt's drawing of the Swan Theatre as Malvolio's wooing of Olivia is a recent 'howler', 5 July 1957, p. 142.) Similarly the pleasure I derive from the almost uniform adequacy of the writing is partly a matter of *not* having to stop and mentally rewrite the reviewer's sentence, as I often find myself doing when reading other reviews, especially the American ones.

And there are positive rewards too. The scholar in me was grateful for the expert correction of some transcriptions of Clare's MS poems (25 May 1956), though I should like to have known who this learned reviewer was. (Was it Blunden?) And I was fascinated with the unpublished details about Hopkins's family and relations (21 December 1956), though again I was distressed not to know who my informant was. (Was he perhaps Mr Gerard Hopkins, of the Oxford University Press, who is, I believe, a nephew of the poet?) And, as a professional literary historian, I found myself reconsidering cherished opinions after reading the reviews of R. L. Sharp's *From Donne to Dryden* (25 March 1955) and Clay Hunt's *Donne's Poetry* (16 March 1956). Even if one disagreed, one had at least been critically stimulated.

The cumulative effect of the polish and general literary elegance of modern *TLS* prose—in which it would be churlish not to recognize the influence of the present editor—is more difficult to analyse. Without signatures to help the reader to distinguish between Reviewer A and Reviewer B, the total final impression is of a diffused perfection that approaches a mechanical monotony. This might be called the stylistic argument against the anonymous review. The anonymity obliterates the personal differences that are of the essence of a good prose style. On the other hand, if the reviews are taken singly and the book under discussion is one that engages the reviewer's sympathy, the writing does often come to admirable life in the urbane, sophisticated, slightly mannered prose the typical *TLS* reviewer seems to favour today. Three recent examples, each in its respective way a model of the well-informed and well-expressed book review, are the notices of A. N. L. Munby's *The Formation of the Phillipps Library* (21 September 1956), Humphry House's *Aristotle's 'Poetics'* (5 October 1956), and J. R. Hale's edition of *The Italian Journal of Samuel Rogers* (31 May 1957). And it would be easy to extend this list.

Per contra, it must be admitted that if the book he has been allotted *fails* to engage the reviewer's sympathy, the style may degenerate into covert sneers, the paraphrase that verges on parody, and similar weapons of sophisticated denigration. It is easy to be irritated, perhaps unfairly irritated, by such reviews. It is after all the proper corollary of that much-prized, much-laboured lucidity and elegance of his own style that a *TLS* reviewer should underrate a book without such virtues, even if it possesses more solid qualities. The prejudice against the *Scrutiny* group—sometimes, it is only fair to add, heroically overcome—is a case in point. Another is Waldock's *Paradise Lost and Its Critics* (reviewed 1 November 1947), a really seminal work—even if some aboriginal Australian brashness has survived in it —which the reviewer, when challenged by F. R. Leavis (22 November), could only sum up as 'clever and readable, but not important'. Fortunately on this occasion C. S. Lewis, one of the critics under Waldock's fire, was able to confirm Leavis's protest (29 November).

Anti-Americanism is also often charged against *TLS*, and one cannot deny the thing altogether, of course, though it is, I think, a less sinister phenomenon than is sometimes alleged. Fundamentally it amounts to a collision, inevitable if occasionally painful (but a recognition of the inevitability should diminish the pain), between two very different philosophies of literature. The *TLS* reviewer—because of the special (to most of us, excessive) importance that he himself attaches to the scrupulous use of English—*must* resent and deplore the uncouth jargon of much modern American writing, if he is to be true to his own literary ideals. The barbaric yawps—and the culture that they seem to express or typify—are a challenge to his whole scale of values. To the American scholar, however, conscious only that hard work and hard thinking have been rejected with jeers, *TLS* may well seem to have entered into a conspiracy to deny Americans the recognition they feel, often with justice, their work deserves. As S. Le Comte, of Columbia University, put it recently in an angry but effective letter (9 March 1956):

> . . . For the rest, one should be used by now to *The Times Literary Supplement* tradition that nearly all the critical perception is on one side of the Atlantic while the dull, blundering 'scholars', the dogged gatherers of 'withered sticks and pebbles', are, massively but let us not hope impenetrably, congregated on the other.

The sticks and pebbles are from the last sentence of a review (20 January 1956) of three American books on Milton, including one by Le Comte himself. It is that sort of witticism—not, I think, altogether undeserved in this particular case—which has made *TLS* so odious to the English Departments of the United States.

But the case against *TLS* is not often properly stated by its American critics. The anti-Americanism—which, though sincere in a kind of way (as I have tried to indicate), *can* be purblind, for instance, in the failure to recognize the special importance of *Theory of Literature* (24 February 1950) or the critical essays of W. K. Wimsatt (10 December 1954)—is only one aspect of what, at its worst, can amount to cultural snobbery. I was struck by a phrase used by the Editor in introducing the Special Autumn Number of 1953: 'the range of variation permissible to a civilized judgment'. He was repeating a formula, the definition of the ideal *TLS* reviewer, that he had already used in the Fiftieth Anniversary Number ('. . . a voice which is we hope that of a civilized man . . . the civilized man does not change with fashion'). The definition is thrown out as if self-explanatory, but what, I found myself asking, *is* a civilized judgment? *Who* is this civilized man? And then I suddenly remembered Clive Bell's *Civilization* (1927), in which the United States came very low in the scale of civilized life. And Clive Bell's name immediately suggested those of Virginia Woolf and Lytton Strachey, and I realized that the judgment and the man were really the judgments and men that would have commended themselves to interbelline Bloomsbury; that it is in fact—to simplify, perhaps oversimplify—the old Bloomsbury flag, repaired at the edges and re-dyed blue, that now flies over the *TLS* office.

The sin of Bloomsbury was complacency, and complacency is the temptation a typical *TLS* reviewer of the 1950s finds the most difficult of all to resist. He has style, he has taste, he has scholarship, how can his critical verdicts ever be less than infallible? And the long-established, time-honoured *TLS* tradition of anonymous reviewing, how can *that* be questioned—especially since the general level of the reviews is so high, higher perhaps than it has ever been. The two questions are interdependent, and I suppose the ultimate answer to both is that no effective substitute has been found so far for the Christian values. It is an answer that the critics of *TLS* are entitled to press to its logical conclusion. The reason why Bloomsbury civilization looks so silly today (I am thinking particularly of the ideal society projected in the last chapter of Clive Bell's book) is because, at any rate in its relations with the barbarous external world, it *repudiated* Christian charity and Christian humility. And so we remember it, appropriately, by the fatuously self-satisfied Mr Mercaptan—of the snouty look and the delicious middles—of Aldous Huxley's *Antic Hay* rather than by the nice, historical Mr Bell, who is, incidentally, a *TLS* reviewer himself.

The application to *TLS* will be best made by way of a particular example. Because of the episode's notoriety and because it raises one aspect of the Anglo-American issue in a clearcut form, the brilliant and devastating review of Tom Burns Haber's *The Manuscript Poems of A. E. Housman* (29 April 1955) is a good one to select. The gist of this review, as summarized by the reviewer himself (1 July 1955) in a rejoinder to Haber's ineffective reply, is that Haber as an editor was 'lacking in candour, overconfident, not a dependable transcriber, incapable of fully appreciating the tone and idiom of his author, and not literate in his writing of English'. Just that! And the reviewer then proceeded to prove it, meticulously, over and over again. To the onlooker it was a fascinating spectacle, but all the same most of us came away feeling a little unhappy. No doubt Haber had deserved every word of it; of the 'animosity' of which he accused the reviewer he was not able to produce any evidence at all. But one had an uncomfortable feeling, nevertheless, that something had gone wrong. As a fellow human being, however guilty, brazen and uncivilized, might not Haber have been permitted to *see* who this strict inquisitor was? The thick curtain of anonymity was disturbing somehow to one's sense of democratic justice. If the reviewer was in fact John Sparrow, the Warden of All Souls, as is now known, the fact is surely relevant. It would certainly be considered so in every other journal in the English-speaking world in which a similar review might have appeared. In a matter of so much importance, a criminal charge practically, the prisoner has the right to know who is prosecuting him. And the *TLS* reader, who is, as it were, the jury, has the same right. A Voice from the Cloud—with no name attached to it because it claims to speak with the collective wisdom of 'civilization'—is necessarily suspect in a democratic community. And the reviewer's sentence carries less weight than it might merit objectively *because of* the anonymity. Rightly or wrongly we suspect it as a part of the apparatus of a fundamentally non-Christian 'Establishment'—one that does not love its neighbours as itself.

A fundamental critical principle is also involved. If the reader had known that Sparrow was to reprint the review under his own name in his *Independent Essays* (1963), it would have clinched the case against Haber. A reviewer, by the nature of his trade, can only present the reader with part of the evidence from which he has reached his conclusions. In *TLS*, where most of the reviews are compartively short, the reader does not really expect much more than the reviewer's considered opinion. But the worth of an opinion varies with the degree of respect we have for the holder of the opinion—which in its turn depends upon our knowledge and approval or disapproval of whatever other opinions he or she may have already expressed. Now to anyone who knows his way about modern English literature, a name such as Sparrow's at the foot of a review is a virtual guarantee in itself of the reliability of the verdict reached. In other words, *the reviewer's name is an essential part of the meaning of the review.* The principle is a corollary of the commonplace that a saying must imply a sayer and a sayee. That is to say, the more one knows about both the writer of a work of literature and the audience he is explicitly or implicitly addressing, the less likely one is to misunderstand it. In the absence of such information, the reader is reduced to constructing—on the basis of the internal evidence to be extracted from his text and whatever external evidence he may possess—a hypothetical author and audience. In the case of *TLS*, as we have seen, we tend to assume that the review will be 'out of' Bloomsbury, as it were, 'by' scholarship, an assumption that is then modified or corrected as we read on. But the margin of possible error is always considerable, and the canny reader tends to reserve his judgment. In the absence of a signature, he cannot be sure where he is in relation to either author or audience. An anonymous review cannot, therefore, be as trustworthy as a signed one of the same quality—not because anonymous reviewers are wickeder than others (though they are perhaps likelier to be, since they have a better chance of escaping detection), but because an important determinant of its meaning has been suppressed.

The point is an easy one to establish. Every reader of defunct journals will sometime or other have read an anonymous review or article which he discovers the authorship of later. Is it not a fact that the discovery of the author's identity almost always alters and enriches its meaning for us? And the closer the review approaches to a critical article, the greater the difference between our first and second readings? A good example of the process is the long and, in every sense of the word, critical review of Leavis's *D. H. Lawrence: Novelist* (28 October 1955), which I am told, on good authority, was by Middleton Murry. I read the review originally without knowing who wrote it, and on rereading it I find the knowledge makes all the difference in the world to the way I react to it. It is a much more interesting critical document, and I am no longer worried by the firm, though understanding, way in which Leavis's enthusiasms and overstatements are pulled up. Murry had earned the right to talk like that.

Three pleas are sometimes offered on behalf of the unsigned review. It is said (i) that experts in official positions, or literary men invited to review books by friends or influential acquaintances, will often agree to contribute anonymously, though they would find it embarrassing to have to sign the review; (ii) that every reviewer has to begin sometime, and the knowledge that his fledgelings will not be formally distinguishable from those of more experienced hands gives the beginner confidence; (iii) that an anonymous reviewer is not so likely to show off or play to the gallery like the man who can wave his name before the reader. The apologies seem to me, I must say, all three of them, more moral (or immoral) than literary. To (i) we must surely say quite firmly that the truth can never embarrass the Good Man, and if the *TLS* expert is not prepared to show us the literary object as in itself it really is to *him*, an individual identifiable human being, we do not want his reviews; to (ii) that beginner's confidence, alias cheek, is one of the worst features of anonymous reviewing, and its immediate elimination from *TLS* would do much to repair Anglo-American academic relations; and to (iii) that nobody minds a little innocent exhibitionism *à la* John Wain or John Raymond, so long as the reviewer does his duty by the book he has in front of him. It is (i), of course, that is the real bone of contention. The literary world is a comparatively small one, and sooner or later the book comes along to every reviewer which is complicated by personal relations.

Leslie Stephen, in the shrewd 'Thoughts on Criticism' recently disinterred by S. O. A. Ullmann (*Men, Books and Mountains*, 1956), saw in this fact a practical justification of anonymous reviewing. 'Why should I not condemn a man's work without telling him that I personally hold him to be a fool? Why

should literary differences be embittered by personal feeling?'
Stephen's questions were, of course, rhetorical, and they invite
a similar retort. Why on earth should the relationship between
reviewer and reviewed be subject to a different morality from
that which rules in every other public relationship in a democratic society? In a collision on the road both drivers are required
to disclose their identity; in the head-on collisions that often en-
liven *TLS* only one party, the one that has been run into, gives
a name and address. Why? Is it not a kind of favouritism, which
is liable to breed in the favoured a superman morality? And any-
how, morality apart, such literary class-divisions are bad for
criticism. Let me quote—to make up for calling him an exhibi-
tionist—the excellent definition in John Wain's *Preliminary
Essays* (1957, p. 187): 'Literary criticism is the discussion, *between equals*, of works of literature, with a view to establishing
common ground on which judgments of value can be based' (my
italics). *TLS* reviewing would be better than it is if the discussion was more fully one between equals. As it is, the effect of the
anonymity, whatever the particular reviewer's intention may be,
is to seem to exalt him to a status of superiority over both reader
and author. It pulls against equality, so that when an author
defends himself the anonymous reviewer is never, or hardly
ever, able to admit that he was in error. Instead we get that un-
edifying performance, much too common in *TLS*, in which the
reviewer concentrates on the weak points in an author's retort
and turns a conveniently blind eye to the matters in which the
author has the best of the argument. Such intellectual dishonesty
is not inevitable in anonymous reviewing, but it is noticeably
more frequent in *TLS* than in such a journal as the *Review of
English Studies*, where the reviews are all signed.

As I see it, then, the weaknesses of *TLS* are almost all traceable
to this survival from its pre-critical Edwardian days. Today, except as providing the material for guessing games in Senior Common Rooms, the practice seems to me to serve no reputable
purpose whatever. Is it over-optimistic to hope that the time may
soon be ripe for a Down-with-Anonymity Deputation to Printing
House Square? Might not Mr Eliot, for example, be persuaded
to head it? *TLS* is too indispensable a feature of our culture to be
allowed to remain less good than it might be simply because of a
demonstrably defective procedure of presentation. In the meantime, the conscientious reader can follow the lead given by

Leavis and Lewis with *Paradise Lost and its Critics* and submit letters of protest whenever they feel serious injustice has been done. The Editor and his Assistant were kind enough to check my facts in an earlier draft of this article, and I feel sure they will always allow the voice of reason to be heard. In my time I have written many letters to *TLS*, and they have always been printed in full. On one memorable occasion (1 March 1941), what I wrote as a letter was promoted to the status of a signed article, and I was *paid* for it!

23

A TLS Postscript•

Nunquamne reponam? The question Juvenal asked in the first line of his first satire had been provoked by the *Theseid* of Cordus, a now unknown epic by an equally unknown poet. A parallel with *The Times Literary Supplement* today may well seem forced. Juvenal was the captive audience of his long-winded poet; we, on the other hand, can always stop reading our infuriating rag—and even, in the last resort, cancel our subscriptions. (I have only done this once—when an ode by Edmund Blunden lauding the Munich Agreement had occupied its front page.) But Juvenal's helpless, hitherto suppressed indignation, even if it was only assumed for rhetorical effect, is not really so very different from the bubbling rage that *TLS* occasionally inspires. I at least, though not strictly a captive, cannot do without my *TLS*. The reviews are generally fair, level-headed, well written, and it covers the whole field of literature and scholarship in a way none of its rivals—not even the excellent *New York Review of Books*—can claim to do. But if indispensable for all of us whose business is literature its policy of impenetrable anonymity in the reviews is as intolerable to many

• *Essays in Criticism*, April 1971.

of us as the 'raucousness' of Cordus was to Juvenal. The defect
is always there, a running sore that its readers are never permitted to heal. As we turn the pages from one judicious *TLS*
review to another we simply cannot help asking ourselves 'Who
wrote that?', or at least 'What kind of person will have written
that?' Perhaps this reaction, which must always be that of any
anonymous *reviewee*, explains the tendency *TLS*'s regular readers
have of always turning first of all to the 'To the Editor' pages.
Here at least, however foolish they may be, are creatures with
faces. And though in the frequent clashes the reviewer is usually
given the last crushing word, a certain sympathy attaches to his
victim because he is at least an identifiable human being with a
name and an address.

The editor must properly refuse some of the letters submitted
to him for publication. He is clearly right to defend his columns
against the crackpots, and even the best scholar may sometimes
lose his head on these occasions. I was once shown a long
unprinted leter directed against my own views on early un-
authorized editions of *The School for Scandal*. The writer, an
éminence grise of the Yale English Department, had devoted an
acutely embarrassing first paragraph to my various virtues, laying
them all on with a trowel, before turning then to rend me. 'If
gold rusts,' as he chose to put it, 'what shall iron do?' What
indeed, as I happened to be his 20-carat gold? And all because
we had disagreed about whether a text was a 'reported' one or
not.

Unfortunately, editorial censorship in Printing House Square is
liable to the corruptions of any censorship. The editor of *TLS*
(Arthur Crook since 1959) is particularly sensitive to any criticism
of the traditional policy of anonymous reviewing. An almost
comic case has just been reported to me by Professor Barbara
Hardy of Birkbeck College. It seems that *TLS* had reviewed
unfavourably a book in an area in which she is known to be
especially interested. The author came to the false conclusion
that she *must* have been responsible for what he considered a
grossly unfair notice, and in due course news of his distress
reached Mrs Hardy. What was she to do? The author was unknown to her personally, and she decided that the proper way to
scotch what had now become an academic rumour was a short
letter in *TLS* denying her authorship of the review. But this was
returned to her by Mr Crook. She then tried again at greater

length and in more solemn tones. But Mr Crook wouldn't print this letter either, and in her despair she has now turned to me. Professor Hardy now authorizes me to announce publicly that she has not, does not and will not ever review for *TLS* as long as its reviews remain anonymous. I have no doubt that other potential *TLS* reviewers feel very much as she does.

An elaborate historical and critical assessment of *TLS* that I wrote in 1957 (now printed above, pp. 225–37) discussed the whole question of anonymous reviewing at some length and I need not repeat here what I wrote then. My own article sparked off leading articles and letters in *TLS* itself, including one of masterly non-committal from T. S. Eliot. The editor then was A. P. Pryce-Jones, but I have a suspicion that the two leading articles that initiated and closed the correspondence were the work of Mr Crook, at that time the assistant editor. Mr Crook has since proved himself a much better editor than his predecessor, but on the question of anonymity he has what I can only call a bee in his bonnet. The one serious argument to which he returns again and again is that if a reviewer is allowed the luxury of a signature this is bound to tempt him into 'showing off'. As a hypothetical possibility this may be conceded, but its solution is surely simple: the editor returns the review and instructs the reviewer to remove the egotistical fireworks. And then, if the worst comes to the worst, the reviewer is dropped.

TLS is now the only reputable journal in the English-speaking world in which the longer reviews are *not* signed. In our special English circumstances, as when the reviewer is in the Civil Service, a *nom de plume* may sometimes be necessary. But such exceptions are rare; even *The Times* has broken with its aboriginal tradition and now signs the reviews. Has not Mr Crook noticed, as Canute may be presumed to have done, that the tide has turned? We are no longer in the nineteenth century.

And there is another special objection to *TLS* anonymity: it has unquestionably exacerbated Anglo-American literary relations. Although the Crook epoch has been a great improvement in this respect over the Pryce-Jones period, an anti-American bias still lingers in some *TLS* reviews. (Even when it is not really there a suspicion of its continuity persists.) As it happens, Professor Hardy's non-victim was an American. And the only letter I have ever had rejected by *TLS* was one in defence of a distinguished American scholar. What I wrote, regrettably undated, follows verbatim (the reference is to a letter in *TLS*, 18 May 1967, p. 424):

> Sir,—Professor L. P. Curtis's generalizations about the anti-American bias of English literary scholarship are, of course, much too general. As far as *TLS* is concerned, there has been an enormous improvement in this respect as in others over the last ten years. Unfortunately, however, as Professor Curtis's letter itself demonstrates, the tradition of unremitting *TLS* hostility against all things American lingers on in the campuses—*because* it still finds its occasional justification.
>
> For this, Sir, your policy of anonymous reviews—a practice now unknown in any other equally reputable journal (except *The Economist*)—must, I am afraid, be held largely responsible. A regular reviewer who can be immediately identified by his signature (or if it is preferred by his initials or by a consistent pseudonym) soon becomes a living personality for his readers. If he has prejudices we know they are *his* prejudices, and we do not ascribe them to editorial policy or Oxbridge iniquity. We know where we are with him. On the other hand, the sort of wild guesses to which Professor Curtis resorts ('judging from the waspish tone, alliterative style, and malice aforethought I suspect the hand of someone who took his first in the honours school of English at Oxford about twenty years ago') are almost inevitable when a discomfited reader is shooting an unseen enemy in the dark. Anonymity breeds suspicion. (As it happens, Professor Curtis's reviewer read 'Greats' at Oxford and not English.)
>
> *The Times* has shown us recently that it is possible to be contemporary without any loss of dignity whatsoever. Is not this perhaps the moment for *TLS* to abandon for ever its obsolete adherence to faceless reviewers? I know myself from the dozens of letters I received when I raised this issue some years ago that the reform would be welcomed by very many of your old friends and admirers. And, because only two or three of the *TLS* regulars can possibly be called anti-American today, it would lay for ever the unhappy ghost not altogether unreasonably alleged by Professor Curtis.

But the letter was not printed and the indefensible practice remains unchanged.

24

The Novel's Original Sin: A Lecture

It is announced from time to time—by V. S. Pritchett, for
example, or Lionel Trilling, or some other critical bigwig—that
the novel is dead. Or if not actually dead as good as dead, in its
last painful and pathetic agonies. The process of dissolution set
in, it seems, with Gustave Flaubert, became more acute in Henry
James's later novels and short stories, and was completed without
possibility of cure by the great experimentalists of the first
quarter or third of this century—Gide, Proust, Mann, Joyce,
Lawrence and the decidedly less great Virginia Woolf. After their
masterpieces, or all-but masterpieces, a failure of nerve set in;
apparently there was nothing significant left for the novelist to
say and no interesting new way in which to say it. I need not
elaborate the familiar obituary notice. Alas, poor Yorick! I knew
him well, too well—especially when I was in my twenties and
(critically) deplorably liable to be led by the nose.

My own attitude to the novel today is rather different from the
tale of literary decline and fall I have just summarized, though
perhaps it is even more disparaging. The thesis that I am
proposing to advance, put as bluntly as possible, is not that the
serious novel is dead but that, with the exception of the satiric

novel, it *ought* to be. It is certainly true that would-be serious
and non-satiric novels continue to be written and even read, but
I deplore both facts. In a word, I regard the novel as *per se* an
inferior art form, one hopelessly vitiated by an internal technical
self-contradiction.

I begin with the aesthetic problem posed by the length of the
average novel. It is impossible for the human memory to retain in
its original freshness and detail each episode in the preceding
chapters as a novel progresses. At best we retain a vague outline
of what occurred before, and though it is theoretically possible
no doubt to refer back to a related passage in an earlier chapter,
how often do we do so? Unlike the historian the novelist does
not even provide indexes; the list of characters at the beginning
of a Dickens novel is the nearest we get to one.

Sometimes the chapters have headings or brief outlines, but no
novelist that I can think of gives us the detailed summaries that
Milton added to each book of *Paradise Lost*. Unlike the lyric too
—which is continually sending us back to earlier stanzas by its
repetitions of phrasing or imagery—the novel is in effect a One-
Way form of literary traffic. Poetry has been defined as memorable words; a novel on the other hand, consists of immemorable
words. *Qua* novel it makes little or no difference whether the
writing is finished or slovenly. Novels after all translate, and
within certain limits it does not seem to matter how competent
the particular translation is. No doubt that is why the translator's
name is so often omitted.

But the crucial self-contradiction implicit in the novel form is
not the deficiency in any unity of impression that its immemor-
ability imposes. I want to dig deeper into the hideous, ultimate
nature of the novel. Before doing so, however, let me throw at the
novel-addict a dictum of E. M. Forster's in *Aspects of the Novel*.
According to Forster, who was after all as such things go not at
all a bad novelist himself, a novel can *never* achieve the final
beauty of form that is obtainable in a play. Never, never, never—
however much you struggle with *le mot juste* or some subtle and
delicate shade in your characterization or plot. The remark is
made more or less *en passant*, and Forster shows no awareness of
its devastating implications. He may not perhaps have realized
the strict critical consequences of his admission. For surely if a
literary genre is necessarily, by its very nature, incapable of the
sort of perfection that is attainable in such a closely related genre

as the drama its life cannot be expected to be a long one. Is it not even our duty, as responsible literary critics, to administer forthwith the fatal destructive *coup de grace*?

As I have already admitted, I am prepared to allow one species of the genus an exemption from this universal condemnation. But with this one exception the rigour of my Puritanic logic will not allow me to condone the practice either of serious novel-writing or of serious novel-reading. Frivolous novels are, of course, another matter. It is not a sin to read or to write a thriller or a detective story. I am myself a P. G. Wodehouse fan. But we are not concerned with such sub-literature. I am shooting now at the big stuff—*War and Peace, Moby Dick, David Copperfield, Middlemarch, The Ambassadors, Women in Love, Ulysses—et hoc genus omne.*

Let us begin, then, by asking what a novel is—or is supposed to be. A novel is first of all, I suppose, a narrative in prose of a certain length (40,000 words has been suggested by Forster as the minimum); it is also, obviously, something more. 'Realism' must be superimposed on 'story'. 'The first thing we normally ask of a novel', Walter Allen has said, 'is that it shall give us a recognizably faithful picture of the life of its times.' A novel, then, is a kind of social history. But that history must be pseudo-history. For the second thing that we normally ask of a novel is that it shall be *fiction*, a 'life of the times' enacted by characters who have never existed, proceeding from situation to situation that are all equally unverifiable historically.

The contradiction could hardly be more complete: the untrue masquerading as the true! Or, to put it in another way, an omniscient narrator disguising himself as a biographer or social historian, but without the historian's limitation that his researches will always be incomplete. Now it is precisely in attempting to persuade us to suspend our disbelief in the reality of its characters by providing them with a background and a setting that are recognizable and familiar that the novel commits what I call its original sin. The reader ought surely to be convinced of the quasi-reality of a novel's characters from his own social or introspective experience, as he is convinced of it in a good play, narrative poem or romance. But the novelist adds to the evidence from intersubjective human probability the objective minutiae of real life—landscapes, houses, costumes, professions, incomes, etc. And the effect of the latter is supposed somehow to confirm the former. 'Improbable, my dear reader, though my heroine's behaviour may seem', the novelist insinuates, 'it did really happen. I know, because I can tell you how many windows there were on each floor of my heroine's uncle's house, the Rectory of Hogsbottom Episcopi, in the county of Somerset in the year 1867.' But in fact the one kind of knowledge (the illusion of psychological probability) has no necessary connection with such information as is provided in the *Victoria County History of Somerset* or Pevsner's *Penguin Guide*. The knowledge provided by a novelist is really a mode of rhetoric; it is only by rhetoric, the art of persuasion, that he can hope to convince us he does know all about the windows of Hogsbottom Rectory in 1867. But this rhetorical omniscience, though it is intended to look like history, is not history because it is not verifiable from historical documents. You can explore every acre of Somerset without finding a Hogsbottom Episcopi in any one of them. In other words, *the novel is fiction posing as fact*.

The point is worth elaborating. The novel is distinguished from other narrative genres—such as drama or the epic—by its wealth of plausible incidental detail, their general function being to encourage the reader to believe himself in a world similar in all its external aspects to that in which we have our daily being. Instead of the mere willing suspension of disbelief that poetry or fantasy demands from its readers, the novel-reader finds himself cajoled into accepting the events described in a novel as of almost the same order of reality as the events he meets in the newspaper. The two worlds become co-terminous. That at least seems to be the novelist's ambition.

Consider the case of the first English novelist—Daniel Defoe. Having begun as a genuine journalist in his *Review* he had no difficulty in concocting his *Journal of the Plague Year*, which was for a long time considered an authentic contemporary account of the Great Plague of 1665—just as he had no difficulty in passing himself off as a Whig in Edinburgh when he was in fact a Tory spy in the pay of Harley. *The Journal of the Plague Year* is now classified as a historical novel. On the other hand, Defoe's *True Relation of the Apparition of Mrs Veal*, after having been first accepted at its face value as a journalist's report on certain psychic phenomena at Canterbury and then reclassified as just one more of Defoe's fabrications ('the first ghost story in English'), has recently been vindicated as an accurate account of what his

Canterbury informants believed to be literally true—though presumably the ghost's recommendation of *Drelincourt On Death* was an advertising trick devised by Defoe to push the sales of that dreary treatise.

The history of the novel is full of similar episodes, some of them involving highly respected scholars. Thus George Sherburn's excellent article in *Modern Philology* on early appreciations of Milton's minor poems instances Edmund Waller's recommendation of *Lycidas* to Saint-Evremond, which he dates *c.* 1673. His source, however, is *Letters supposed to have passed between M. de St Evremond and Mr Waller*, which was only published in 1769 and is in fact the work of the poet John Laughorne and is a sort of historical novel. More recently a Miss King-Hall wrote an orthodox historical novel, largely based on Horace Walpole's letters, called *The Diary of a Young Lady of Fashion*, which several reviewers, including one in the *Spectator*, absurdly mistook for the authentic memoirs of an eighteenth-century aristocrat. Though surprised, Miss King-Hall (who had not intended to deceive anybody) was naturally delighted. For a historical novelist such an error constitutes the sincerest form of flattery. And even when a confusion with history proper does not occur, a near-miss, as it were, will be chalked up by the critics in the novel's favour. Consider this tribute that Max Beerbohm once paid to Trollope's novels: 'Reading him, I soon forget that I am reading about fictitious characters and careers: quite soon do I feel that I am collating intimate memoirs and diaries. For sheer conviction of truth give me Trollope.'[1] And here is an extract from a review in the *New York Times* of a novel called *The Kentuckians*: '...consistent and persuasive: instead of a current novel by Janice Holt Giles, it might almost be a word-for-word printing of a manuscript found by her among the archives.' The logical implication of such eulogies is clear: the closer the novelist gets to persuading his readers that what they are reading is not *his* invention but solid historical fact, the more satisfied they ought to be.

The standard reply to such objections as I have been making is that the novel's realism is a literary convention. It is only children, or simple souls like Partridge in *Tom Jones*, who confuse the actors on the stage with real men and women in a real human situation. And no doubt there *is* an element of

[1] From the essay on 'Servants' in *And Even Now* (1920).

convention in even the most naturalistic novel. But the convention that the novel uses is different—in degree if not in kind—from any other literary convention: it is *the convention of doing without conventions*—one that minimizes the aesthetic distance between the world of art and the world of things. 'Illusion' trembles in it on the edge of 'delusion'.

A useful parallel might be drawn with the conventions of the painter. An 'academy' portrait often approximates to a photograph in colour. The difference between Queen Victoria as she was seen by her subjects and a portrait of her by Winterhalter or Herkomer was that they immobilized the Queen, eliminating the real-life complexities imposed by time, and at the same time reduced the three spatial dimensions of phenomenal actuality to two, a certain area surrounded by a gilt frame. But the virtual identity of such pictures with a large photograph is certainly critically disturbing. Take the frame away and you get the *trompe l'oeil* French and Dutch painters of the seventeenth century. (You know the sort of thing. The fly that you instinctively brush from the cake in the corner of the room is not a real fly but a painted one—and the cake isn't real either!)

No doubt a great painter is able to create the illusion of actuality by his pigments as a medium for non-representational statement; that is, abstract patterns in colour and shape, what used to be called 'significant form'. But the novelist's original sin will remain a constant temptation for the painter too. Aristotle would clearly have been a great novel-reader if only he had had the opportunity. Chapter 4 of the *Poetics* gives him away:

> Imitation is natural to man from childhood, one of his advantages over the lower animals being this, that he is the most imitative creature in the world. . . . And it is also natural for all to delight in works of imitation. . . . Though the objects themselves may be painful to see, we delight to view the most realistic representations of them in art, the forms for example of the lowest animals and of dead bodies.[1]

Zeuxis, the painter whose grapes were so much like the real thing that birds pecked them, was a contemporary of Aristotle's, and the latter's doctrine of *mimesis* seems to me to confirm Aristotle's obvious lack of real literary sense. In any case, a painter usually puts a frame round his picture, and the viewer cannot see the painting without seeing the frame. The effect is to remind us that

[1] Ingram Bywater's translation (1909).

we are not looking at real cakes or grapes. And the painter will not insert real cakes and grapes into his pictures, except for those occasional modernistic experiments which are rarely successful. But this is just what in effect the novelist does do. If he does not disguise his novel to look like biography (the Defoe formula), he may unblushingly insert large chunks of unacknowledged history, as Shorthouse inserts extracts from Lady Fanshawe's *Memoirs* in *John Inglesant*. Or he may try and pass off autobiography as prose fiction. If in *The Way of All Flesh*, for example, you substitute 'Samuel Butler' for 'Ernest Pontifex', the book stops being a novel and immediately becomes an unusual auto-biography. And similar substitutions can be made in parts of some of the best English novels, among them *David Copperfield*, *The Mill on the Floss*, *Sons and Lovers* and *A Portrait of the Artist as a Young Man*.

The case against the novel's realism, then, is that it deliberately confuses, or at best juxtaposes, two orders of reality—the world of art and the world of things. The reader is never certain whether he is looking at painted grapes or real grapes. And this means that he does not know what criterion of value he is entitled to apply. Is an autobiographical novel to be read as autobiography or as a novel? An autobiography is a kind of biography, which is a kind of history; the names are real, the dates can be authenticated, the places can be found in an atlas. In a novel, on the other hand, real names, dates and places—the '1831' of *Middlemarch* for example—tend to be embarrass-ments because they distract the reader's attention from the sequences of internal causes and effect in the characters' impres-sions and evolution that the narrative art is principally concerned with.

Sons and Lovers provides an elementary example of such con-fusions. When Paul wins the first prize in the winter exhibition at Nottingham Castle, are we to treat this as historical fact (D. H. Lawrence had after all been an undergraduate at Notting-ham University, and he was also a painter of some talent), or as an episode in the career of the fictitious hero? Or is it perhaps both—in which case we should like a date provided so that we can check the historical accuracy of the event, e.g. in a contem-porary Nottingham newspaper? An episode near the end of *Sons and Lovers* raises a similar problem as it were in reverse. This is the curious friendship that is supposed to develop between

Paul and the ailing Baxter Dawes. In terms of the necessary and probable I do not believe in this episode. Nothing that Lawrence has told us about either Paul or Baxter makes the reconciliation plausible. But if the episode is *autobiographical*—a reflection perhaps of some ultimate reconciliation between Lawrence and Frieda's first husband—I shall have to believe in it, improbable though it seems in terms of the novel, because Lawrence can presumably be relied upon on such a point as a historian of his own life.

I need not labour this point. *Madame Bovary*, to take another example, is a great novel, but *le Bovarysme*, the real-life psychological equivalent produced by a diet of sentimental romances such as those Emma Bovary subsisted on, is fact. Edith Thompson, one of the most celebrated of modern English murderesses, was a clear case of *le Bovarysme*.

I have admitted that one kind of novel evades the general criticism I have levelled against the genre. Why should there be no similar theoretical objection to the satirical novel? *Gulliver's Travels* exhibits the proliferation of pseudo-factual detail that characterizes the common-or-garden novel, but the alleged facts are continually being disproved by Swift's overriding formulas. The elaborate descriptions of nature and social life in Lilliput and Brobdingnag defy credibility because we do not believe for one moment that their inhabitants and physical objects are respectively one twelfth and twelve times the dimensions of their European equivalents. In Book IV the formula is not an arithmetical but a moral or cultural ratio: the Houyhnhnms have the rational qualities of human nature in animal form, the Yahoos who look like human beings have the animal without the rational. Swift, however, does not ask us to *believe* in the curious worlds he creates (Book III is muddled), but to accept his formulas simply as satiric premises. And the abstractness of the premises continuously permeates the concrete 'realistic' examples by which they are illustrated.

Animal Farm operates in much the same way. The animals never achieve zoological actuality because the reader is aware all the time of the human political forces that they represent. And in satiric novels generally the more a character is conceptualized, the more a sort of allegory is approached, the less the danger grows of fiction being confused with fact. The realistic novel's original sin lies in its accumulation of things at the expense of

values: the satiric novel reverses the process: values deflate
things.

Jane Austen will provide an example. You will remember
Sir Walter Elliot *of Persuasion*. Like myself he was not a great
reader of novels, but he did do some reading. His peculiar habits
are described in the first sentence of the first chapter:

> Sir Walter Elliot, of Kellynch-Hall, in Somersetshire, was a
> man who, for his own amusement, never took up any book
> but the Baronetage. . . . [And] this was the page at which the
> favourite volume always opened:
>
> ELLIOT OF KELLYNCH-HALL.
>   Walter Elliot, born March 1, 1760, married July 15, 1784,
> Elizabeth, daughter of James Stevenson Esq., of South Park,
> in the county of Gloucester; by which lady (who died 1800) he
> has issue Elizabeth, born June 1, 1785; Anne, born August 9,
> 1787; a still-born son, Nov. 5, 1789; Mary, born Nov. 20, 1791.

Jane Austen always knew when to stop, and from this point the
entry is only summarized: 'first settled in Cheshire . . . mentioned
in Dugdale . . . dignity of baronet, in the first year of Charles II
. . . [etc.].' What or whose this *Baronetage* was is not specified,
but the various phrases and formulas are exactly those used by
John Debrett in his *Baronetage of England* (2 volumes, 1808); and
the detailed exactness of the fictitious entry provides a large part
of the satirical point. The genealogical minutiae supplied by
Jane Austen from this imaginary entry in a real book exhibit
Sir Walter's beginning and end in vanity, and so they acquire an
implicity symbolic character. The days of the month on which
Sir Walter's four children were born serve no narrative purpose,
but the implication clearly is that they interest him not as
birthdays, the occasions of family festivals and the distribution of
presents, but as satisfactions of his vanity from their tabulation
in print in the Baronetage. The gap between the importance he
attaches to the 9th August, Anne's birthday, as two printed
words, and its natural human importance to Anne as one frus-
trated 9th of August followed another, neatly impales Sir Walter's
moral inadequacy on Jane Austen's satiric pin. The realistic detail
is here serving a serious literary purpose as a comment upon
human society. No reader of *Persuasion* ever finds himself con-
sulting an early Debrett to see if the Elliot entry is really there;
but the meticulous accuracy with which Debrett's style is copied
is a part of the satire. Sir Walter may be a fictitious character,

but there are plenty of people in the real world whose self-importance finds a similar reassurance—though today it is more likely to be in the pages of *Who's Who* or *The Landed Gentry*—and who deservedly share in the ridicule the reader will continue to bestow on their fictitious exemplars.

Unlike a mere 'story' ('Yes—oh, dear, yes—the novel tells a story'), the satiric novel points to a verifiable external world. The non-satiric novel, on the other hand, though it may *use* aspects of the external world, is essentially subjective, appealing primarily to the reader's curiosity ('What happened next?'), or the reader's latent sentimentality or escapism, all of them self-indulgent mental habits. An escape route from such self-indulgences may be thought to be provided by what is loosely called symbolism. If the satirical novel may be—indeed, must be—symbolical, why should symbolism not be permissible and respectable in other forms of the novel?

A general answer to this question might be that the atomized fragments of phenomenal reality upon which the novel depends to achieve 'realism' cannot bear the moral weight that the non-satiric novelist must put on them. They have to be both casual and significant, trivial and supremely important. The contradiction between what the symbols seem superficially to be—mere brick and mortar, so much physical or organic matter—and the moral immensities that they are supposed to represent is too gross.

E. M. Forster's *Howard's End* will illustrate the point. The book is concerned with serious themes and its epigraph 'Only connect . . .' has almost become a slogan for a cure of the ills of the modern world. The England that it describes is divided between four disconnected classes—an almost extinct peasantry (Howard's End had once been a farm), the philistine world of London business (represented by the Wilcox family), a cultured class (represented by the Schlegel sisters), and a lower middle-class with aspirations to higher things (represented by the clerk Leonard Bast). On the plot level 'connections' are certainly made, though often in defiance of psychological probability. Thus the first Mrs Henry Wilcox is the last surviving member of the family who had actually farmed Howard's End. The marriage is not a happy one, but Mrs Wilcox becomes the intimate friend of Margaret Schlegel who on Mrs Wilcox's death in due course marries a humbler Henry as his second wife. At the same

time Helen Schlegel has a child by Leonard Bast, much to the
annoyance of the lesser Wilcoxes. But the plot has to be desperately reinforced by symbols. Thus the garden of the old farm-
house has an ancient wych-elm in which pigs' teeth have been
imbedded—the relics, we are given to understand, of some
primitive cult that somehow authenticate the mystical powers of
the first Mrs Wilcox. An even more grotesque symbol of the
urban nature of the other members of the Wilcox clan is their
liability to hay fever—an allergy from which the Schlegels are
significantly free. The book ends with Helen's baby by Leonard
Bast being carried triumphantly through the hay-field: ' "The
field's cut!" Helen cried excitedly—"the big meadow; We've seen
to the very end, and it'll be such a crop of hay as never!" ' Poor
Bast is dead by now, but he has 'connected' through his baby
and the hay-field both with the Schlegels' rather affected London
culture and the primeval wisdom of the countryside.

There is more to be said for *Howard's End* than this. It has
brilliant passages, and in Tibby, the Schlegels' absurd brother,
satire is achieved of the highest comic character. But the pigs'
teeth and the symbolic hay-fever were a mistake. No doubt other
novelists have done better—Dickens's fogs, Melville's white
whale, the silver in *Nostromo*. But even at its best symbolism
seems to be uncomfortable in the novel—forced, unnatural, an
invasion from the territory of poetry. An image can only become
a symbol by continuous verbal repetition. And prose, the natural
linguistic medium of the novel, resists verbal repetition, whereas
poetry thrives on it. Forster's wych-elm has therefore to be given
encore after *encore* as though it was an albatross. It soon becomes
a nuisance.

What are we left with? Let me count the survivors. The satiric
novel is safe. I read every novel by Aldous Huxley and every
novel by Evelyn Waugh as they came out—from the first page to
the last. The frivolous novel, what used to be called 'railway-
reading', is also safe if it is well enough done. If there were really
such a thing as what Leavis calls 'the dramatic poem in prose'
I would be glad to salute it too, as the drama and poetry clearly
constitute the highest peaks of European literature; but I suspect
that the only dramatic poem possible in prose is the short story.
The human memory cannot retain more than at most 10,000
words at a single reading without such aids as metre or rhyme
—just as the human eye can only register a limited area of paint-

ing at one glance, however prolonged the glance is. As for the historical novel, the intercultural novel (*à la* Henry James), the documentary novel, or the autobiographical novel, I prefer my history, my clash of cultures, my reporting and my autobiography to be 'straight'—the real thing and not fact mixed with fiction. After all, as the great Bishop Butler once put it, 'Things are what they are; their consequences will be what they will be. Why then should we deceive ourselves?'

But the novel-addict *wishes* to deceive himself.

DATE DUE